CABO VERDE AND THE CREOLE SOUTH ATLANTIC

MALYN NEWITT

Cabo Verde and the Creole South Atlantic

A New History

HURST & COMPANY, LONDON

First published in the United Kingdom in 2026 by
C. Hurst & Co. (Publishers) Ltd.,
New Wing, Somerset House, Strand, London, WC2R 1LA
© Malyn Newitt, 2025
All rights reserved.

Distributed in the United States, Canada and Latin America
by Oxford University Press, 546 Fifth Avenue, New York,
NY 10036, United States of America.

The right of Malyn Newitt to be identified
as the author of this publication is asserted by him in accordance
with the Copyright, Designs and Patents Act, 1988.

A Cataloguing-in-Publication data record for this book
is available from the British Library.

ISBN: 9781805264293

EU GPSR Authorised Representative
Easy Access System Europe Oü, 16879218
Address: Mustamäe tee 50, 10621, Tallinn, Estonia
Contact Details: gpsr.requests@easproject.com, +358 40 500 3575

Printed and bound in Great Britain by Bell & Bain Ltd, Glasgow

www.hurstpublishers.com

CONTENTS

Maps		vii
Abbreviations		xi
Preface		xiii
1.	The Creole Islands in Context	1
2.	The Settlement of the Cabo Verde and Guinea Islands in the Sixteenth Century	23
3.	The Slave Trade and the Formation of an Atlantic Culture	57
4.	The Creole Islands: The Uncertain Years	87
5.	The Nineteenth and Early Twentieth Centuries	117
6.	The Cabo Verde Nation Comes of Age	155
7.	Independence	187
8.	Some Aspects of the Cultural Life in the Cabo Verde Islands	219
9.	The Changing Creole World of the South Atlantic	253
Glossary		273
References		277
Index		291

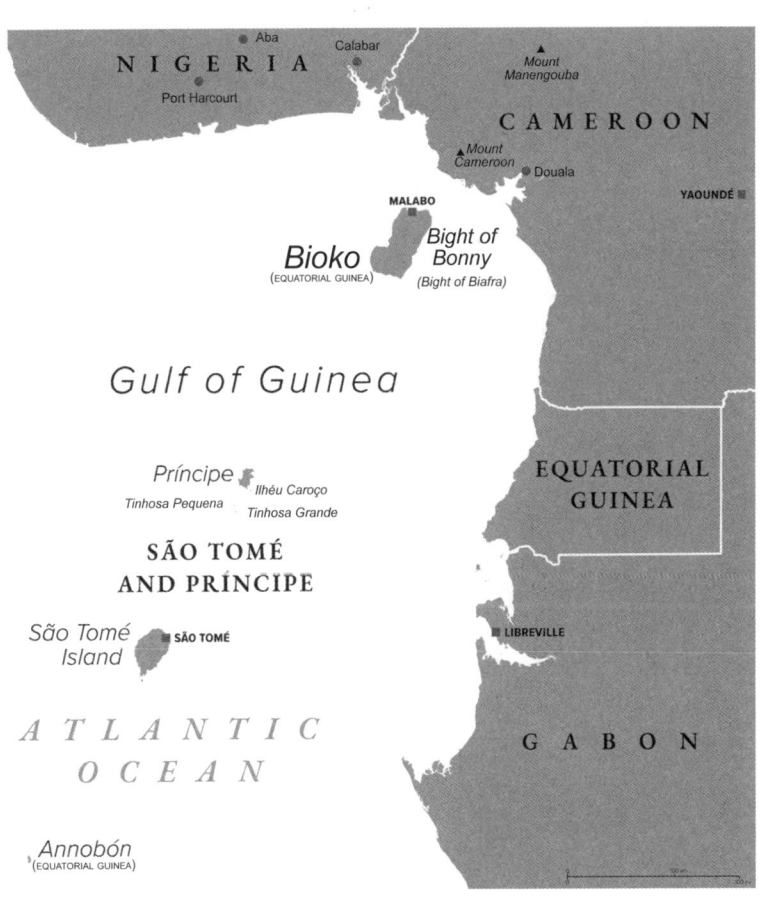

Volcanic islands off the Gulf of Guinea. (Alamy)

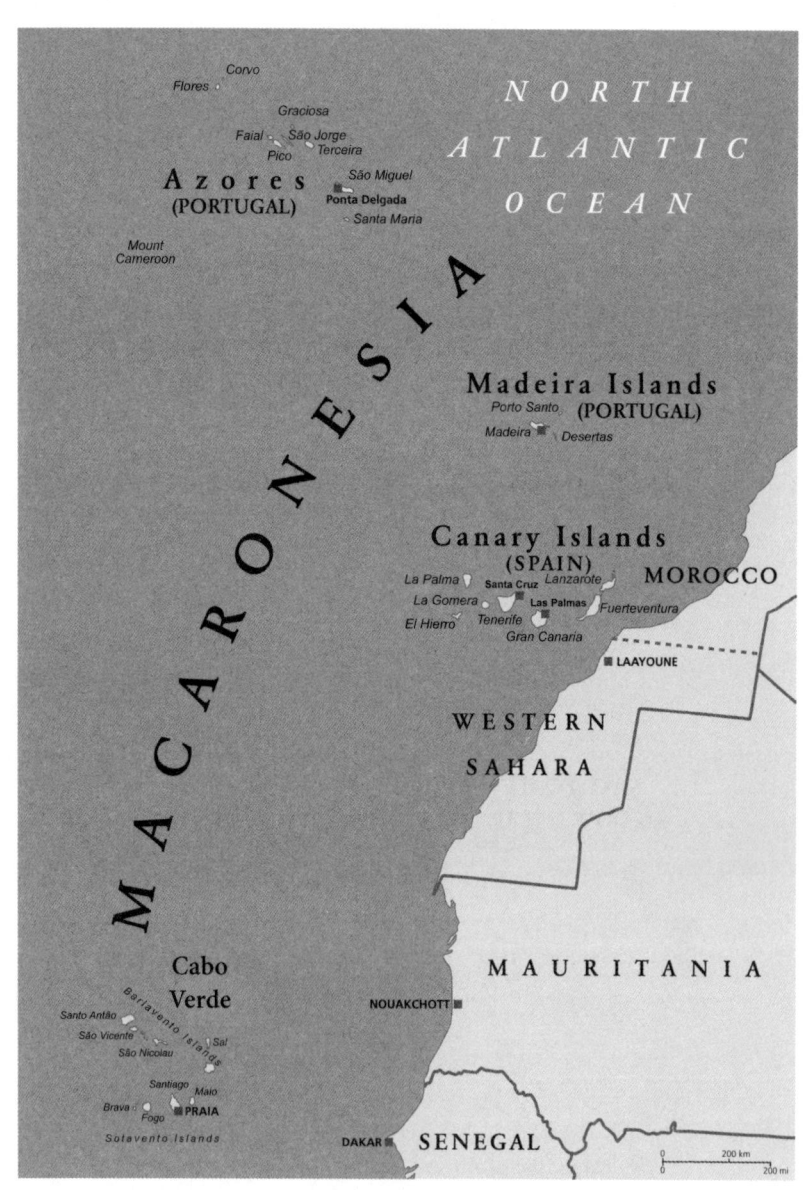

Macaronesia political map: the Azores, Cabo Verde, Madeira and the Canary Islands. The four archipelagos in the North Atlantic Ocean. (Alamy)

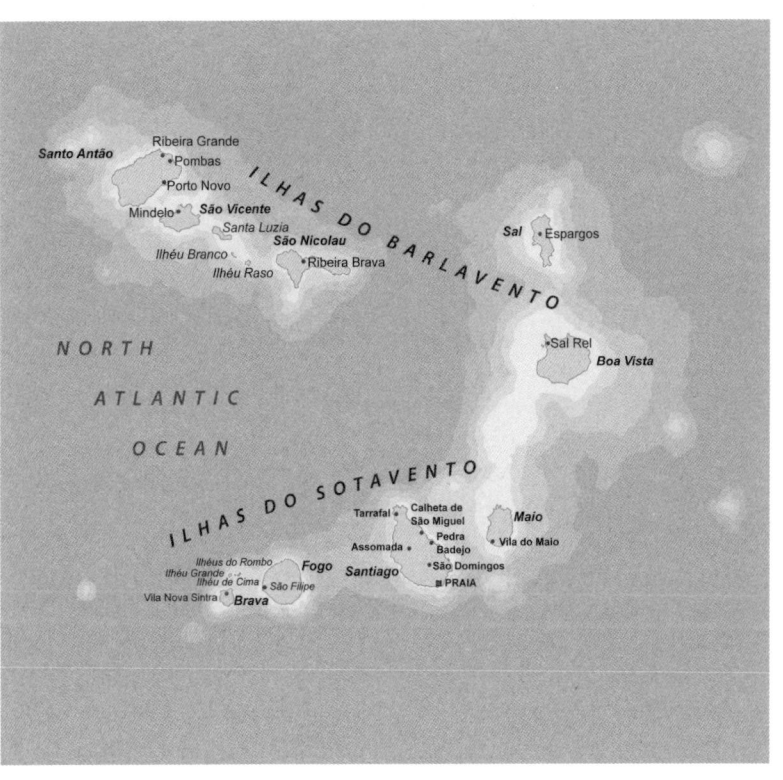

Cabo Verde. (Alamy)

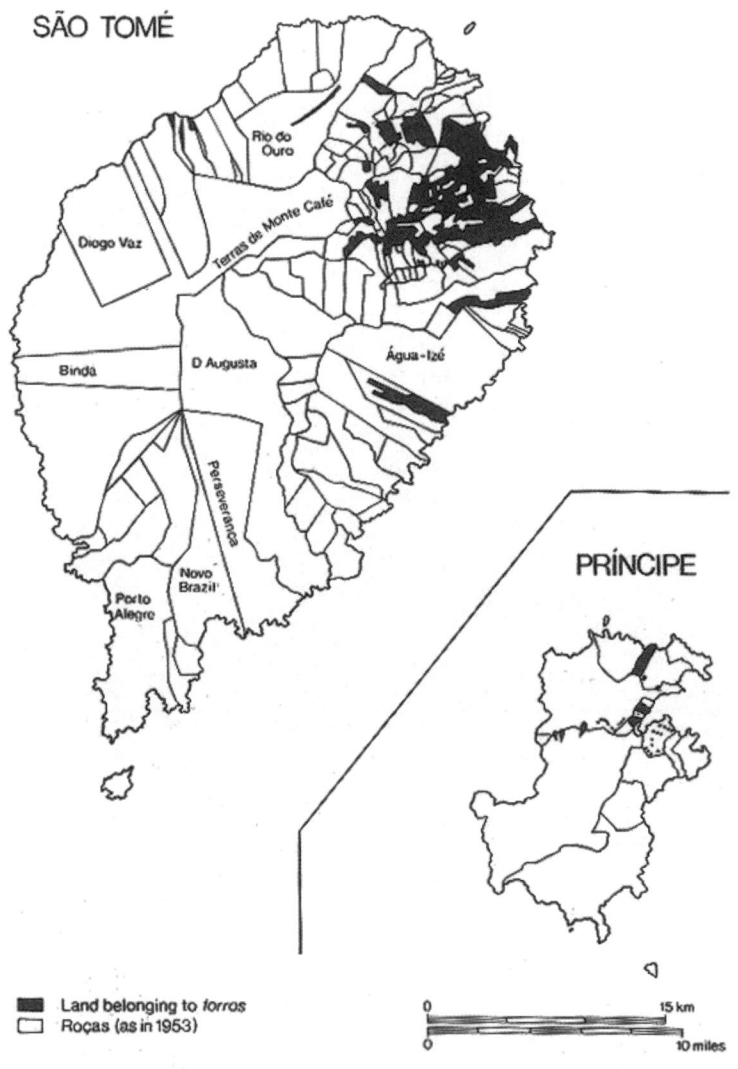

Land ownership pattern in São Tomé and Príncipe before independence.
(Malyn Newitt)

ABBREVIATIONS

ECOWAS	Economic Community of West African States
EEZ	exclusive economic zone
FDI	foreign direct investment
HDI	Human Development Index
HGCV	*História geral de Cabo Verde*
LDC	least developed countries
MFA	Movimento das Forças Armadas
MLSTP	Movimento de Libertação de São Tomé e Príncipe
MpD	Movimento para a Democracia
MPLA	Movimento Popular de Libertação de Angola
ODA	official development assistance
PAICV	Partido Africano da Independência de Cabo Verde
PAIGC	Partido Africano para a Independência da Guiné e Cabo Verde
PIDE	Polícia Internacional e de Defesa do Estado
SOE	state-owned enterprises

PREFACE

Writing the histories of individual countries is a very artificial enterprise as every society in the world is embedded in a historical ecosystem that comprises its immediate neighbours and the wider influences of climate, environment, human migration and cultural and economic exchange. Although the main purpose of this book is to outline the history of the Cabo Verde islands, and although these islands are exceptional and in many ways unique, they have to be seen in a context that includes the Guinea islands of São Tomé and Príncipe, the other creole islands off the coast of western Africa. These two archipelagos were discovered and settled by the Portuguese at the same time and in many ways their histories follow a similar trajectory—except for the influence of climate and geographical location. These two factors drove their histories in different directions, only for them to converge again when both became independent nation states in 1975.

As the story of the Cabo Verde and the Guinea islands is the story of the evolution of creole identity, it is important to place this in the wider context of the history of creolisation in the South Atlantic. This is needed to prevent the history of the islands becoming simply that of two small colonies dragged along in the wake of Portugal's historical journey. As the history of the islands is tied so closely to the history of the slave trade, the wider context of the South Atlantic is once again necessary to understand this trade and how it has affected the cultural development of the countries on both sides of the ocean.

1

THE CREOLE ISLANDS IN CONTEXT

Islands

The history of the Cabo Verde islands is inextricably linked to the more general history of the Atlantic Ocean itself: the islands have played an important part in the development of Atlantic trade and in the cultural interactions of the inhabitants of the countries bordering the ocean. This history is not primarily one of the relations of sovereign states, nor are states on each side of the Atlantic even the major participants in this story. Rather, as the *História geral do Cabo Verde* puts it, "There are also the contractors, illegal traders, pirates, ethnic minorities and many others. We are dealing with actors whose identity resists geographical, political or social categorisation" (Albuquerque and Madeira Santos 1991: I, 2).

The importance of the Cabo Verde islands in Atlantic history has ebbed and flowed; at times the islands have been central to the maritime networks and the strategic thinking of the Atlantic states, at other times they have been relegated to comparative insignificance. However, throughout their history they have been at the crossroads of the sea routes to and from Europe, Africa and the Americas, and have had cultural and commercial relations with all three continents. They have received immigrants from Africa and Europe and have exported population, slaves and emigrants, to the Americas. They have experienced a unique flow and counterflow of cultural influences, which are reflected not only in the creole language and rich musical traditions, but also in the appearance (phenotype) of the islanders and the evolving consciousness of a unique island identity. Cabo Verdeans are neither European nor African nor American but have a mid-Atlantic creole personality which reflects the diversity of all three continents.

Today the Cabo Verde islands, together with the other islands of the north-east Atlantic (the Azores, Madeira and the Canary Islands), are geographically grouped together under the name of Macaronesia. However, although the Cabo Verde islands share much of their history with these other islands, there is another island group, the so-called Guinea islands (Bioko, São Tomé, Príncipe and Ano Bom—or Annobón), with which they share a cultural history in a much more intimate way. So, throughout this book the affinity with those islands is discussed to highlight similarities and contrasts in the development of creole island identities. How these unique creole societies came into existence and evolved is the subject of this book. Like all communities, their character has been to a large extent conditioned, if not determined, by their environment. This chapter will describe the special features of the island environment and how it influenced the long-term development of the human communities there.

The Cabo Verde islands received their name in the fifteenth century from the Portuguese, who referred to them as the Ilhas de Cabo Verde—Cabo Verde (or, in French, Cap Vert) being a point on the African coast which had been discovered and named by Portuguese navigators in 1443. Since then the islands as a group have retained this name, being today called officially the República de Cabo Verde.

When T. Bentley Duncan wrote his book *Atlantic Islands*, which was published in 1972, the Second World War was still a vivid memory, the Cold War had not yet begun to thaw, and the Portuguese empire was still intact, commanding the Atlantic seaways to southern Africa. The book drew attention to the importance of the island groups of the central and eastern Atlantic—their role in provisioning and supplying sailing ships, their commercial importance as entrepôts of maritime trade, their strategic importance in aviation and in warfare, and their role as producers of exportable commodities in their own right.

For Duncan the most important island groups were those of Madeira, the Azores and the Cabo Verde islands, all at that time part of Portugal, and the Canary Islands, the group nearest to Europe and, since the fifteenth century, an important part of Spain's maritime empire. Of the four islands of the Gulf of Guinea, two of them, São Tomé and Príncipe, were still part of the Portuguese empire and, although mentioned, were not accorded much importance in the book. Duncan did also recognise the strategic value of two British Islands: St Helena and Ascension (though the scope of the book did not take into account the other British islands scattered in the South Atlantic: Tristan da Cunha, Gough Island, the Falkland Islands and South Georgia). Because the Macaronesian islands serviced international shipping, their populations tended to be ethnically mixed and cosmopolitan, while the smaller, less frequented islands experienced various degrees of extreme isolation.

Returning to Duncan's book fifty years later, perspectives have inevitably changed. Two of the island groups, the Cabo Verde islands and the Guinea islands, have become independent states in their own right. Although international aircraft now overfly the islands, the strategic importance of the Azores and Ascension has remained. Sailing ships have long gone and commercial shipping no longer depends on bunkered coal, while submarine cables, at one time relayed through the Cabo Verde islands, are being superseded by satellite communications. What is new, however, is mass tourism, especially important when considering the Cabo Verde archipelago and the Canaries. Comparatively new also is a growing interest in island culture. Although the shipping of slaves to the Americas from the Cabo Verde islands was for a long time seen simply as a crime against humanity, it is now being appreciated that this diaspora of peoples, of which there are still so many examples in the globalised conditions of the twenty-first century, can create rich and vibrant creole cultures.

In the past much of history has been written by Europeans and North Americans and has been seen from their point of view. This is reflected in the maps of the world, with the north shown at the top and the meridian running through London, making it somehow seem to be the centre of the world. How different our perceptions would be if the map of the world was shown with the southern pole at the top (as it was in ancient Islamic world maps) and the meridian running through Cape Town or Mumbai. If the map of the world was indeed turned upside down, the Cabo Verde islands would still occupy more or less the same place towards the middle, but there would be a change of perceptions. What is now the South Atlantic would take pride of place at the top, and the creole cultures that grew up in this region might not be so easily forgotten and dismissed.

In 1992 Helen Hintjens and I edited a collection of papers entitled *The Political Economy of Small Tropical Islands* (Newitt and Hintjens 1992). This was not a study of the Atlantic islands as such—indeed the only South Atlantic islands discussed were the Guinea islands (largely neglected by Duncan) and St Helena—but it focused on the strategic, political and economic situation of island communities generally, whether they have taken the path to independence or have remained attached to, or integrated with, their former colonial masters. The book highlighted deep historical contradictions—how islands could assume huge economic and strategic importance as way stations, only to be sidelined when technological advances made them redundant; how being surrounded by the sea acted for them as a defence but at the same time opened the way for an enemy to attack them; how islanders could be at the same time extremely isolated but also part of an unusually diverse mixture of peoples arriving or passing through. The contradictions even extended to their geography. Volcanic tropical islands are exposed to devastation caused by eruptions, earthquakes and hurricanes, but the eruptions and tropical rains leave behind them rich and fertile soil. Finally, the islands experience extraordinary population movements as tourists and maritime visitors arrive in numbers and islanders leave, also in great numbers, to escape overpopulation, the pressure on limited resources and the lack of opportunities at home.

Small islands have also given rise to a new idea of what constitutes a state. The old idea, often traced back to the Treaty of Westphalia of 1648, was that a state had defined borders within which it exercised full sovereignty and its citizens were those who resided within those borders. This definition, still in many ways employed today, never fitted comfortably with the European colonial empires, where subjects of the European states might be found in far distant outposts and colonies, and territorial extensions of the nation state could be located anywhere in the world. Today it is common for small island states to cling to the Westphalian notion of statehood while recognising as citizens large extra-territorial communities that live elsewhere (Lowenthal 1992; Borges 2022).

Meanwhile, in the twenty-first century, it has become clear that small islands are not as small as they look on the map. As independent states they can claim extensive rights over the sea and its resources, extending conventionally to 200 miles from their coasts. The Cabo Verde islands' land surface is approximately 4,033 square kilometres, but its EEZ (exclusive economic zone) is 790,000 square kilometres. Even more extreme, the Seychelles, with a land area of 455 square kilometres, has an EEZ of 1.4 million square kilometres. With the development of deep sea drilling and mining and the growing importance of the conservation of marine life—not to mention the long-term consequences of climate change—small island states have become major participants in these particular areas of international diplomacy.

Islanders have had to be endlessly adaptable. As David Lowenthal put it, "I see islands as special and different, unlike continental areas in their societal, cultural and psychological make-up. One difference is that even seemingly beneficial changes can have catastrophic effects in highly vulnerable island societies ... They do well to view development options with grave reservations" (Lowenthal 1992: 19).

To jaded northern Europeans fretting under their grey skies, tropical islands still evoke ideas of paradise and escape from the real world—and the tourist industry assiduously markets this idea. In one form or another this is a very old idea. The eighteenth century revelled in such escapism, which enabled its writers to imagine a world inhabited by the Noble Savage. Paul and Virginie, the innocents of Saint-Pierre's novel, inhabit their tropical isle where they aspire to live the simple life, and the Cabo Verde island of Brava has its own foundation legend of a couple escaping to live together in an island paradise (Irwin and Wilson 2001: 176–7).

To readers of English literature, tropical islands evoke the experiences of Robinson Crusoe. The apparent simplicity of Defoe's novel continues to throw up complex interpretations. The island on which Crusoe is stranded changes from a tropical paradise, where he is saved from death and destruction, into a prison, where his faith and virtue are sorely tried, and from there to a testing ground for the ingenuity and strenuous work ethic of a Protestant Englishman, who turns the raw material of a desert island into a prosperous and thriving colony and becomes by implication a protagonist of empire.

The story of Robinson Crusoe has prompted a scholarly search for the inspiration behind Defoe's tale. Various real shipwrecks have been advanced as providing Defoe with his raw material, and the experiences of Alexander Selkirk are widely held to have been his principal influence. However, there is a closer connection with the Cabo Verde islands than might at first seem to be the case. As well as writing the fictional story of Robinson Crusoe, Defoe is believed to have ghost-written a whole series of books of adventure on the high seas. Among these are the travels of Robert Drury in Madagascar (Drury 1729); the book entitled *A General History of the Pyrates*, attributed to Charles Johnson (Defoe 1972); *The Life, Adventures and Piracies of the Famous Captain Singleton* (Defoe 1720); and *The Four Years Voyages of Capt. George Roberts* (Defoe 1726). Defoe, it is maintained by some of his biographers, was mining a rich seam of travel literature, which allowed his readers the vicarious experience of the thrills and adventures of the pirates who haunted the Caribbean islands, Madagascar and the Cabo Verde islands, and the trials of Englishmen shipwrecked or otherwise stranded in hostile countries who survived through a mixture of ingenuity, good luck and their own courage. It was a genre of which the public of early eighteenth-century England could never get enough.

Of these stories *The Four Years Voyages of Capt. George Roberts* is of particular interest. This is an account of an Englishman marooned in the Cabo Verde islands by pirates, who had to survive through his wits in a very hostile environment. In 1975 Manuel Schonhorn summarised the book as "a tale of shipwreck and survival among the

Cabo Verde islands that recapitulates in many obvious, recognisable ways the hardships, perseverance and little tragedies, and final victory of Robinson Crusoe" (Schonhorn 1975). This book, which was published in 1726, not only tells of Roberts' adventures but includes a long and detailed account of the Cabo Verde islands themselves, their geography, their settlements and the lives of their inhabitants—by far the richest and most wide-ranging account of the islands that had been written up to that time. Maria João Soares, in her article on the English in Cabo Verde, wrote: "The sources in Portuguese which relate to this colonial space are quite poor ... As a result, we must turn to information in non-Portuguese sources. English authors like the privateer Dampier and the small trader George Roberts wrote more about Cape Verde and Cape Verdean people in a few pages than we can find in dozens of Portuguese documents" (Soares 2011: 129–30).

It should be added that the *General History of the Pyrates*, also at one time attributed to Defoe, contains a long account of the islands of São Tomé and Príncipe. These accounts have not been extensively used by historians, no doubt influenced by their attribution to Defoe and the belief that they were works of fiction. More recently the general assumption that the author of *Robinson Crusoe* was at work inventing a whole canon of shipwreck adventures (a sort of eighteenth-century G. A. Henty) has begun to crumble. The *General History of the Pyrates* is now thought to have been the work of Nathaniel Mist, not Defoe (Bialuchevski 2004), while critics tend to believe that Drury's travels in Madagascar are the authentic experiences of a real man. George Roberts still poses a problem. However, his alleged writings were widely believed at the time to be authentic and were used extensively by John Green in his *New General Collection of Voyages and Travels* alongside other well-known authors like Dapper and Dampier (Green 1745–7).

It may be that George Roberts is a fictional character and his *Voyages* a figment of the imagination of Defoe or some other writer, but the description of the Cabo Verde islands reads as wholly authentic. As Schonhorn (1975) wrote, "all the materials that went into the making of the story can be found in documents of the period: newspapers, trials, travelogues, and geographies". In their

Dictionnaire encyclopédique et bilingue. Cabo Verde / Cap-Vert, published in 2001, Françoise and Jean-Michel Massa describe Roberts' account as "*un document de grand intérêt*" (2001: 196).

For all these reasons I believe that historians are making a mistake if they ignore George Roberts, and I have made extensive use of the information contained in his book.

Geography of the Cabo Verde Islands

It is tempting to be deterministic about the geography of the Cabo Verde islands, for there can be few countries in the world where geography has imposed such a straitjacket on human activity. The main determinants of the island geography have been, on the one hand, their position relative to the wind and pressure systems of the Atlantic and, on the other, their geological formation.

There are ten Cabo Verde islands as well as a number of islets. The islands all lie between latitudes 15°N and 17°N but are conventionally described as forming two groups—the windward (*barlavento*) and the leeward (*sotavento*) islands. The windward group includes Santo Antão, São Vicente, Santa Luzia, São Nicolau, Sal and Boa Vista; the leeward group consists of only four islands: Brava, Fogo, Santiago and Maio. All the islands have a volcanic origin, and one of them, Fogo, still has an active volcano, which last erupted in 2014.

The islands were formed by a so-called hotspot located at the edge of the Africa tectonic plate. The hotspot appears to be forked, so that, as the plates moved, two strings of volcanic islands were formed instead of the usual single line of islands, as in the Gulf of Guinea or the Canary Islands.

The first islands to be formed were the eastern islands (Sal, Maio, Boa Vista and Santiago), while the younger (Santo Antão, São Nicolau, Brava and São Vicente) were formed during the Miocene, and Fogo, the youngest of all, during the Quaternary.

This outline of the geological history of the islands is subject to academic argument over whether the islands are the result of deep or shallow seismic activity. The hotspot has given rise to the so-called Cape Verde Rise, a huge dome in the seabed some 500 miles in diameter. Most of the islands' rocks are of volcanic origin, but because of their great age there are also sedimentary rocks to be found in the older islands. Although the islands are conventionally divided into the *barlavento* (northern) and *sotavento* (southern) groups, this division does not make sense geologically. The oldest of the islands are Boa Vista, Sal and Maio—the three easternmost islands and the three that have experienced the most erosion. Today they are low-lying, highly eroded and bear every resemblance to extensions of the Sahara. However, it should be noted that this largely waterless world of sand and salt has nourished the tourist industry, which thrives on nothing better than sea and sand (Ramalho 2010).

The westernmost islands, especially Santo Antão, São Vicente and São Nicolau in the *barlavento* group and Fogo in the *sotavento*, are rugged and mountainous. These islands have spectacular scenery with deep gorges scoured out by rain, green fertile valleys and rocky coastlines. The mountainous interior of Santiago, the largest of the islands (383 square miles in extent), is so barren and inaccessible that from early times it became a refuge for escaped slaves and in more recent times for dissident minorities like the so-called *rabelados*. The contrast with the low-lying eastern islands could not be more pronounced.

Fogo island has an active volcano. Its frequent eruptions have left the centre of the island scarred with black lava flows. The central cone rises from a massive caldera, caused by the collapse of a magma chamber. This caldera is breached on the western side so that the whole forms a deep, crescent-shaped valley.

The eruptions of the Fogo volcano have, not surprisingly, been much studied. The Portuguese first became aware of the volcanic nature of the Atlantic islands when they discovered, and later settled, Pico in the Azores. It was then that the term *caldeira* (Portuguese for a "boiler") was first used and it was later adopted in international parlance. Some time before 1503 there must have been an eruption of Fogo because the name of the island was changed from the earlier name of São Filipe, which became the name of the island's principal settlement. The first detailed description of an eruption was given by Valentim Fernandes in 1507 (Ribeiro 1997: 207). There are descriptions of eruptions in 1564, 1596, 1604, 1664, 1675, 1680, 1689, 1697, 1713, 1761 and 1774, although it is not always clear from these descriptions exactly when the eruptions occurred (Ribeiro 1997: 209–12). Ribeiro concluded from this information that there were two long dormant periods, from 1500 to 1564 and from 1604 to 1664. The eruption of 1785 was described in detail by the Brazilian naturalist João da Silva Feijó. There were further eruptions in 1799 and 1816. The first known ascent of the volcano occurred in 1826 when a Spanish *degredado* (convict) climbed it and gave a report to the governor. After this there were frequent visits to collect sulphur. There were further eruptions in 1847, 1852 and 1857. After this there was nearly a hundred years of dormancy. There was a weak eruption of ash in 1909, but it was only in 1951 that another major eruption occurred (Ribeiro 1997: 245–76). There were subsequent eruptions in 1995 and in 2014, when part of the town in the caldera was buried in lava, leaving only the tops of the houses visible.

Although the black lava flows scar the land, Fogo is nevertheless one of the most fertile islands and, together with Santiago, was the earliest to be settled. Vines thrive in the mineral-rich rock and can be seen pushing up through the blackened lava flows. So successful has vine growing proved that from quite early times the Cabo Verde islands produced their own wine and continue to do so today.

If geology is one determinant of the islands' story, climate is the other. The islands lie due west of Dakar, more or less in the same latitude as Mauritania and northern Mali. Rainfall is very irregular and occurs mainly between August and October. The northern *barlavento* islands, like São Vicente, receive on average only 3–4 inches of rain a year. The southern islands can receive as much as 7 inches of rain, but there are many years when the rains fail altogether. The islands that regularly receive the most rain are Santiago, Fogo and Santo Antão, due in part to their high mountains, while Sal, Boa Vista and São Vicente receive the least. Prolonged droughts can last three or four years, though there have been occasions when dry phases have lasted for ten years or more. Rain, when it comes, can fall in heavy downpours, the resultant flooding accounting for the deeply scoured valleys. Such heavy rain means that much of the water flows directly into the sea, carrying topsoil with it. Although rainfall is meagre, the mountains of the western islands are often cloud-covered and the moisture from the clouds has allowed trees and agriculture to thrive on the upper slopes of the mountains. This can be seen on the so-called Monte Verde (Green Mountain) on São Vicente, where little plots of land were traditionally cultivated by the inhabitants of the coastal towns, and on Santo Antão, where trees flourish on the mountain tops, in contrast to the barren coastal lowlands, and perennial streams run down from the higher slopes.

The wayward climate was picturesquely but quite accurately described in 1726 by the author of the *Four Years Voyages of Capt. George Roberts*.

> This Drought has continued for this Sixteen or Seventeen Years at *BonaVist*, and the Isle of *May*, and longer at the Isle of *Sal;* and none of them of late have had the rainy Seasons so kind as formerly, but the high Lands have always the most, and the Natives will tell you, that the Mountains draw, and gather the Clouds together, 'till they are so ponderous, that the Air being unable to bear their Weight any longer, they break and fall down in Rain; but the low Islands, such as *Sal*, *BonaVist*, *May*, etc not having such high Mountains to detain and gather the Clouds together, they blow over, which, they say, occasioned the Drought there, more than at the other Islands. (Defoe 1726: 386–7)

It has been suggested that when the islands were first discovered in the middle of the fifteenth century, they were covered with light Sahelian forest. The islands' original flora is likely to have included savanna at lower elevations, with semi-desert plants growing on the drier portions of the archipelago. The higher islands with more moisture and rainfall probably supported dry woodlands or forests. Native tree species include the dragon's blood tree (*Dracaena draco*), the fig trees *Ficus sycomorus* ssp. *gnaphalocarpa*, the tamarisk (*Tamarix senegalensis*), the marmulan (*Sideroxylon marginatum*) and the Cabo Verde date palm or *tamareira* (*Phoenix atlantica*) (Wikipedia n.d.).

Human settlement, which began in 1462, resulted in rapid changes to the precarious ecological balance which had allowed the islands to develop drought-tolerant species. The Venetian explorer Alvise Cadamosto, who visited four of the islands in 1456, described Santiago as "well wooded" (Crone 1937: 64–5). Fifty years later, in

1509, the German printer Valentim Fernandes published an account of the Cabo Verde archipelago which he obtained from mariners who had visited the islands. In this account the islands are still described as well watered and some had plenty of trees, but already the story of the islands is beginning to unfold in a rather more sinister fashion.

> Boa Vista is the island nearest to Cabo Verde from which all the islands get their name … it is bare without trees and without any people.
>
> Sal Island … is so called because of a great salt pan or *marinha* which is in the centre of it, where there is much salt which all the ships that go there can load. This salt is made by itself from the sea water that enters [the salt pan]. This island has no people. It has many wild goats and few trees. This island does not have water and the goats who live there drink the sea water.
>
> The island of Mayo … is so called for it was first discovered on the first day of May … it has some brackish ponds. It is populated by goats and not people and is bare and without trees.
>
> The island of Santiago … is populated with many people. It has two captaincies and good anchorages. This island has many streams of good, fresh water. In this island much cotton is grown and the cotton bushes when watered give two harvests a year … and those which are not watered give only one crop. In this island of Santiago there are three months of winter, June, July and August. And this is called winter not because of the cold but because of the rains. This island produces all the fruits of Portugal and if one plants figs, grapes, melons, sugar cane and all other fruit, they produce throughout the whole year. It does not have wheat or barley but millet and rice as in Guinea. There are a lot of animals and cattle.
>
> The island of Fogo … is so called because in the middle of it is a very high mountain, higher than any other in these islands. In this mountain there burns a fire which can always be seen but which flares up at certain times of the year and the rocks round about fall into it and then a great quantity of stones and ash and other things come out. In the year 1500 a great piece of the mountain fell into it so that the fire appeared also in the side of the mountain where previously it had never been seen except

at the top. And then came so much ash and rocks that it almost covered the whole island and sea round about ... This island is populated. Here there are no houses made with stone and lime or of wood but only of *pedra emsonsa*. In this island a lot of goats are bred. There is little water which is brackish but which the people drink. A lot of cotton grows here ...

The island of Brava ... is so called because it is very rugged and does not have a good port. This island has streams of good water and a lot of goats breed there. There are no people.

The island of São Nicolau ... is bare and high [mountainous] with many trees and much good water. There are in this island many large dragon trees [*Dracaena draco*] from which they make "dragon's blood". The island is populated with goats and not people ...

The island of São Vicente ... has few trees and little water. It is populated by goats and not people ...

The island of Santo Antão is high and rugged. It has much good water and large dragon trees. It is populated by goats and not people. (Baião 1940: 119–21)

This is the first full and detailed description of the islands and shows that at one time many of them had a good water supply and a healthy vegetation of trees and wild cotton. Santiago and Brava in the southern group and Santo Antão and São Nicolau in the northern group are still reported to have supplies of good water, and São Nicolau and Santo Antão have trees producing "dragon's blood". Santiago and Fogo have been settled, though in Fogo the water supply is brackish. The other islands have no water, and Boa Vista and Maio have no trees. Boa Vista, Maio, Sal, Brava, São Nicolau, São Vicente and Santo Antão are described as being populated "by goats and not people". The goats had been introduced by the Portuguese, along with cattle and horses, which were allowed to run wild. The destruction of the fragile ecosystem by wild goats and cattle had begun (Albuquerque and Madeira Santos 1991: I, 180).

The islands, particularly the eastern islands (Sal, Boa Vista and Maio), are exposed to a constant wind that blows from the Sahara, a dry wind that often carries sand particles and is responsible for much of the erosion of the ancient rocks. In spite of the scanty rainfall, it seems that in the past these islands may also have supported typical Sahel woodland. There are still patches of ancient trees— like the giant tamarind growing in the desert heart of Boa Vista. The natural environment was in a very delicate balance, and the crude cultivation methods of the earliest settlers, the clearing of the land and, in particular, the unregulated grazing of cattle and goats, were the cause of the rapid degradation of the island environment. In the early nineteenth century José Joaquim Lopes de Lima, who compiled a massive statistical record of all the Portuguese colonial possessions, forcefully maintained that it was the lack of tree cover that had led to the desiccation of the islands. He added the interesting comment that there was "resistance on the greater part of proprietors to the planting of trees" because, they said, it contributed to the drying out of the soil (Lopes de Lima 1844a: 8).

Over a period of five centuries, the irregular rainfall pattern has had profound consequences. First, it has meant that the islands were never able to develop a purely agricultural economy like Madeira, the Azores or even the Guinea islands. Although sugar and other crops were grown, Cabo Verde was never home to a classic plantation society. Instead the islands developed an economy based on trade with western Africa and the services provided to visiting ships. The commercial orientation of the economy also led to small-scale manufacturing, especially the weaving of cotton cloth (*panos*), the production of sugar and rum (*grogue*), and the building of boats for local trade.

The rainfall pattern also had a direct impact on the settlement of people in the islands. Because agriculture was difficult and the islands were months distant from Portugal, there was a reluctance on the part of emigrants from Europe to settle. Instead slaves were imported from the West African mainland, and some Cabo Verdeans in their turn settled in trading ports on the African rivers. As the islands suffered over the centuries from recurring droughts and famine, emigration from the islands to the mainland was resorted to as a survival strategy. This was, until very recently, actively encouraged by the government of the archipelago as the default policy for dealing with famine.

The Guinea Islands

Ten years after the Cabo Verde islands were discovered, Portuguese sailors sighted another group of islands, this time in the Gulf of Guinea. There were four of these, and the Portuguese named them Fernando Pó (after the captain who first found them), São Tomé, Príncipe and Ano Bom. These names have stuck, all except the first, which has been decolonised and is now known as Bioko. The Portuguese also began to plant settlements on these islands, and after an uncertain start, São Tomé and Príncipe overtook the Cabo Verde islands in the growth of a prosperous plantation economy. Both island groups developed a distinctive creole culture, but they differ considerably in their physical endowments. The geography and the related historical development of São Tomé island were studied in depth by Francisco Tenreiro, a native of the island and a poet associated with the *Claridade* poets of Cabo Verde, who became São Tomé's deputy to the Portuguese Cortes. His book *A ilha de São Tomé* was published in 1961, and is possibly the most important example of a scientific study of one of the creole islands produced by a native (Tenreiro 1961).

The Guinea islands are peaks of a volcanic mountain chain which continues on to the African mainland, where Mount Cameroon is still active. The islands lie in a straight line bisecting the angle formed by the Gulf of Guinea. The largest of the islands, Bioko, is only 20 miles from the African coast and is 779 square miles in extent, which makes it twice the size of Santiago in the Cabo Verde islands. It was never settled by the Portuguese, although they came to claim sovereignty over it. The lack of settlement is probably due to the fact that the island was already inhabited and lay too close to the African mainland for safety. Moreover, ships sailing south from the Gold Coast and Niger delta towards the Zaire river and Angola would naturally bypass Bioko, access to which was dangerous for sailing ships. The smallest of the islands is Ano Bom. It lies 200 miles from the African coast and is only 7 square miles in extent. The whole group of the Guinea islands is much closer to Africa than the Cabo Verde islands, and this proximity is reflected in their history. By contrast, the Cabo Verde island nearest to Africa is Boa Vista, which is 280 miles from the mainland. The whole Guinea archipelago is strung out over 200 miles from 4° N to 2° S, and the equator passes through the small islet of Rolas, which lies off the island of São Tomé. São Tomé island is 330 square miles in extent, which makes it comparable in size to Boa Vista and Santiago in the Cabo Verde group. The four islands consist of rugged mountain terrain. The tallest peak on Bioko rises to 9,480 feet and the Pico of São Tomé to 6,638 feet. Príncipe and Ano Bom are also mountainous, rising to 3,109 and 2,438 feet respectively. By contrast, Pico do Fogo in Cabo Verde is 9,282 feet, and the highest peak in Santo Antão is 6,506 feet.

The little island of Ano Bom lies beyond the reach of the tropical winds that regularly bring heavy rain to the other three islands. As a result it is arid like the Cabo Verde islands and unsuitable for agriculture. It was, however, settled at an early date because its waters were rich in fish, and it was leased out by the Portuguese Crown in the same way that the Cabo Verde islands were granted to favoured individuals to exploit their wild cattle.

The Guinea islands were formed during the Upper Cretaceous, but the platform through which the volcanic peaks pushed has since tilted the islands towards the south-west. They now share a geological formation which makes the southern parts of the islands high mountains rising from deep sea while the northern faces of the islands slope gently towards much shallower seabeds. On São Tomé island the seabed off the south of the island is 3,000 feet lower than that off the northern coast.

With the exception of Ano Bom, the islands have plentiful rainfall. The southern parts of São Tomé and Príncipe receive up to 100 inches of rain spread over the year, with up to 160 inches falling on the São Tomé Pico. There are perennial rivers and, when first discovered, the islands were covered with dense tropical rainforest. The constant rainfall has led to the breakdown of the softer basalt rocks, producing a highly fertile soil and exposing the so-called phonolite necks, which are much harder, resulting in the extraordinary mountain peaks, like the Cão Grande, that thrust up from the surface. The English merchant William Towerson, who saw the island of São Tomé in 1557, described how "on the western side of it you shall see a very high pike, which is very small and streight, as it were the steeple of a church which pike lieth directly under the line" (Hakluyt 1913: IV, 126).

It was the constant rainfall and the temperatures, which varied from extreme heat at sea level to the temperate climate thousands of feet up the mountains, that produced the ideal conditions for tropical agriculture and that distinguished the Guinea islands from the desert-like conditions of the Cabo Verde archipelago. The contrasts in the geography of the two archipelagos go a long way towards defining the parameters of their historical journeys.

The Long History of the Cabo Verde Islands

The Cabo Verde islands have experienced to the full all the contradictions that small islands face. The islands lie 280–400 miles off the coast of Senegal and in the path of maritime navigation heading from the northern to the southern hemispheres. Once a sea route from Europe to the Indian Ocean and the Americas had been opened up in the early sixteenth century, the islands ceased to be small settlements at the end of extended trading voyages from Europe to western Africa and found themselves at the centre of a network of shipping lanes. For sailing ships on the long haul to South America or the Indian Ocean they were essential points of call where water, food and fuel for their onward journeys could be obtained, and where they could land the sick and find fresh crews. When steamers began to replace sail in the nineteenth century, ships stopped to take on board supplies of coal. Atlantic whaling ships also made the islands a base and sought crews among the experienced seamen of the islands. Submarine cables, laid during the second half of the nineteenth century, came ashore at a relay station in the islands before completing the networks connecting to Africa and South America. Then in the twentieth century, before long-distance flights became possible, international aviation made use of refuelling facilities in Cabo Verde.

In this way the geographical location of the islands placed them at the centre of global communications, and these in turn brought a wide variety of immigrants who settled for shorter or longer periods. However, the importance of the islands as nodes in the global communication networks came to an end shortly before the islands became independent. Oil-fired cargo vessels do not need to take on coal; satellite communications have gradually replaced the submarine cables; and long-distance aircraft do not need to refuel but can now complete the longest flights without touching down. Ship repair facilities on São Vicente island are now all that is left of the importance that the islands once had for international shipping and communications.

However, the Cabo Verde islands are not just part of maritime history. Placed less than 400 miles off the African coast, the islands early became entrepôts for trade with West Africa. Their locations gave them security from the perennially disturbed conditions on the African mainland but placed them near enough for there to be regular commercial contacts. Goods from Europe were channelled to West Africa through the islands, and the islands themselves produced horses, cotton cloth, salt and rum to add to the list of trade goods. Traders from the islands established ports on the Guinea rivers and exported to the mainland the creole culture that evolved in the islands. There it underwent further changes and accommodations with long-established local traditions and practices.

The relative security of the islands at first gave them an important role in the development of the slave trade. Consignments of slaves traded on the coast, often in quite small numbers, were kept securely on the islands before being re-exported to Europe or the New World.

Although the islands did not immediately attract many settlers from Europe, they soon became a refuge for Jews and the so-called New Christians (converted Jews) expelled from the Iberian peninsula, while the ease with which slaves could be imported led to the emergence of a mixed population made up of African, Jewish and Christian Portuguese elements, with individuals from visiting ships periodically adding to the mixture. During the sixteenth century the island populations grew and a local creole language evolved. However, from the early importance which the islands had acquired in the commerce of the Atlantic region, they sank into relative obscurity in the seventeenth and eighteenth centuries, though it was during these centuries that permanent settlements were finally established in all of the islands.

While the islands continued to be of some importance to sailing ships, their role in the slave trade was largely taken from them by the growth of the trade from Angola and the emergence of the Dutch, English and French as the dominant influences in West African trade. Because only two of the islands had permanent settlements during the sixteenth century, there was nothing to hinder foreign ships from stopping at the other islands to kill the wild cattle or load up with salt or water. The archipelago was a virtually undefended and tempting target for interlopers of all kinds. The raids by English, French and Dutch were not designed to seize possession of the islands so much as to undermine their commerce with West Africa. At the same time these attacks imposed huge defence costs on the Spanish Crown during the period of the union of the crowns of Portugal and Spain (1580–1640). After 1640 the costs fell on the newly independent Portuguese Crown, and much of it was passed on to the islanders themselves. The raids also contributed to the decay of the few urban centres that had grown up on the islands and to the decline of the growing of cotton and the manufacture of cotton cloth (Albuquerque and Madeira Santos 1991: II, 10–11, 125–6).

The small size of the islands and the precarious nature of their climate resulted in another development which was to contribute to the unique position that Cabo Verde has come to occupy in the modern world. While periodic droughts and famines afflicted the population and led to high levels of mortality, the island populations proved amazingly resilient and their numbers continued to grow. When famine struck, the most obvious recourse of the islanders was emigration. Ever since the fifteenth century there had been close ties with the Guinea region, and emigration to Guinea became common, with islanders establishing permanent settlements or making arrangements with the African societies of the mainland to grow crops on a seasonal basis. Otherwise emigration meant seizing the opportunities presented by visiting ships, particularly American whalers, which began to frequent the islands in the eighteenth century. When these vessels returned to their home ports, many of their Cabo Verdean crews settled on the eastern seaboard of the United States and opened the way for further emigration from the islands. This emigration increased in the late nineteenth and early twentieth centuries, some enterprising islanders investing in sailing vessels, which gave them access to their own means of transport. By the later twentieth century there were communities of Cabo Verdean origin not only in the United States but in Argentina and increasingly in Europe—in Luxembourg, Switzerland, Italy and, of course, Portugal. These widely dispersed communities retained ties with their islands of origin and made Cabo Verde once again the centre of a network of international communication.

Early in the twenty-first century the islands entered a new phase of their existence with the boom in tourism. The story of twenty-first-century holiday islands where hundreds of thousands of tourists can enjoy the luxuries of sun, sand and sea is also the extraordinary story of a population which is enjoying a measure of prosperity after surviving four centuries imprisoned on tiny islands where the same relentless sun, sand and sea had frequently meant drought, famine, emigration and death.

Slave Trade, Cultural Exchange and Creolisation

The settlers who came to the Cabo Verde islands imported slaves to provide the labour they required, and for about a century and a half the islands were an important clearing house for the international slave trade. However, this trade cannot be seen in isolation from the wider political, commercial and cultural developments in the southern Atlantic region. During the period 1500 to 1822 Portuguese influence on both sides of the southern Atlantic was very strong, and this influence continued even after Brazil became independent in 1822. Over a period of 500 years the Portuguese established settlements and had a major commercial presence not only in the Cabo Verde islands but also in Upper Guinea, on the Gold Coast, and in the Guinea islands, the kingdom of Kongo and Angola. On the other side of the Atlantic there were Portuguese settlements in Brazil, from Amazonia to the Rio de la Plata, while Portuguese Jewish and New Christian mercantile networks spread into Spanish America, the Caribbean and North America.

The slave trade early became by far the most important branch of commerce linking these settlements on the coasts of the South

Atlantic land masses. It was a three-way relationship between Europe, Africa and the New World, and in geographical as well as economic terms the Atlantic islanders were middlemen. Merchants and rulers of the coastal states of Africa were as eager to sell slaves as the Portuguese were to buy them, and slaves were treated simply as commodities in the often complex commercial exchanges of the region. African societies retained many of the slaves that were not sold on to overseas buyers, and these provided a labour force and were incorporated in one way or another into local societies. In the same way, the non-African buyers of slaves employed their purchases in different ways—the majority were sent on to the Americas or Europe while others were incorporated into island society.

Although there was a formal Portuguese presence in various ports on the coast of Upper Guinea and in Elmina, Axim and the Kongo kingdom, Portuguese commercial influence extended far beyond the area directly under Lisbon's control. Commercial relations led to cultural exchange and the process of creolisation, as religious practices, marriage customs and commercial and material cultures were exchanged and evolved. New creole dialects and languages emerged in the cultural cross-currents. These influences extended deeply into the African societies of the mainland with which the Portuguese came into contact, while African cultural influences not only profoundly influenced island society but were carried across the Atlantic with slaves and helped to determine much of the culture of Brazil.

Some historians have claimed that the term "creole" should only be applied to the communities that were formed in the Cabo Verde and Guinea islands, where creole languages became permanently established (Seibert 2012), but this seems an unhelpfully restrictive definition. Creolisation was not just an end product but a complex process of cultural interaction and change that could influence and, in some cases, transform the lives of individuals and elite groups as well as slaves and their descendants (Newitt 2017). Creolisation, sometimes referred to as "transculturation", is essentially a dialectical process that occurs when different cultures come into contact (Naro 2007: 1). There is a spectrum of creolisation. At one end there are limited cultural interactions, like the incorporation of loanwords and the adoption of material goods from another culture. At the other end is a more or less complete adoption of a new culture and language with the retention of only vestiges of an original way of life.

To understand how Africa has been affected by globalisation it is important to recognise that cultural hybridity has always been a feature of African history, even when no European or Islamic outsiders were involved. It was this long-established and recurring pattern of political and social change that allowed Islamic and Portuguese outsiders to insert themselves relatively easily into African society and enabled them to begin their own process of creolisation. It was largely through the creolised populations which emerged through the meeting of Islamic and European outsiders with the indigenous African populations that sub-Saharan Africa was made part of the intercontinental systems of commercial and cultural exchange of the Atlantic and Indian oceans.

2

THE SETTLEMENT OF THE CABO VERDE AND GUINEA ISLANDS IN THE SIXTEENTH CENTURY

Overview

This chapter will give an account of the early settlement of the Cabo Verde islands (at first only two of them) and the Guinea islands by Portuguese and Sephardic Jewish immigrants, the import of African slaves and the attempt to establish a plantation economy. By the second generation a society had emerged based on seigneurial landholding, local self-government and a flourishing trade with the African societies of the Guinea coast. This early period of settlement was marked by the emergence of the creole language and was accompanied by the spread of Portuguese influence along the whole coast as far south as Sierra Leone. At the same time the role of the Cabo Verde islands in the supply and servicing of long-distance oceanic voyages developed as a result of their strategic position, and this made them increasingly vulnerable to attacks from pirates and from the enemies of Portugal and Spain.

Discovery and Early Settlement

It is possible that the Cabo Verde islands had been visited by shipping in classical times and that they were known to Islamic seamen and even to the Wolof inhabitants of what later became known as Senegal. Mysterious islands appear on early maps, and in the eighteenth century strong assertions were made, supposedly based on oral traditions, that Wolof canoemen had visited the islands (the nearest of which, Boa Vista, is 280 miles from the African coast) and may have settled there (Carreira 2000: 295–300; Santos 2017: 72–5). All this is possible but is of little importance, as no permanent population had ever been established in the islands, and they were uninhabited when first visited by Portuguese and Italians in the 1450s. By that time traders were leaving Portugal each year to trade along the western coast of Africa as far as modern Sierra Leone. These traders brought manufactured goods from North Africa and the Iberian peninsula and especially horses, which were stabled in the central cargo space of the caravels over the long, sometimes two-month journey from Portugal. From Africa the traders sought primarily gold, which had for centuries been a staple of the trans-Saharan trade, but from the 1440s onwards their return cargoes were increasingly made up of slaves, who were sometimes captured on raids ashore but more usually were obtained through trade with the African communities of the Guinea rivers.

A number of confirmed sightings of the Cabo Verde islands were made by various ship's captains between 1456 and 1460, the earliest apparently by the Venetian trader Alvise Cadamosto, who claimed to have visited four of the islands in 1456. Sailing along the coast of the island that he named "Isola de Bonauista" (Boa Vista), he sent a party ashore

> to climb a mountainous and high part of the island, to see whether they could find anything, or catch sight of other islands ... From the farther shore they had sighted three other large islands which we had not seen ... They could also see in the western quarter, far out to sea, what appeared to be other islands, but they could not make these out clearly because of the distance ... Then sailing along the coast of one of them, which appeared well wooded, we discovered the mouth of a river issuing from it. (Crone 1937: 64–5)

In spite of this detailed account, most Portuguese historians seem to consider 1460, not 1456, as being the year the islands were first discovered, and this has become the date of the discovery officially recognised in Portugal (Albuquerque and Madeira Santos 1991).

In 1462 the Portuguese king, D. Afonso V, granted the islands to his brother Fernando, who was the heir to their uncle Henry the Navigator, who had died in 1460. At this time not all the islands had been explored, but landfalls had been made on the largest, Santiago, and on neighbouring Fogo. Fernando decided to follow the precedent set during the settlement of the Madeira and Azores archipelagos and to establish two captaincies on the island of Santiago—the north being granted to Diogo Afonso, described as *contador* of the island of Madeira, and the south to António de Noli, a Genoese, in recognition of his service in making the first landfall and exploration of the island.

As captains, António de Noli and Diogo Afonso were granted a wide range of seigneurial rights over the island of Santiago and had the obligation to undertake its settlement, Fernando retaining for the Crown the ultimate jurisdiction in capital crimes. This had been the system that had worked well in the case of Madeira and rather less successfully in the case of the Azores. Because those islands were well watered, had fertile volcanic soils and were comparatively close to Portugal, it had proved easy to attract settlers. By the middle of the fifteenth century a successful agricultural economy had been established, Madeira in particular producing sugar and wine for export to Portugal. The Cabo Verde islands would prove to be more difficult to colonise. Not only were they a two-month voyage from Portugal, but it soon became apparent that the meagre rainfall would make agriculture difficult, while the disease environment of the tropics would take its toll on settlers from Europe.

After Fernando's death in 1470, overlordship of the islands passed to his heir, the duke of Viseu. He was murdered by the king, D. João II in 1484, after which the islands were granted to his cousin, who in 1495 succeeded to the throne of Portugal as D. Manuel I. From that time the islands became part of the patrimony of the Crown. As it was some time before a viable royal government was installed, the islands continued to be administered by their donatary captains.

By 1466 little progress had been made in attracting anyone to settle in the northern captaincy, which had its centre at Alcatrazes. Meanwhile the southern captaincy established its base at the mouth of the river, which was optimistically given the name of Ribeira Grande. It also struggled to attract many settlers other than the immediate Genoese colleagues of António de Noli, who had brought with him his brother, his nephew and their followers.

Nevertheless, it was considered important that the islands should be occupied because already non-Portuguese interlopers were sending ships to trade on the West African coast and Castile was disputing Portugal's claims to a monopoly of commerce in the area. So, in 1466, in an attempt to attract colonisers, the Crown formally granted anyone who settled in Santiago the right to trade freely on the African coast south of the area that had already been granted to the merchants contracted to trade at Arguin on the coast of modern Mauritania. The grant stated that "Dom Fernando my very dear and beloved brother tells me that it is four years since he began to populate his island of Santiago ... that its being so far distant from our kingdom, people do not want to go to live there unless with very great liberties and franchises and expenditure" (Albuquerque and Madeira Santos 1991: I, 350). The settlers would have to pay a royal tax amounting 25 per cent on the goods they brought from Africa but would be exempt from customs payments and from the necessity of obtaining a royal licence for each individual voyage (Almeida 1998: 52).

This concession seems to have attracted a number of traders anxious to take advantage of what was, in effect, an open door to African trade. Evidence of the success of this "open door" can be deduced from the action taken by the Crown only six years later to modify the terms of the grant, as the "open door" was threatening to complicate the Crown's longer-term plans for its own relations with western Africa.

In 1469 the king had decided to lease the royal trade monopoly with West Africa to Fernão Gomes, a Lisbon merchant, in exchange for an annual payment. The 1466 concession posed a threat to the monopoly rights which Gomes hoped to enjoy, and in 1472 the Crown decided to impose limitations on the "open door" which it had

THE SETTLEMENT OF THE CABO VERDE AND GUINEA ISLANDS

granted in 1466. The new arrangements limited where the people of Santiago could trade, and stipulated that only bona fide settlers could make use of the provision and that they must trade only in products of the island. However, it was already too late to close the door which the 1466 concession had opened. Traders not only from Portugal and Genoa but now from Castile and other European ports had begun to bring their goods to Santiago and to use the island as a jumping-off point for trade in the West African rivers. For the next fifty years the Portuguese Crown would try in vain to reassert its monopoly rights in the West African trade.

The island of Santiago had now become a base for African commerce, and its future would lie in that rather than in plantation agriculture. The neighbouring island of Fogo had also begun to attract some settlement. The island had an abundance of wild cotton, and this could be collected, shipped across to Santiago and from there sent to markets in West Africa, in this way allowing the Fogo settlers to benefit from the Crown's concession. After a shaky start a small town, called São Filipe, was established, the archipelago's second urban settlement.

There is no record of attempts to settle the other eight Cabo Verde islands, but the Portuguese did land cattle and goats in the islands to run wild and they apparently multiplied successfully. By the early part of the sixteenth century these islands were being leased to those who wanted to exploit the wild cattle, and hides and tallow were added to the products of the islands. To cure the hides salt was needed, and salt was readily and cheaply obtained from the island of Sal and especially from Maio (Albuquerque and Madeira Santos 1991: I, 223–4). Cattle ranching attracted those who wanted to make quick profits with the minimum amount of investment—and naturally it appealed to absentees who were able to use their influence to obtain contracts from the Crown. The cattle industry effectively prevented attempts to settle any of the islands apart from Santiago and Fogo. Planting settlements, even on islands like Brava, São Nicolau and Santo Antão where agriculture would certainly have been possible, would have required extensive investment and they would not have been able to compete with the easy profits of the trade in hides and tallow (Albuquerque and Madeira Santos 1991: I,

27

213–14). Salted goat's flesh was also sent to São Tomé and later to Brazil (Carletti 1964: 8). The breeding of cattle allowed the islanders to produce quantities of butter, which was a commodity sold to passing ships; it was a substitute for olive oil, which the islands did not produce (Albuquerque and Madeira Santos 1991: I, 91).

As already suggested in the previous chapter, the wild cattle and especially the goats did long-term damage to the frail ecology of the islands and, by destroying the natural vegetation, contributed to the long-term increase in desert-like conditions.

Castilian Bid to Control the Islands

Less than twenty years after their discovery, the Cabo Verde islands were almost torn from Portugal's grasp. In 1474 D. Afonso V decided to make a bid for the crown of Castile. His niece Juana, who was a minor, was the presumptive heir to the Castilian throne, and Afonso proposed to marry her and assume the crown himself. War broke out between Portugal and Castile, and although the fighting was focused on the European battlefields, the Castilians, encouraged by Isabella, the half-sister of the previous king and Juana's principal rival, decided to challenge the Portuguese in West Africa. In 1475 a large Castilian expedition reached the Cabo Verde islands and took António de Noli and many of the settlers in Santiago as prisoners back to Castile. Behind-the-scenes negotiations led to de Noli returning, this time as Castile's governor of the island. It seems clear that Castile had no master plan to supplant the Portuguese, and in the years that followed, Portugal gained the upper hand on the African coast, defeating and capturing a large Castilian fleet of trading ships in 1478.

In the Treaty of Alcaçovas, which ended the war in 1479, the Portuguese king abandoned his claim to the Castilian throne but secured for Portugal uncontested sovereignty over Madeira, the Azores and the Cabo Verde islands, along with the monopoly of trade with western Africa. Only the Canary Islands were left to Castile.

The Discovery of São Tomé and the Foundation of Elmina

Meanwhile, the Portuguese presence in western Africa had increased significantly. As a result of the efforts of Fernão Gomes's captains, another group of islands had been discovered. Two captains, João de Santarém and Pero de Escobar, discovered the islands of São Tomé, Príncipe and Ano Bom between December 1470 and January 1471, Ano Bom being sighted on New Year's Day and named appropriately. The following year (1472) another captain, Fernão do Pó, sighted the island of Bioko, which was named after him until its name was changed in 1973. Although Bioko/Fernando Pó was probably populated and therefore not attractive to the Portuguese for settlement, the other three islands were eventually granted as captaincies just as the Cabo Verde island of Santiago had been. Six months' sail from Portugal and situated on the equator, the islands may have been even less attractive than the Cabo Verde islands for settlement. However, lack of rainfall was not their problem. Instead the tropical climate of the islands, although it bred disease, proved ideal for growing sugar cane, and after the first attempts at settlement in 1485 failed, São Tomé was granted to another captain, Álvaro de Caminha, who energetically rounded up settlers, including numerous Jewish children taken from their parents, and moved to the island with his family. Investors were then found to take up concessions of sugar-growing land on these remote islands, which they planned to turn into another Madeira (Seibert 1999: 19).

Portuguese sovereignty in the Cabo Verde and Guinea islands had been confirmed by the Alcaçovas peace treaty, but the Castilian threat, as well as the activities of other interlopers hoping to strike it rich in African trade, was ever present in the mind of the king, D.João II, who had succeeded his father, D.Afonso V, in 1481. Shortly after the peace had been signed, the king organised a new exploratory voyage (as Fernão Gomes had done so successfully), which was dispatched under the command of Diogo Cão in 1482. At the same time the king ordered the building of a royal trading factory on what was later to be known as the Gold Coast. Diogo de Azambuja, a trusted servant of the king, was sent with a fleet to build a fort and factory, subsequently known as Elmina (The Mine).

This was strictly a trading post, similar to that at Arguin, which had been established in the 1440s, and it was to be under direct royal control. It was administered by a fort captain and a royal factor, who traded gold on the king's behalf. Although it was intended to be a trading station and not a settlement, Elmina, as well as its satellite trading station at Axim (founded in 1515), became a centre from which Afro-Portuguese creole culture was to spread along the coast.

In 1486 the king had attempted to establish another trading post in the land of the *bumi* Jeleén, ruler of Waalo on the lower Senegal river, which would have resulted in another royal fortress. That year the *bumi* came to Portugal and was feted by the king, but the return expedition ended in a fiasco, with the African prince being murdered. More successful was the establishment of relations with the Kongo kingdom, which lay south of the Zaire river. After the first contact made by Diogo Cão in 1484, an embassy was sent from Portugal and a permanent mission was established in the country.

These developments were to lead to the emergence of four parallel but distinct centres of Portuguese (and later creole) culture and economic activity. While the island settlements were controlled by their donatary captains, the royal trading factories were trying to maintain the Crown's monopoly of trade with mainland Africa. By the end of the fifteenth century it was apparent that there was a deep contradiction at the heart of royal policy, as settlers from the islands who traded with the African states of the mainland were often in direct competition with the Portuguese Crown and in contravention of its monopolies. The tensions caused by these rivalries would characterise the first hundred years of European contacts with western Africa.

The years immediately following the Alcaçovas treaty saw the commerce with West Africa grow and the beginning of a new development, as traders based in the islands began to settle on the mainland, establishing commercial relations with African lineage heads and rulers among the coastal communities. Portuguese traders found that, although some African peoples made large ocean-going canoes, their own capacious caravels were able to capture the market in local coastal trade, shipping bark cloth, *cori* beads, slaves and, later, kola nuts from one coastal port to another. The Portuguese also brought many things from Europe that the West African market needed, among them horses, and brass and iron, which was in short supply in some of the West African communities. They also traded raw cotton from the islands. As well as gold and slaves, they bought carved ivory objects, which had a market in Europe.

The Settlement of Fogo and Santiago

Only a few scraps of information have survived that describe the earliest settlers in the Cabo Verde islands. A number of Genoese came in the wake of António de Noli, but they would have been interested in trade rather than settlement, and it was reported that they were collecting wild cotton for export. As early as 1469 two Castilians obtained a concession to collect orchilla (*Roccella tinctoria*), a lichen used by European cloth manufacturers in the dyeing industry. The collecting of orchilla later became a royal monopoly, which continued until the end of the eighteenth century, a monopoly that the Crown leased out on a regular basis to syndicates willing to collect the lichen.

A group of Franciscan friars settled early in Santiago, and some men of noble status (or who could claim to be *fidalgos*) obtained land concessions, anxious as this class always was to extend its patrimonial lands. Curiously, the rumour spread that the blood of turtles, which, then as now, bred on the islands in large numbers, was a cure for leprosy and some sufferers made the journey and presumably settled at least for a time to take the turtle-blood cure (Russell 1995: s. XIII, 10). Some convicts (*degredados*) were sent to the islands to serve out their sentences or to have the death penalty commuted into life exile. These were the first of thousands of convicts who were sent to the islands over the next 400 years, most of whom died without leaving much of a trace but some of whom formed partnerships with local women and mixed their blood with that of the islanders and imported slaves.

Few if any of the early settlers who came from Europe to Cabo Verde were women. However, the first limited census of the population in 1513 did record four single women, who were probably *degredadas* and most likely prostitutes. In São Tomé some women settlers are recorded, and there were females among the Jewish children sent to the island. However, the scarcity of women settlers from Europe in the population was made up for by importing female slaves, and in São Tomé surviving documents make it clear that these slaves were imported with the specific intention of providing wives for the male settlers.

The 1513 census provides the first statistical information about the Cabo Verde island population, though slaves and minors were not included in the count. There were fifty-eight "*vizinhos homens honrados brancos*" (honourable white citizens) and sixteen "*vizinhos negros*". A *vizinho* was a permanent settler and property owner, and the *vizinhos negros* would have been *forros* (free black people), already apparently a well-established class in the islands. Then there were fifty-six "*estantes estrangeiros*". These were people resident in the islands who were not deemed to be permanent settlers. This category would include Crown officials and merchants. In addition there were the four single women already mentioned and ten black women, twelve clerics and three brothers (*frades*), presumably friars. The ten black women are also noteworthy. They may have been female slaves manumitted by their owners, but they may also have been important women from the African mainland who were involved in trade with the islands. Writers have sometimes given the impression that, from the first, Cabo Verdean society was one structured in a crude binary of masters and slaves. However, from this early description it is clear that there was a substantial group who did not fall into either category—what might be crudely described as a middle class who were neither masters nor slaves. This census is the first indication of the complex ethnic make-up of the Cabo Verdean population, which has been such a marked characteristic up to the present.

The fifty-eight *vizinhos homens honrados brancos* were the great property owners. The regime of landownership that had been adopted was that of *vinculação*. Land granted under this system might be either a *morgadio* or a *capela*. The *capela* carried with it obligations to support the Church financially but was otherwise the same as the *morgadio*. These were entailed estates whose ownership descended through primogeniture. They were inalienable and could not be sold, divided or gifted from the family who had obtained them.

The Crown was anxious to protect the interests of this class, some of whose estates included land in both Santiago and Fogo, and to guarantee the continuance of a social structure securely headed by white landowners—a sort of feudal nobility. This prospect proved attractive to some of the wealthy and noble families of Portugal who obtained *morgadios* in Santiago and Fogo. Although the *morgadios* could not be alienated from the family that possessed them, there was no condition that the owner had to be resident in the islands, and as the history of the islands unfolded, many of the biggest landowners were absentees living in Portugal, their estates farmed or rented out by local agents.

While the Crown was granting *morgadios* to favoured individuals, there was another system of land law that was being employed—*sesmarias*. These were smaller grants made to settlers on the condition that they farmed or otherwise developed their land. If they had not done so after ten years, the land would revert to the Crown. The system of *sesmarias* had been used in Portugal to bring wastelands into cultivation and was much more flexible than that of the *morgadios*, allowing a class of small proprietors to establish itself.

By the early sixteenth century a number of royal decrees show that the Crown was attempting to regain greater direct control over island society in order to prop up the social hierarchy. At the head of this society were the Portuguese *fidalgo* landowners, who not only controlled the land but also occupied all official positions in the royal bureaucracy. However, the Crown was aware of the creolisation that was rapidly taking place with the growth of the mixed-race *mestiço* population. A *morgadio* granted in 1531 excluded "clerics, religious, friars or bastards even though those might have been granted legitimacy". In this case there was an interesting exception that if no legitimate heir was living, "bastards might inherit as long as they were white" (Albuquerque and Madeira Santos 1991: I, 162).

The Crown also knew that settlement in the islands was proving attractive to Jews and New Christian emigrants from Portugal. A number of royal decrees sought to prevent not only the New Christians but also the Castilians from settling. There were also decrees against the so-called *lançados*, Portuguese who were living permanently on the African mainland. However, although these decrees are strong evidence of the Crown's concerns and of its long-term policy objectives, they are at the same time evidence that none of these goals was being achieved. New Christians continued to settle, and wealthy Castilians were still mentioned as being house owners in the second half of the century.

As for the *lançados*, the Portuguese authorities, and especially the missionary priests, came to see them almost as the arch-enemies of Portugal's interests. The Jesuit Manoel Álvares, writing in the early seventeenth century, described them in this way: "They are all that is evil, idolaters, perjurers, disobedient to Heaven, assassins, debauchees, thieves of the reputations, credit and names of innocent people and of their goods, casting themselves into the way of danger like pirates, sending their ships to places where boats used to come to trade, lawless men without respect for anything except their own appetites, the seeds of hell" (Boulègue 1989: 11).

Nevertheless, in spite of the opposition of the landowners, New Christians and *lançados*, the Crown began to consolidate its direct administrative control in the islands. In Santiago, the settlement of Alcatrazes had not prospered. Diogo Afonso never came to his captaincy and by 1516 "the houses had begun to disappear, abandoned by their inhabitants who had moved to Ribeira Grande and to a new settlement: Praia" (Amaral 1964: 172), which remained for a long time in the shadow of Ribeira Grande. The northern captaincy seems to have been discontinued after the death of Diogo Afonso, and the lands were distributed under various tenures to the settlers. António de Noli had died in 1483, but his captaincy was inherited by his heir, though his jurisdiction was severely limited when the Crown sent officials to oversee justice and revenue.

The king also began to appoint *corregidores*, permanent senior royal officials, who were to strengthen the hand of royal justice, to make more secure the Crown's fiscal rights and to see that royal decrees were carried out and justice implemented. As a consequence there were continual confrontations between these royal officials and the powerful landowners. In 1580, after the union of the kingdoms of Portugal and Castile under Philip II of Spain, there was opposition in the island of Fogo, allegedly organised by New Christians. Consequently, after the devastating raid by Francis Drake in 1585, the decision was taken to appoint a governor who would have overall responsibility for the islands, though the right to draw revenues from the uninhabited islands continued to be granted to favoured noblemen or courtiers.

In 1647 the administration of the Crown's commercial monopolies was transferred to the settlement of Cacheu on the Guinea coast, and in 1650 the responsibility of the governors of Cabo Verde was extended to cover Cacheu and the Guinea coast as well as the islands. The governors were to have this dual responsibility until 1879, when the government of Guinea was separated from that of Cabo Verde (Agência-Geral do Ultramar 1960: 17).

New Christians

At first the Cabo Verde and Guinea islands struggled to attract colonists, but an unexpected turn of events led to a major influx of settlers. In 1492 the Genoese captain Christopher Columbus, sailing under Castilian colours, had discovered another group of islands in the Atlantic. Although the Portuguese at first tried to claim sovereignty over them, in 1494 D. João II's diplomacy eventually secured the Tordesillas treaty, which famously partitioned the world between Spain and Portugal for the purposes of exploration, trade and evangelisation. D. João meanwhile had been angling for a Castilian marriage. A betrothal between his son Afonso and Isabella, the daughter of Queen Isabella of Castile, had been agreed as part of the Alcaçovas settlement in 1479, and the marriage finally took place at the end of 1490. However, the young Afonso died in a riding accident in 1491 and his father followed him in 1495, leaving the kingdom to his cousin Manuel. In the twisted, not to say incestuous, dynastic marriage politics of the time, the new king now sought to marry Afonso's widow, who was also his niece. But there was a price to pay. In 1492 the Catholic monarchs had decreed the expulsion of the Jews from Spain. Since many thousands of these had taken refuge in Portugal, pressure was put on the Portuguese also to expel the Jews.

With his eye on a Castilian marriage, D. Manuel proceeded with further measures against the Jewish population. All Jews, including those from Spain, were given the choice of converting to Christianity or leaving the kingdom. Many Jews took the option of going abroad while others converted. It soon became apparent that many of those who nominally accepted conversion had also decided to leave, and the opportunity to settle in possessions of the Portuguese Crown overseas provided a possible destination. In fact the Crown saw the exodus of New Christians as one way of encouraging settlers to go to the Moroccan towns under Portuguese control or to the remoter Atlantic islands to increase the population. It is not known how many New Christians went to Cabo Verde, but they soon formed a significant element of the islands' population. It was also alleged at the time that around 2,000 Jewish children were taken from their parents and sent as colonists to São Tomé (Baião 1940).

Once established in the islands, many New Christians moved from there to settle on the African mainland, where they could practise their religion and where they became active in the development of trade, residing among the creole population that was growing up around the trading ports. Jews remained a significant element in the *lançado* population well into the seventeenth century, when Judaism went into decline, partly, as Jean Boulègue points out, because "according to Mosaic law, *mestiços* could not be real Jews because their mothers had not been" (Boulègue 1989: 57).

It is possible, as Toby Green has claimed, that because New Christians were accustomed to the cultural ambiguity of being of Jewish heritage while claiming to be nominally Christian, they could make further cultural adjustments and adopt many of the cultural practices of the African societies where they lived and of the African women they took as their wives. It also seems that, once in Africa, many New Christians felt they were able to be much more open about their former Jewish faith. So while the New Christians added significantly to the population of the islands, they were also a major factor in the emergence of a creole society on the African mainland (Green 2012). They also played a significant role in the slave trade, which began to expand rapidly after about 1510 to meet the growing demand from Spanish settlements in the New World.

After 1536 royal government was greatly strengthened by the establishment of the Inquisition, and although there was no branch of the Holy Office in Cabo Verde or São Tomé, in 1551 the islands were brought under the jurisdiction of the Lisbon court and reports on the islands were sent to Lisbon in 1563 and 1567 (Green 2012: 167). There followed a stream of cases brought against New Christians, who were also the most prominent of the clandestine traders.

Suspicion and tensions between Old and New Christians remained an important factor in creole culture and in the growth of creole society in both the Cabo Verde and the Guinea islands well into the seventeenth century. It was a division that cut across and significantly complicated divisions based on race and social status (Green 2009).

Mestiços and Free Blacks

The steady arrival of slaves traded from Africa meant that these soon became the largest section of the population, and the children of female slaves began to form a population of mixed race who were free and who were known in Portuguese as *forros*. At first these were excluded from the European settler community, but this segregation soon broke down as many children of mixed race were recognised by their fathers, who treated them as family members and, in some cases, sought to have them declared legitimate so that they could inherit property. As evidence of this change, in 1546 a petition was sent to the Crown to allow *mestiços* and free black people to hold municipal offices.

Contemporary accounts refer, often in a positive way, to the mixed liaisons which became characteristic of the island settlements and gave rise to the *mestiço* population. The settlers in São Tomé all had wives and children, said the anonymous pilot who described the island in the middle of the century. "But it sometimes happened that if their white wives died, the merchants took black women. There was no difficulty in this as the black inhabitants were intelligent and rich and bring up their children in our manner both with regard to customs and to dress, and those who are born to these black women are of a brown (*parda*) colour and are called mulattos" (Anon 1960: 52).

Francesco Carletti, writing of Santiago as he had known it in the 1590s, expanded on this theme in a way which he knew would appeal to his patron, the Grand Duke of Tuscany. Ribeira Grande, he says, "has its bishop and inhabitants numbering about fifty houses of married Portuguese men, some with white women from Portugal, some with black women from Africa, and others with mulatto women born there of white men and Moorish (or black, as we should say) women. These Portuguese men love these black women more than their own Portuguese women, holding it as a certain and proved fact that to have commerce with them is much less harmful and also a much greater pleasure, they being said to have fresher and healthier natures" (Carletti 1964: 6). Such comments by writers in the sixteenth century were later to feed the carefully nurtured mythology of Luso-tropicalism, which occupied much interpretative space in twentieth-century writing about Portugal and its empire.

By the end of the century, in both Cabo Verde and São Tomé, those of mixed race had already become numerically the largest group in the free population. They were now occupying municipal and ecclesiastical offices and were on the way to becoming the largest group among the landowners.

Another element of growing importance in the population were the free black people, often referred to as *forros*. As a result of the practice of manumission, the numbers of free black people on the islands grew. To these were added children of the next generations and some immigrants from the mainland of Guinea. From time to time Africans from the mainland came to the islands as traders or as refugees from mainland wars or even, on occasion, to seek an education or to receive baptism. Africans, some slaves but others free, were also employed as interpreters (*linguas*) and were able to establish themselves among the *forro* population (Albuquerque and Madeira Santos 1991: I, 163).

By the middle of the sixteenth century the population of Fogo and Santiago was already assuming its distinctive creole character. The island culture was not homogeneous but reflected a population already very diverse and stratified according to class, religion, occupation, ethnicity, slave or free status, and also increasingly characterised by the experience of living apart and in isolation on separate islands.

THE SETTLEMENT OF THE CABO VERDE AND GUINEA ISLANDS

Prosperity and Growth

During the first part of the sixteenth century, Ribeira Grande on Santiago experienced considerable prosperity as an important commercial centre and a hub for transoceanic shipping. Trade with the African mainland grew and flourished, and the port developed as a place where ships bound for India or Brazil could assemble to take on provisions, wood and water before heading out into the South Atlantic.

In 1533 Ribeira Grande, which had had an acting town council since the end of the fifteenth century, was formally raised to the status of a city with its own *senado da câmara*. The same year a bishopric was created and the islands were separated from the diocese of Funchal in Madeira. The new bishop was given jurisdiction over the whole western coast of Africa, though the following year a bishopric was also created for São Tomé. At the same time a structure of parishes was established on Santiago and Fogo. In 1556 work began on a cathedral in Ribeira Grande, though, like cathedrals elsewhere in the world, it took a 150 years before it was completed. The bishops, when they could be persuaded to take up their appointments in person, were in many respects agents of royal authority, administering the Crown's rights under the *padroado real*—the privileges granted to the kings of Portugal by papal bulls in the 1450s—which regulated the government of the Church in Portugal's half of the world.

A Misericórdia was also founded. This charitable brotherhood, which had been created under the patronage of Queen Leonor, the wife of D. João II, at the end of the fifteenth century, was a sign that Ribeira Grande was now recognised as fully part of the expanding realm of the Portuguese king. The Misericórdia performed a range of vital social services, and branches were set up wherever a major Portuguese settlement was established.

The first settlers from Europe had brought not only cattle, goats and horses, which were let loose to roam and multiply on the islands, but also a range of European fruits and sugar cane. During the first century of settlement horses were bred for export to West Africa, where they were highly valued for military purposes but also for the prestige that their ownership conferred. Apparently, even when horses died, as they rapidly did in the Guinea climate, their tails were kept as prestige symbols. Early English traders who visited the Guinea coast soon appreciated that horse tails were an item of commerce that was highly valued (Albuquerque and Madeira Santos 1991: I, 186–7; Hakluyt 1913: IV, 129).

Although in the early days some sugar was produced and orchilla lichen was exported to Castile, cotton was the only island product that was successfully exploited on a large scale. Cotton, which grew wild in some of the islands, was cultivated, particularly in Fogo, and was exported not only to Africa but also to Flanders. Between 1460, when the islands were officially discovered, and the early sixteenth century, it seems that the market for Cabo Verde cotton grew as the wearing of cotton clothing spread in Wolof society (Albuquerque and Madeira Santos 1991: I, 185). By the mid-century a weaving industry had been established in the islands, using traditional narrow African looms to produce indigo-dyed, patterned cloths, known as *panos*, which replicated the styles that were in demand in the African market.

Traders from the islands also bought cloth woven in the Casamance region of what is now Senegal to trade in other parts of Guinea where there was a market. In this way Cabo Verde traders took part in local exchange, their larger boats giving them an advantage over the local canoes, which had a much smaller capacity. Later this coastal trade came to include dye stuffs and kola nuts bought in the Sierra Leone region and sold further north. This local trade linked Cabo Verde traders with the *lançados* settled in the river ports and in turn aligned the economy of the islands with those of the African peoples of the Guinea region (Albuquerque and Madeira Santos 1991: I, 280–1).

Cotton apart, agricultural production in the islands was not able to expand due to the lack of rain. As wheat would not grow, African millet and rice were introduced, but these never produced enough to feed the population, and food had to be imported from mainland Africa to supply the growing island population. The only crop grown with some success was sugar, much of it made into rum for the African market.

In spite of the generally unfavourable geographical conditions, Santiago and Fogo began to prosper as the demand for slaves rose steeply in the early sixteenth century. Contemporary reports mention Ribeira Grande as one of the richest cities of the Portuguese kingdom. In 1549 the *contador* André Rodrigues had complained that the Portuguese Crown was not paying sufficient attention to developing the island (the first complaint of many that were to be made over the next centuries), and claimed with some exaggeration that "apart from Lisbon, there were not two cities in the kingdom that returned as much as [Ribeira Grande] because it was experiencing so much growth" (Albuquerque and Madeira Santos 1991: I, 138).

By the 1540s the population of Santiago had grown considerably. The anonymous pilot who wrote an account of Cabo Verde and São Tomé asserted that there were 500 Portuguese and Castilian households, suggesting a free population of between 3,000 and 4,000 (Anon 1960: 26). In 1572 an ecclesiastical census listed nine parishes on the island of Santiago with a total of 1,058 households and 2,239 people seeking confession (Albuquerque and Madeira Santos 1991: I, 141). It is clear from this census that there were now settlements throughout the island, including one where the city of Praia would eventually be built and one at Tarrafal, a coastal settlement and small port at the other end of the island, which was to become notorious in the twentieth century for its concentration camp. Ten years later another writer estimated the population of Santiago as 13,408 and that of Fogo as 2,300. A rough calculation also suggests that 55 per cent of the population of Santiago lived in the cities of Ribeira Grande and Praia (Albuquerque and Madeira Santos 1991: I, 232–6). However, these various estimates of the population are very uncertain and not always consistent—not least because it is usually unclear to what extent these are counts of free males only or whether they include women, children and slaves.

Sixteenth-Century Descriptions of Santiago and Fogo

When Santiago was described by the anonymous Portuguese pilot in the 1540s, his picture of general prosperity may reflect a period of unusually good rains.

This island is seventeen leagues long and has a city on the sea with a good harbour, called Ribeira Grande, because it is situated on two hills and through the middle runs a large river of fresh water which rises two leagues in the interior. From the start of the river to the city on both banks there are numerous gardens of orange trees, lemons, citrons, pomegranates and figs of all qualities and every few years they plant palms which produce coconuts, commonly called nuts of India. Here they also grow and cultivate perfectly all kinds of vegetables though the seeds they produce are not good to sow the next year and each year it is necessary to bring fresh ones from Spain.

This city is open to the south and has good houses of stone and mortar inhabited by numerous Portuguese and Castilian gentlemen (*cavalheiros*) amounting in all to 500 households. There is a royal *corregidor* there and each year they elect two justices. One of them deals with cases related to seamen and the sea and the other administers justice to the inhabitants of this and the neighbouring islands.

The whole of the land is mountainous and has many places that are rough and stripped of all trees. The valleys, however, are widely cultivated. When the sun enters into Cancer which is in the month of June, it rains almost continuously and the Portuguese call this time the moon [month] of waters. In the first days of August they begin to sow the grain which they call *milho zaburro* and which in the western isles [Azores] is called maize; white peas (*chícharo*) are common in all the above-mentioned islands and in the whole coast of Africa and with it all its inhabitants sustain themselves with only forty days between sowing and harvest. They also plant rice and cotton which grows very well, and after it has been collected they make with it various kinds of cloth striped with various colours which afterwards they sell throughout the African coast, that is in the land of the blacks, and in exchange they are given slaves. (Anon 1960: 25–7)

In the final years of the century, between 1586 and 1590, Gaspar Frutuoso, a Portuguese priest who had served for many years in the Azores, wrote an important description of the western Atlantic islands which he called *Saudades da terra* (Nostalgia for the land). He does not seem to have visited Cabo Verde, but he tried to describe the islands in detail, presumably from the accounts of those who had been there. Again the description is one of fertility and fruitfulness, another indication that, although the 1580s had seen a period of severe drought, the islands did not suffer from the desiccation of later years.

> The island of Santiago is the metropolis and headquarters of the bishopric of the islands of Cabo Verde ... [Ribeira Grande] is a city of two hundred *vizinhos* through the middle of which runs a river. The Bishop resides there ... The island of Santiago produces a lot of sugar from which they make very good conserves although not as good as those of Madeira, and it has many palm groves which produce coconuts. It also produces cotton which comes from trees as big as apple trees (*macieiras*) which produce bolls from which they obtain cotton when they open. These trees and their fruits continue three or four years after they are planted. They have many banana trees which produce the figs like cucumbers (*pepinos*), which are called bananas and which are like crooked green peppers. And when the figs or bananas are cut into slices, in each slice can be seen the figure of the crucifix or cross which leads the natives of the land and the residents to say that this is the forbidden fruit of paradise. Wheat does not grow in this land but there is much white millet and cobs and so plentiful that they load the ships for all destinations. There is also another, *milho miudo* [baby corn], plenty of *fruta de espinho* [pitaya or dragon's fruit] and other fruits, figs, melons and grapes which are found ripe all the year. (Frutuoso 1939: 117)

Fogo was described less often, but in 1566 George Fenner, who commanded three English trading ships, gave an account of a stop there which was included in Richard Hakluyt's *Voyages*. At this time English and French traders like Fenner routinely stopped at Madeira and the Canary Islands, where their trade and purchases of provisions were welcomed. Fenner then proceeded to the Cabo Verde region of the mainland, where three of his men were detained on shore by Africans in retaliation for earlier raids by slavers. Having failed to secure the release of his men, Fenner sailed for the Cabo Verde islands, where he hoped to be able to trade as he had at Madeira. He recorded that, after their poor reception in Santiago, they sailed on to Fogo and anchored by a "white chappell in the West end of the sayd iland". Eventually they moved to "within halfe a league of a little towne". He mentions the volcano and how "three yeeres past the whole Island was like to be burned with the abundance of fire that came out of it". The English found a spring of good water and obtained as much as they needed. The islanders had no wheat but grew millet from which they "maketh good breade ... Their merchandise is cotton which groweth there" (Hakluyt 1913: IV, 151).

The Other Islands

During much of the sixteenth century, only Santiago and Fogo had a permanent settled population. In the other islands, the right to deal in hides and tallow from the wild cattle and goats was granted to nobles or other favourites of the king. Sometimes an island would be granted by the Crown to a petitioner for a number of years. Those receiving the grants engaged contractors to hunt and slaughter the animals. The hides were sold especially to Castile and paid for the import of European foodstuffs (Albuquerque and Madeira Santos 1991: I, 190). This was a very prosperous trade. For example, in 1504 it was reported that 7,980 hides were exported from São Nicolau and São Vicente and 12,687 from Santo Antão (Albuquerque and Madeira Santos 1991: I, 211).

The trade involved cattlemen and slaves setting up temporary camps in the islands and ships calling to take away the hides and tallow. *Degredados* were sometimes sent as members of the parties that went to slaughter the livestock and prepare the hides for export. However, it does not seem that there were systematic attempts to establish permanent settlements in any of the islands except Santiago and Fogo.

Boa Vista was visited by George Fenner in 1566. Here he found "the Northside of the sayde Iland is full of white sandie hils and dales and somewhat high land". They cast anchor on the west side and, going ashore, "found five or six small houses, but the people were fled into the mountains". Next day they met two Portuguese "who were but poore & simple, and [Fenner] gave each of them a paire of shoes and so set them ashore again" (Hakluyt 1913: IV, 151).

In the 1540s the anonymous Portuguese pilot wrote of Sal: "It is uninhabited and barren and there are no animals there except wild goats … In all these islands of Cabo Verde, which are ten in number, the goats have three or four kids at a time and give birth every four months. These kids are very delicate to eat for they are fat and full of flavour, the goats often drinking the sea water."

> [The island] is low-lying and when there is a small storm the sea water rises up into some lakes and swampy places so that when the sun is in the tropic of Cancer and passes perpendicularly overhead, all this water congeals and forms the said salt. The same thing happens in all the islands of Cabo Verde and in some of the Canaries but much more in this one than the others and for this reason it is called Ilha do Sal, although Boa Vista also has it and not far from there Maio in which there is a lake more than two leagues long and as much wide, all full of salt congealed by the sun from which they can load a thousand ships. And it is common [free] to all who come there because it is just sea water. And although they [the islands] are subject to the king of Portugal nothing is paid for the export of this product. (Anon 1960: 19–20)

George Fenner also visited Sal and

> went ashore in the Baie to the houses where [they] found 12 Portugals. In all the Iland there were not above 30 persons, which were men banished for a time [*degredados*], some for more yeeres, some for lesse, and amongst them there was one simple man which was their captaine. They live upon goats flesh, cocks, hennes and fresh water; other victuals they have none, saving fish which they esteeme not, neither have they any boats to take them. They reported that this Iland was given by the King of Portugall to one of his gentlemen, who hath let it foorth to rent for one hundreth dukats a yeere, which rent is reared only in goats skinne. For by their speaches there hath bene sent foorth of the sayd Iland into Portugall 40,000 skins in one yeere. (Hakluyt 1913: IV, 147)

Fenner reported that the English were made welcome and were offered as much goat's meat as they wanted, the islanders "bringing them from the mountains upon their asses". He went on to say that "they have great store of the oyle of Tortoises [turtles]" and that he was told that cattle had been introduced "but by reason of the heate and drought they have died".

Brava was first granted to a New Christian, Francisco de Fonseca, in 1509 and produced cattle and cotton for export, but in 1545 the island was transferred to a member of the royal council after members of the Fonseca family were found to be practising Jews (Green 2012: 136). According to George Fenner, it had "good store of goates and many trees, but there are not passing three or foure persons dwelling in it" (Hakluyt 1913: IV, 151). Because it had no population Brava was increasingly visited by English ships in search of water. In 1578, at the beginning of his famous circumnavigation, Drake stopped in the Cabo Verde islands, where, having seized the ship in which Nuno da Silva was the pilot, he called at Brava and "being there they filled certaine vessels with fresh water" and left the crew of Silva's ship (Hakluyt 1913: VIII, 75).

Santo Antão, the second-largest island after Santiago, was still uninhabited when it was granted in 1548 under terms which made it a donatary captaincy, but there was little sign that the captain ever exploited his concession and the island remained virtually uninhabited until the following century (Carreira 1982: 20). According to the Azorean priest Gaspar Frutuoso, Santo Antão "is very lush, has a lot of water and fruit and cattle … the *senhor* [of the island] is a *fidalgo* from Evora called Gonçalo de Sousa" (Frutuoso 1939: 117, 118).

São Vicente, the Azorean priest reported, is larger than the island of Faial [in the Azores] and belongs to the count of Portalegre, the king's *mordomo-mor* (chief steward). "In this island are many white crows and numerous doves and many green lizards which eat them … Many goats breed there." São Nicolau "is large and very high and also belongs to the count of Portalegre. A lot of goats and cattle are bred there and it has many orange and citron trees and many thickets of strange trees [*arvoredos estrangeiros*] and has a lot of ambergris. These islands are all healthy and grow all the fruits and vegetables that you can get in Portugal. Horses, mules and asses are bred there."

He concludes in a moralistic vein by saying that the islands are "very healthy for those who regulate their eating and drinking but the lustful die from infection of the blood" (Frutuoso 1939: 117–19).

In 1582 it was recorded that there was a church in each of the islands and a priest would be sent annually by the bishop to minister to the few people resident there, though the islands were still for the most part uninhabited.

São Tomé and Príncipe

While the Cabo Verde islands developed as a base for supplying ships on long-distance voyages and prospered through their trade with western Africa, their society developing a marked creole identity, Portuguese settlements had also been established in the Guinea islands on the equator. As even fewer people came forward as settlers than had volunteered for the Cabo Verde islands, the captains sought to boost the population by encouraging the settlement of New Christians and even unconverted Jews. At first the prospects for the Guinea islands did not look good, but two factors worked to turn their fortunes round. The first was the rapid growth of Portuguese trade in the Gulf of Guinea region, with the royal fort at Elmina and the official Portuguese embassies to the Kongo king giving the region a very high priority in the royal councils. São Tomé became an important port of call for royal ships sailing to and from these destinations and a centre for regional commercial activity. Diogo Cão is known to have stopped at the islands, and Duarte Pacheco Pereira, the author of *Esmeraldo de situ orbis*, took refuge on Príncipe after having suffered shipwreck near the island. Boats were built in the islands to be employed in coastal shipping, making use of the fine tropical hardwoods in the island forests.

The second factor that gave a huge boost to island settlement was the discovery that the climate was ideal for the growing of sugar. Soon sugar growers from Madeira, who had been disappointed in their efforts to grow the cane in Cabo Verde, were marking out sugar plantations and setting up mills (*engenhos*) in the lowland region of São Tomé.

In 1509 Valentim Fernandes published a long and rambling account of São Tomé which he had compiled from the reports of Gonçalo Pires, "a mariner who went to this and other islands many times". This account was accompanied by a series of sketch maps of the Guinea and Cabo Verde islands. Too long to reproduce in full, this early account of São Tomé is rich in detail. It was Pires who provided the information that 2,000 Jewish children of eight years or younger were sent to the island, "of whom many died so that at present only 600 both male and female are alive". The two-thirds who died within a short time of arrival were probably victims of the tropical climate, which proved lethal for people from Europe with no immunity to Africa's diseases. The island captain, he says, "married them but the only marriages that produced offspring were the marriages between white females and black men and black females and white men" (Baião 1940: 122).

It is difficult to assess this information. Certainly, 2,000 children seems a very high number, and 600 survivors in 1506 would mean that the island was relatively well populated. The implication that these young Jewish exiles, male and female, were provided with black partners, presumably slaves, with whom to mate again seems to challenge probability. This is the only mention of women being provided with male slaves for this purpose.

Pires says that the captain, Álvaro de Caminha, built a fortified tower in which he lived with his wife and children. Was this a European wife brought out to São Tomé by her husband? He also had two churches built. The main island settlement had a population of 200 (no mention of the 600 children), who were mostly convicts whose death sentences had been commuted, and he says that each *degredado* was given a male or female slave "*pera sua ajuda e servijço*" (for their help and service). Many of them now had as many as fourteen slaves, who grew yams and millet for them. He then goes on to say that the island had 2,000 slaves who worked the land, apart from the 5,000 or 6,000 slaves who were sold on. Again, these figures seem carelessly exaggerated.

Cattle were brought from Cabo Verde and grew very large, as did sheep, pigs and goats. Horses on the other hand lived only for one year. Rats, he says, grow as big as rabbits and are eaten there. A lot of

Pires's account describes the birds, animals and plants of the island, but he is especially impressed by the great trees and mentions one which it took fifteen men to cut down and from which planks 25 palms wide were made and used to build two caravels for trading to Guinea. These trees were no doubt the giant okoumés.

Pires also describes the island of Ano Bom, which he says was settled in 1503 and in 1506 had nine inhabitants. The Portuguese had also let pigs and goats roam wild on this island. About this island he tells a very interesting story. When the Portuguese first arrived they found one African living there. He was the only survivor of a group of three men who had been fishing off the African coast when they were blown out to sea by a storm. They lived four years on the island, during which time two of them died. The survivor had lived there for three years until the Portuguese boat arrived and he was rescued. What is significant about this story is that it seems quite possible that Africans from the mainland could have reached the islands before the arrival of the Portuguese (Baião 1940: 129).

In other respects São Tomé grew in parallel with Cabo Verde. In 1522 an investigation by the Crown into the conduct of the donatary captain resulted in his donation being cancelled and royal government instituted. São Tomé's main town and seaport was granted city status in 1525 and the diocese of São Tomé was created in 1534, only a year after that of Cabo Verde. From the first, the town council (*senado da câmara*) was dominated by the great landowners, and as there were frequently long periods when there was no governor, the *câmara* became in effect the government of the islands. From that time, there were frequent conflicts between the governors, the *câmara* and the bishops, although the last-mentioned seldom came to the islands to take charge of their dioceses. Again, these conflicts reflected similar confrontations in Cabo Verde, where the interests of the landowners and the Crown frequently clashed.

By the 1530s sugar production was well under way, and shipping from Europe regularly called at the island, bringing much-needed supplies and taking away the sugar. In 1555 there were reported to be sixty to eighty *engenhos*, and 2,150 tons of sugar were being produced. Twenty ships a year carried sugar to Antwerp (Garfield 1971: 52).

The anonymous Portuguese pilot gave a detailed account of São Tomé, Príncipe and Ano Bom, which he said he had visited five times since 1520. Ano Bom, he says, was famous for its fisheries, and the inhabitants of São Tomé went there for fish, but "there are an infinite number of crocodiles and poisonous snakes" (Anon 1960: 50). São Tomé was covered with trees when first discovered and many of these had now been felled to build the main town, which went simply by the name of Povoação (Settlement). The town was made up of between 600 and 700 houses—which made it larger than Ribeira Grande—and had a *corregidor* who was responsible for royal justice. The inhabitants were mostly merchants; among them were Portuguese, Genoese, French and Castilians and all "were accepted with good will" (Anon 1960: 51).

The inhabitants were mostly involved in the manufacture of sugar and imported all that they required "because they are not accustomed to the food of the blacks" (Anon 1960: 53). There were sixty cane-crushing mills already in the island, powered by water, though where there was a lack of water the machinery was operated either by hand or by horses.

The pilot describes how during the hottest times of the year four or five families came to take a meal together and shared the burden of food preparation. Fever was common and the first onset was very often fatal. It was treated by bleeding followed by a regimen of soup, salt and chicken flesh. Venereal disease and scabies were also common and were treated in the African manner, but he says the black women are not concerned about it and have medicines to treat it. However, they do not escape fever. Few Europeans lived beyond the age of 50, and "it is seldom one sees a man with a white beard". However, the Africans, he thinks, live to be over 100.

As in Cabo Verde, this account shows a creole society in the process of formation around the interlocking lives of slaves and slave owners. The slave owners brought their European foods and clothes, technology and buildings but adapted these to the climate, and adapted also to the black women with whom they formed partnerships, and whose medical skills were employed to deal with fevers and other complaints.

THE SETTLEMENT OF THE CABO VERDE AND GUINEA ISLANDS

Like Cabo Verde, the Guinea islands lay close to the African mainland, and in spite of attempts by the Crown to impose its control over the activities of the islanders, there was soon a flourishing contraband trade with various mainland communities. Like the traders of Cabo Verde who settled on the mainland to form the nuclei of creole communities of *lançados*, the São Tomé islanders were also establishing a creole presence at various points on the mainland.

In one other respect the development of São Tomé and Príncipe resembled that of Santiago and Fogo. Settlers from Europe were mostly male traders and sugar growers. There were few European women, workmen or artisans. This element of the population had to be supplied by importing slaves from the African mainland, with the result that by the second generation there was a class of people of mixed race, who soon became numerically the largest element of the population (Caldeira 1999).

The Creole Islands under Threat

In 1521 the Cabo Verde islands found themselves caught up in the growing dispute between Portugal and Spain over the Moluccas in the Far East. Ferdinand Magellan's fleet had set out in 1519 to discover a western route to the spice islands and in the process found a sea passage through what became known as the Magellan Strait. After armed clashes in the Philippines that resulted in the death of Magellan, and the failure to find a viable route back across the Pacific, a single ship, captained by Sebastián del Cano, headed home for Spain round the Cape of Good Hope. Desperately short of supplies, the ship, the *Vitoria*, stopped at the Cabo Verde islands to get food and water. There sixteen of the crew were arrested by the Portuguese on suspicion that they had infringed the Portuguese king's monopoly in the Moluccas. With half his crew in Portuguese custody, del Cano had to make his way back to Seville with his ship only manned by sixteen survivors. The release of the captives in Cabo Verde became one of the issues in the negotiations between Portugal and Spain that arose from this famous voyage, and led eventually to the Treaty of Saragossa in 1529.

Although during the early part of the sixteenth century the Cabo Verde and Guinea islands prospered, this prosperity was not securely based. The barren Cabo Verde islands found it difficult to provide food and water to the fleets bound for India and Brazil, and by the middle of the sixteenth century the India fleets began to call at ports on the Guinea coast rather than at the islands. After 1530 there are virtually no records at all of ships bound for India calling at Cabo Verde (Hall 2019: 32; Albuquerque and Madeira Santos 1991: I, 317).

By this time, the islands were coming increasingly under attack, and the Portuguese seem to have been slow to take any serious measures to protect the island communities. In front of Ribeira Grande lay an open roadstead that led immediately to the town square and to streets and churches built along the river towards the interior. In São Tomé the plantations also backed on to an open roadstead, although the captain, Álvaro de Caminha, had built a defensive "tower" where he resided with his family. In São Tomé the Portuguese began the construction of a fortress in 1566, named after the king D.Sebastião, but no such fortifications were built at Cabo Verde. The undefended towns were an open invitation for pirates, and in the 1540s an increasing number of attacks were launched first by the French and then by the English on Portuguese shipping and then on the island towns themselves.

However, the French and English who appeared in the islands and off the Guinea coast were not all pirates bent on plunder. They were also carrying on clandestine trade in contravention of the monopoly claimed by the Portuguese king, and their growing trade would be one of the causes of the long-term commercial decline of Ribeira Grande. For example, in 1542 a French ship was reported to have taken on a cargo of cotton from Fogo for sale in Flanders (Albuquerque and Madeira Santos 1991: II, 129). Clandestine traders and corsairs would also call secretly at one of the islands for water or provisions—as in 1553, when the *Primrose* and the *Lion* "arrived at the Iland of St Nicholas, where they victualled themselves with fresh meat, of the flesh of wild goats whereof is great plenty in that Iland, & in manner of nothing else" (Hakluyt 1913: IV, 40).

These English traders were not welcome. When in 1566 George Fenner visited Ribeira Grande, where he hoped to trade, "we saw a faire road, and a small towne by the water side, and also a fort or platforme by it". There they were not made welcome, and after guns were fired on them they sailed a few miles further along the coast to a bay where they found "two or three small houses". There the English were met by a large troop of horsemen who urged them to come ashore to trade. Meanwhile, a bit further along there was "a towne behinde a point fast by the sea side [presumably Praia]", where there were caravels and brigantines. The Portuguese then mounted a night attack on the English ships, which only escaped by cutting their anchor cables (Hakluyt 1913: IV, 149–51).

The English were also trading in slaves in defiance of another monopoly claimed by the Portuguese Crown. The three slaving voyages of John Hawkins between 1562 and 1569 are the best known, but there were others. On some of these voyages there were Portuguese pilots and crew members, as many skilled Portuguese seamen and navigators took well-paid positions serving rival monarchs. Often these were New Christians: such was António Eanes Pinteado from Porto, "a wise, discreet and sober man ... being as well an expert Pilot as a politike captaine" (Hakluyt 1913: IV, 39). If Portuguese pilots were to be found working for the English and French, the *lançados* of the Guinea coast, mostly Portuguese in origin, were also now acting as commercial agents for the foreign traders, advising on the trade goods and commercial practices along the coast.

The monopolistic policy pursued by the Portuguese Crown also contributed to the decline of the commerce of Santiago and Fogo. The Crown increasingly leased out the collection of customs dues and other Crown revenues while at the same time granting the Crown's trading privileges to contractors and awarding captaincies over the other islands to courtiers and favourites. As a result there were a number of people, all with concessions from the Crown, competing for commercial advantage in the islands. This policy of trying to abstract revenue from the islands in whatever way possible was to be the mark of official Portuguese policy towards Cabo Verde well into the eighteenth and even nineteenth centuries. The confusion only served to promote the practice of bypassing the islands altogether, with traders of all nations trading directly with the ports on the Guinea coast (Albuquerque and Madeira Santos 1991: I, 340–5).

Although pirate attacks had not been coordinated and had not received official backing from either the French or English monarchs, the situation changed radically when Philip II of Spain inherited the Portuguese Crown in 1580 and established the headquarters of his naval operations in Lisbon. Philip was engaged in a prolonged war against Dutch rebels, who were supported by the English. Portuguese overseas possessions were now seen as legitimate military targets, and increasingly attacks were mounted by English corsairs on the Atlantic possessions of Portugal, which proved to be almost undefended targets.

Another result of the union of the crowns of Portugal and Spain was that ships from the breakaway Netherlands provinces were no longer able to load salt from the salt pans in Aveiro in Portugal. They now began to visit the islands of Maio and Sal in search of salt cargoes. This was seen by the Portuguese as a major threat, and in the early seventeenth century the Spanish Crown even proposed that an expedition should be sent to destroy the salt lakes on Maio (Albuquerque and Madeira Santos 1991: II, 164–5).

Between 1583 and 1585 the Cabo Verde islands were at the centre of the growing conflict between Spain and the supporters of the Portuguese pretender Dom António, prior of Crato. In 1583 a fleet of ten ships manned by French and dissident Portuguese and commanded by Manuel Serradas reached Santiago. The islanders refused to recognise Dom António, and in the ensuing engagement Manuel Serradas's forces captured and held Ribeira Grande, which they plundered before going on to Fogo. In order to avoid the fate of Ribeira Grande, the inhabitants of Fogo welcomed Serradas and declared for Dom António. Serradas was joined by English corsairs, but another attack on Santiago was a failure and the attackers retired. Fogo was subsequently forced to submit to Philip, and its inhabitants were eventually pardoned (Albuquerque and Madeira Santos 1991: II, 154–6).

Two years later, on 11 November 1585, Francis Drake mounted a major assault on the virtually undefended Ribeira Grande. Drake's men captured the town and plundered it of anything of value. The inhabitants all escaped inland, and Drake marched into the interior hoping to capture the governor and hold him to ransom. He burned the village of São Domingos and then returned to attack the town of Praia a short distance from Ribeira Grande. By 28 November Drake had completed his plunder of the island and left for the Caribbean.

As a result of this experience Philip II authorised the construction of a major fortress at Ribeira Grande, which was laid out on the hillside above the city and is still preserved as a major attraction for tourists. This, however, did not stop the attacks. In 1596 Sir Anthony Sherley commanded a fleet of eleven ships which set out to attack São Tomé. They did not reach that island but instead landed at Praia, "being a very pretie towne, having a small fort in it, with 6 or 7 cast pieces". Finding nothing there, Sherley set out with 280 men from the fleet to march overland to Ribeira Grande. The Portuguese of the island now rallied to resist. "The countrey then being all spred over with people made shew of feare only to draw us into the town … The gentlemen would come galloping by us and viewing us very much … The strength and situation of the towne was sufficient to have daunted a man of very good courage." Sherley nevertheless fought his way into the town, which he occupied for two days. There he was trapped and surrounded by 3,000 men, suffered heavy losses, and eventually escaped in the boats sent from the fleet to rescue him. "So we in a souldierlike order with very good safety departed the towne."

Sherley's fleet went on to Fogo, which he described as "invincible by nature, high cliffed round about, yet by diligent search we found a small path where wee landed our men with exceeding difficulty, and so were masters of the Isle … One night we had a showre of ashes which fell so thicke into our ships from that burning hill of Fuego, that you might write your name with your finger upon the upper decke" (Hakluyt 1913: VII, 213–17).

In 1598 the Dutch attacked Praia and spent ten days marauding around Santiago, taking anything they could (Carreira 2000: 326). However, the English and Dutch were attacking a town whose prosperity was already in steep decline. Although trade with the Guinea coast continued, the slave trade was now increasingly focused on Angola, where the Portuguese had occupied Luanda in 1575 and begun the construction of a city. Over the following thirty years the transatlantic slave trade moved increasingly from Guinea to the coast of Angola, and by the early seventeenth century Cabo Verde was being sidelined in this lucrative Atlantic commerce.

The prosperity of São Tomé began to decline at the same time. With the opening up of settlements in Brazil, many sugar producers relocated from the tiny Guinea islands to the vast expanses of coastal Brazil. This exodus was encouraged by Dutch raids on the island and by increased maroon activity, culminating in the uprising headed by Rei Amador in the 1590s.

As the fortunes of Cabo Verde and São Tomé inexorably declined, so the islands lost their population of European origin, and the local elites, who held the land and filled the public offices, were increasingly made up of the creolised population of free blacks and *mestiços*.

3

THE SLAVE TRADE AND THE FORMATION OF AN ATLANTIC CULTURE

Overview

From the middle of the fifteenth century, the western regions of sub-Saharan Africa played an increasingly important part in the growing commercial world of the Atlantic and until at least the middle of the eighteenth century, the trade in slaves was the principal way in which African societies interacted with the other Atlantic traders. This chapter will look at the part this trade played in creating a distinct South Atlantic creole culture, in which the Cabo Verde islands were deeply embedded. The trade in slaves was a forced migration and became one of the largest and most important migratory movements of the early modern era, only surpassed in the nineteenth century by the mass migrations from Europe itself to the New World and the Pacific.

That this migration had important consequences for both the recipient destinations and the points of departure has given rise to a range of interpretations which place it at the forefront of any understanding of the modern world. To see the trade in slaves essentially as a form of migration offers an angle of interpretation seldom adopted but enables it to be viewed in the wider context of the study of other migrations.

The Early Slave Trade in Sub-Saharan West Africa

By the fifteenth century, the trade in slaves from western Africa to the Mediterranean via the Sahara was already centuries old, as was the slave trade internal to Africa itself. It is impossible to guess the numbers involved in the trans-Saharan slave trade or their impact, because these slaves were only a small part of a much wider trade in slaves from other regions. During the Middle Ages, Christian Europeans enslaved Muslim North Africans, and Muslim North Africans raided European coasts and enslaved European Christians. Slaves also came from the eastern Mediterranean, the Black Sea regions and the Caucasus. The Vikings took many slaves on their raids in Russia and northern Europe, as did the Mongols, whose armies invaded Europe in the thirteenth century.

In the fourteenth century there was a particularly active slave market in Italy, where wealthy Italian families bought slaves as domestic servants. In Florence it was female slaves that fetched the highest prices, with pale-skinned slaves being preferred to dark-skinned Africans. As the Black Death and the subsequent outbreaks of plague led to a sharp decline in Europe's population, slaves became increasingly needed for field labour, while the expansion of sugar production, pioneered by the Genoese in the fourteenth century, meant that slave labour was required in the cane fields in ever greater quantities (Newitt 2023: 106; Tognetti 2005). In North Africa slaves were also widely employed as soldiers.

The market for slaves was already well established in the early fifteenth century, when Portuguese corsairs operating out of Ceuta and the Madeira islands began to bring back slaves captured or traded on the African coast. Numbers remained small until 1444, when a large consignment of African slaves was put on sale in Lagos, an event recorded in some detail by the Portuguese chronicler Zurara. Thereafter, Portuguese slave imports increased, and a total of 50,000 slaves may have been traded from sub-Saharan Africa by the end of the century, most of them being brought to Europe.

As Portuguese influence spread in southern Morocco, the flow of Moorish slaves also increased, and in the early sixteenth century very large numbers were being sold in Europe, in particular women and girls. Vincent Cornell has suggested that during the famine years of the 1520s, as many as 60,000 women and girls from Morocco were sold in the slave markets of southern Spain (Newitt 2023: 206; Cornell 1990).

African slaves accompanied many of the Portuguese trading and exploratory voyages, principal among them being African interpreters. These were men who had been brought to Portugal as slaves. Having learned the Portuguese language, they were sent on board the caravels to interpret for the crews. According to Cadamosto, this was an opportunity for them to earn their freedom: "each interpreter who secured four slaves for his master was to be given his freedom" (Crone 1937: 55). Sometimes slave women fulfilled these tasks, and Bartolomeu Dias had four women slaves with him in 1487 to facilitate contacts with mainland peoples.

What is striking about the early history of the slave trade is the ease with which the Portuguese were able to buy slaves and how cheap they were to purchase. According to António Carreira, the earliest records mention anything up to twenty or thirty slaves being exchanged for one horse (Carreira 2000: 93). This exchange of horses for slaves was already well established when the Portuguese arrived, with horses being brought across the Sahara from North Africa. The horses were highly valued for military purposes but were also esteemed by the rich and powerful as status symbols. Even if a horse died, as many did within a short time of arrival, their tails were often kept as items conferring status. After about 1500 the average price of a slave rose by 50 per cent as the demand from the Americas forced up the price. Even so, between six and ten slaves could still be obtained for a single horse, and there is little indication that there was any shortage of slaves in the market (Albuquerque and Madeira Santos 1991: I, 271). By this time horses were being bred in large numbers in Santiago and had become a staple of the trade of the islands.

Why African societies were prepared to sell slaves so cheaply and in such numbers to Europeans, who, some believed, were cannibals, is hard to know, especially since, as Toby Green observed, "African societies exported large numbers of enslaved captives, whose labour was therefore both lost to the continent and gained by the European empires" (Green 2019: 14).

Slaves were not only cheap to buy but were sometimes given as gifts. Having sold the horses he brought with him, Cadamosto was invited to travel to the residence of a local ruler. "I decided to go with him, but before I left he gave me a handsome negress, twelve years of age, saying that he gave her to me for the service of my chamber. I accepted her and sent her to the ship" (Crone 1937: 36). And there are other examples (Crone 1937: 96).

In the light of the extremely low price asked for slaves, it seems probable that, in the early days, the African slave trade was partly driven by the supply side. There was no shortage of slaves and they were sold very cheaply by the African rulers and merchants. To this there were, of course, exceptions. Cadamosto records that when he visited the Gambia river, he received a very hostile reception. Inquiring after the reason for this, he was told by a local African spokesman "that they did not want our friendship on any terms ... for they believed that we Christians ate human flesh" (Crone 1937: 60).

The societies in western Europe, the Mediterranean and sub-Saharan Africa which made use of slave labour all had laws or customary practices which to some extent mitigated the lot of the slave and made provision for them to be integrated into society. Most had laws against the enslavement of co-religionists, though these may not have been very strictly observed, and most recognised manumission as an act of charity. In Muslim countries and in Africa, female slaves could be integrated into a lineage as junior wives. However, in Africa, even if individuals were often able to escape the most severe aspects of slavery, the status of slave often continued to mark a slave's descendants for generations after the original act of enslavement.

The Atlantic Slave Trade Grows

From the 1440s onwards trade with West Africa was operated as a Portuguese royal monopoly, and slaves, along with other products, were imported by individual ships' captains who sailed to Africa equipped with a royal licence to trade.

When the settlement of the Cabo Verde islands began, ships were able to make the short journey from the islands to the Guinea coast, cutting out the long journey to and from Portugal, Madeira or the Azores. In 1466 the settlers on Santiago were granted exemption from having to obtain a royal licence to trade, though they still had to pay the tax on slaves imported into the islands. From that time the slave trade between the African mainland and the islands grew rapidly, the slaves traded on the coast being either retained in the islands or re-exported to Europe.

During the hundred years after 1460 the island of Santiago was to be at the centre of the Atlantic slave trade. At first the Portuguese Crown tried to insist that all slaves were sent to Portugal, though after 1500 this regulation was increasingly evaded as traders sought markets nearer at hand and tried to avoid paying royal taxes. Slaves were purchased at interior fairs or river ports from the Senegal down to Sierra Leone, including the Rio São Domingos, the Rio Grande and the Gambia. Traders brought raw cotton which grew in the islands, cloth and metalware from Europe, including the brass *manilhas* and barber's basins that feature so often in accounts of the trade, but the most valuable item of trade remained horses.

For most of this period slaves were purchased from African rulers and lineage heads. In the region of Senegal inhabited by the Wolof, slaves were usually obtained in exchange for horses. South of the Gambia river, horses did not survive and trade here focused on brass *manilhas* and iron bars, which were used as a form of currency and whose value reflected the shortage of these raw materials in the region. As trade grew, the demands of the market changed. It was found that trade in local African products like *buzios* (currency shells), *cori* beads and bark cloth was also important. Later in the sixteenth century the Portuguese also became active in the trade in kola nuts, and cotton cloth woven in the islands was added to the trading goods on offer. The cloth was woven, probably by slaves, on traditional narrow West African looms and incorporated traditional designs using thread coloured by the local indigo, which was also an item of commerce. Salt from the salt lakes in Sal and Maio was also traded to Guinea.

As well as slaves, the Cabo Verde islanders bought malagueta pepper and food, especially millet and rice, and there was also a specialist market in carved ivory objects made by African craftsmen, which were a luxury product sent to Lisbon. Gold was also traded, especially after the building of the royal trading factory at Elmina in 1482.

The Slave Trade to the New World

From the time of Columbus's first voyage to the Caribbean, the slave trade became an important part of the Spanish enterprise. At first it was native American slaves that were captured and brought back to Spain, but as the Spanish conquests in the New World proceeded and the native American population rapidly died out, African slaves were in demand for a range of occupations, from agricultural labour and work in the mines to providing soldiers for the campaigns of conquest. Slaves were also employed as replacement crews when the fleets from India and Brazil called at Ribeira Grande to land the sick and take on provisions before completing their voyages to Lisbon. It was the Cabo Verde islands that were able to supply these markets.

The Spanish and Portuguese monarchies tried to control each end of the trade with the object of taxing it. The Portuguese Crown insisted that all slaves should pass through the customs house in Santiago, while the Spanish insisted that import licences had to be obtained to bring slaves to the New World. The Portuguese tax on all cargoes imported from West Africa, including slaves, was 25 per cent, with an additional 5 per cent levied for the Order of Christ, which had responsibility for financing the Church. Initially these taxes were collected by Crown officials, but in 1504 D. Manuel initiated the practice of contracting with individuals (called *rendeiros*) who paid the Crown a lump sum to undertake the profitable responsibility of collecting this tax and all the other taxes on property and sales in the islands. Ships returning to Europe paid 10 per cent on their cargoes, though the Spanish were usually required to pay more than the Portuguese.

However, although both the Portuguese and Spanish monarchies expanded their administrative machinery in their efforts to keep control of the trade, the early modern European state did not have the capacity to control the market in migrant labour, which is beyond even the twenty-first-century state to regulate.

Already by 1500 a large clandestine slave trade was under way, operated by ship owners in the Cabo Verde and Guinea islands. This was facilitated by the agents of the islanders—the so-called *lançados*—who were resident on the African mainland and who were increasingly embedded in coastal society. The *lançados* were effectively beyond the reach of Portuguese officialdom, as long as they did not return to the islands. Moreover, as the reach of royal government was limited to the main towns on Santiago and Fogo, with no officials elsewhere on either island and no settlements at all on the other eight islands, it was not difficult for the contraband trade to flourish.

The rise of the contraband trade was given an added boost by the arrival, after 1506, of large numbers of New Christians and Jews fleeing the persecutions and increasingly hostile environment in the Iberian peninsula (Green 2012: 134). At first the Portuguese authorities allowed the settlement of these refugees because they helped to increase the population of the islands, but the experience of persecution led many of the new arrivals to try to move beyond the reach of royal government by joining unofficial communities of *lançados* in the Guinea rivers area. In this way they helped to initiate a new phase of the Portuguese diaspora, the "unofficial" Portuguese communities beyond the reach of any royal authority, of the kind that later became so important in Asia.

The New Christians soon became deeply involved in the slave trade and brought to it their commercial expertise and the trade networks which had been so important to their survival and prosperity in the Mediterranean in the Middle Ages. It was New Christians who increasingly became the brokers in the clandestine trade with the New World, and the transatlantic networks on which that trade depended were also largely operated by Jews and New Christians.

The importance of New Christian immigrants in the growth of the clandestine slave trade is reflected in the series of decrees issued by D. Manuel's government in the second decade of the century. By these, the king attempted to stop the immigration of New Christians and to control the numbers leaving the islands to settle as *lançados* on the mainland, while at the same time reissuing orders that all slaves should first be sent to Portugal. At the same time the king also tried to stop the export of hides to Castile (Albuquerque and Madeira Santos 1991: I, 190). None of these decrees had any effect at all.

The incentives to evade paying taxes through the clandestine trade networks were large. The voyage to the New World from the Cabo Verde islands took only a month compared with the two-month voyage back to Europe, and the slaves were paid for in gold. At first slaves were sent to Hispaniola, but it soon became necessary for traders who wished to avoid the Spanish licensing and tax system to use other ports, and towards the end of the century Cartagena became a favoured destination.

By the middle of the second decade of the sixteenth century, there were two parallel trades that were well established: an official trade operated with licences from the Portuguese and Spanish crowns, which duly paid royal taxes at the ports of entry and exit, and a clandestine trade that sought to evade the system of licences and taxes altogether. How the official trade was conducted at the end of the sixteenth century was explained by Francesco Carletti.

> One cannot capture Moors, or blacks, of Africa or any other region of Guinea in order to transport them to the Spaniards' places unless one first has purchased licences from the Royal Chamber or from those who have them under lease or have been presented with them by the King. These licences are of two kinds. The first is known as "of liberty", the other as "of the fourth". We bought eighty of the former sort at twenty-five scudos each in money of account. And by each of those licences we had the right to remove one slave from Cape Verde ... and to transport the slave freely, without paying any other fee to the Crown of Castile except a few tiny payments in India [the Indies]. But this did not absolve us from paying the fee owed for those slaves to the

commercial contractors dependent on the Crown of Portugal ... And if the licences are of the other sort, called "of the fourth", which cost less by half than those "of liberty", then one must after reaching India give the King as a customs duty a fourth part of the slaves that one brings there. (Carletti 1964: 10–11)

The volume of the official trade can be roughly calculated and seems to have run at between 1,000 and 2,000 a year, much in line with the trade in the previous century. The customs receipts for the years 1513–16 list a total of 3,166 slaves (Hall 2019: 2), but Toby Green has argued that the level of the clandestine trade must at the very least have doubled this figure, so that between 4,000 and 5,000 slaves a year would have been traded from the Guinea coast. And this would have been on top of the well-established trans-Saharan trade and the internal slave trade.

It is not clear if Green's calculations include the slaves exported from the Guinea islands because there was also an important trade based in São Tomé. In 1509 Valentim Fernandes's account claimed that 5,000 slaves were being held in the islands for the overseas trade. Although São Tomé imported large numbers of slaves to work in its sugar plantations, the islands were also a depot for the transatlantic trade. It is known that 61 ships sailed from São Tomé in the years between 1514 and 1600, 34 in the decade of the 1580s, and a surprising 17 ships sailing in the years 1580–1. In all, in the 131 years between 1514 and 1645, 91 slave ships left São Tomé (Trans-Atlantic Slave Trade Database n.d.).

The Role of Santiago in the Slave Trade

A large part of the prosperity of Santiago, and its principal port town of Ribeira Grande, was based on the slave trade. It was the profits to be derived from this trade rather than income from the entailed estates that was the real attraction for the upper-class Portuguese and Castilians who settled in the island. In the early sixteenth century there was a large mercantile community investing in trading voyages to Guinea, where there were agents who contracted for the slaves with African rulers. The customs returns show that this was a complex system. Numerous individuals invested in each voyage and made small purchases of slaves. For example, when the *Santa Catarina* returned from West Africa in June 1513, the *rendeiro* who fitted out the ship brought four slaves, the ship's captain brought five slaves, the scribe (who kept the ship's log and record of trading) brought two "and retained one as his helper", the pilot brought two slaves, two investors received four and three slaves each, a free black agent brought two, two more investors received one slave each, a trader who had travelled on the ship also brought one "small male child", and another five slaves were delivered to investors, one of whom was the *almoxarife* or customs officer (Hall 2019: 46–8). Trevor Hall has estimated that the customs registers for the years 1513 to 1516 list a total 1,000 individuals involved in the maritime trade of Santiago, though not all these were trading slaves, as there was also a considerable trade in hides back to Europe.

The small scale of individual mercantile activity—numerous individuals importing one, two or three slaves at a time—reminds one of the debate over Indian Ocean trade and the contention that this was essentially trade carried on by small operators or pedlars rather than large investors backed by substantial capital, which only developed with the appearance of the Dutch and English charter companies in the seventeenth century.

Numerous different people were involved in the trade. At the African end, taxes had to be paid to the African rulers at the various river ports and fairs where the trade was conducted. There were also *lançado* agents from whom the slaves were obtained. Many of these had married into the lineages of local rulers or mercantile families and used their position to access slaves either directly through raiding or through purchase in a trading system that had flourished long before the Portuguese arrived and that extended far into the interior. On the ships were the agents of the investors. Sometimes trusted slaves performed this role, and there were African interpreters who were also slaves. There even appear to have been some black African ships' captains, though these were probably not slaves but from the free black population in Cabo Verde (Hall 2019: 19).

On returning to Santiago the slaves would be registered and taxed, the tax often taking the form of 10 per cent of the number of slaves imported. Santiago was used as a holding area for slaves brought from Africa before they were sent on to the New World. The slaves were taken to estates away from the coast with the objective of allowing them to acquire the rudiments of the creole language and a familiarity with Cabo Verdean customs and practices, which greatly enhanced their value in the eyes of traders assembling cargoes for the New World. This process was known as *ladinização*. Large numbers of slaves might be held in this way. António Carreira gives as an example the accounts of the contractor João Soeiro, which recorded that between 1609 and 1613 he imported 1,468 slaves from West Africa but sent 6,642 to various destinations in Spain and the New World (Carreira 2000: 145).

In the 1590s the Florentine merchant Francesco Carletti gave a detailed account of how the trade in the island of Santiago was conducted.

> I was in charge of these slaves and I ordered that one Moor be the head of each ten of them, selecting from among them one who seemed to me more high-spirited and intelligent, so that he might take care of what I would provide for their needs, food in particular. This was given them twice a day, being a certain sort of fat beans that grow there, which they cook simply with water and then flavour with a little oil and salt. And thus, until such time as they would be embarked, they were kept entirely separated in two rooms, the men in one and the women in the other, naked and without clothing, they being content with the skin that Nature had given them and hiding only—by means of a small piece of leather or other skin or rag or tree leaves— that part of the body which Original Sin has made seem more shameful than the other parts. (Carletti 1964: 14)

He then went on to describe the elaborate way some male slaves decorated their penises. The male slaves were placed "below decks, packed next to one another in such a narrow space that when they wanted to turn from one side to the other they scarcely could do so". The females were allowed to remain on deck in the open. On the voyage the slaves were fed with millet and "for breakfast, each of them was given a handful of seeds resembling aniseed in its unripe state". He then admits that a number of his slaves died on the voyage "of a flux of the blood caused by eating certain fish badly cooked or almost raw" (Carletti 1964: 15–17).

By the time Carletti wrote his account in the early seventeenth century, Santiago had ceased to be a principal centre for the slave trade. By that time the trade had switched to Angola and it was largely from Angola that the *asientistas*, who held the contract for supplying Spanish America, obtained their slaves.

Slaves in the Settlement of Cabo Verde

Not all the slaves brought to the Cabo Verde islands in the sixteenth century were shipped to the New World. Some were retained to help with the early colonisation of Santiago and Fogo. The slaves imported assumed a number of different roles. Many were employed as labourers on the estates of the European settlers and helped to establish a typical plantation slavery. Others were employed in the settler households in a variety of occupations, from domestic and artisan work to becoming sexual partners in a society where there were few women of European origin. As we have seen, by the early sixteenth century there were men of slave origin serving on board trading ships, while others became interpreters (*linguas*) and agents in the commercial transactions of the mainland. There were even recorded cases of slaves buying and owning slaves on their own account (Albuquerque and Madeira Santos 1991: I, 268).

The lives of slaves are seldom described in any detail, but Francesco Carletti, in his account of his stay in Santiago in the 1590s, records some details of slavery in the islands. He describes how in one of the houses "their slaves, entirely naked, stand at the head and foot of their table with candles in hand while the masters eat and talk, thus serving as candelabra and valued no less than if they were silver". He also describes fishing and how the fish they catch quickly become rotten "in such a way that they no longer are good for anything except to be given to the black slaves, who eat them as gladly as we eat fresh ones" (Carletti 1964: 7).

Slavery in São Tomé was described by the anonymous pilot in the 1540s. "They [the Portuguese] all have slaves, some as many as 300 who work for their masters six days in the week and grow food for themselves on the seventh day." He was particularly impressed by the cheapness of slave labour, as the slaves fed themselves, made their own huts and did not even need clothes, as they wore only a small strip of cotton or palm mats round their waist (Anon 1960: 60). He explained how the Africans built huts with platforms forming a sort of second storey, which raised them above the area infested by mosquitoes.

Samuel Purchas gives an account of the voyage of Abraham Cocke to the Rio de la Plata in 1589, a typical piratical voyage which nevertheless includes an unusual episode that throws some light on the life of slaves in São Tomé.

> Being in distress for wood and water we went in on the south end betweene San Tome, and the Iland das Rolas ... thinking to have watered but wee found none in the Iland. Heere we had great store of Plantans and Oranges. We found a village of Negroes which are sent from San Tome, for the Portugals of San Tome do use, when their slaves be sicke or weake, to send them thither to gain strength againe for the Ilands are very fruitful; and though there be no fresh water, yet they maintaine themselves with the wine of the Palme trees. Having refreshed ourselves with the fruit of this Iland, we burned the Village. And running on the East side of San Tome, we came before the Towne, but durst not come neere: for this Castle shot at us which have very good Ordnance in it. (Purchas 1905: VI, 368)

The manumission of slaves was a common practice in Portuguese society in the sixteenth century. Slaves of Muslims and other free Africans were allowed to buy their liberty, and this privilege was often extended to the slaves of Christians as well. Some slaves were freed on the death of their owner and others as acts of charity. It is impossible to say how many were freed in this way, but there was a steady process by which slaves and former slaves merged with the poor but free black population. This process was to continue in the seventeenth and eighteenth centuries as it became increasingly common for slaves to escape from their masters and take refuge with the free black population in the remoter rural areas. In this way, although slaves continued to be brought to the islands until shortly before the final end of slavery in the nineteenth century, Cabo Verdean society lost much of its character as a slave-owning society. Slaves became numerically a smaller and smaller proportion of the population, and their way of life was little different from that of the rural poor in general. Cabo Verde had in effect emancipated itself from the inheritance of slavery long before the formal end of the institution.

It is clear that, from early in the sixteenth century, some slaves took the opportunity to free themselves by escaping into the mountains. By mid-century maroon communities existed in Santiago and Fogo, the maroons scratching a living in the arid mountain soils and carrying out raids on the plantations and even the towns. The communities of escaped slaves established in the interior of Santiago were joined by many of the *forros* (free black people) and formed an alternative rural society to that which developed on the plantations and in the seaports.

In São Tomé there were similar escapes from the sugar plantations, but there the maroons provided a formidable threat to the plantations. The first slave revolt is recorded in 1517, and in 1535 the justices in São Tomé wrote to the Crown, "it is true and well known that a *mocambo* [a maroon community] with a large population exists in the forest and they do what damage they can, killing and robbing men and destroying plantations, all of which brings loss and damage to the people of this island and its settlers and a disservice to the king our lord and much loss to his treasury ... We have armed men ready to go against the said escaped blacks and the fortified *mocambo*, but we do not have any money" (Newitt 2010: 64).

There was a slave revolt in 1574, and in 1595 a major insurrection led by a man who went under the name of Amador (later remembered as Rei Amador, or King Amador) placed the survival of the entire Portuguese community in danger. At its height a slave army said to number 5,000 men attacked the main town of São Tomé (Ambrosio 1970: 241, 245–8). Amador was later adopted in the 1970s as the legendary founding father of the newly independent São Tomé republic.

The maroons in São Tomé eventually reached some kind of accommodation with the authorities and acquired over time their own identity, becoming known in the nineteenth and twentieth centuries as Angolares. They survived and even prospered modestly in the west of the island and spoke a creole dialect of their own (Seibert 2007; Caldeira 1999: 93–4).

Ladinização and the Control of the Slave Trade in the Seventeenth Century

During the sixteenth century the slave trade had been the most important commercial activity of the Cabo Verde islands, and in the middle years of the century the islands had been the principal suppliers of slaves to the New World. The slaves were obtained from a range of sources, from the Senegal river south to Sierra Leone. However, in the seventeenth century the Cabo Verde slave trade went into steep decline. In the years 1600–10 there were twenty-one slave ships leaving the islands, in the next decade the number was only nine, and in subsequent decades up to 1690 there were only twenty-six ships recorded, barely one ship every three years (Trans-Atlantic Slave Trade Database n.d.).

The conflict over control of the trade now assumed an unexpected character. In the early days of island settlement there had been little missionary work and the Order of Christ had controlled the ecclesiastical affairs of the overseas territories, but on the accession of D. Manuel in 1495 the Order of Christ was finally added to the patrimony of the Crown. With the creation of bishoprics in Santiago and São Tomé, the Crown began to build a religious infrastructure which in many respects became a form of social control. By the end of the century the spiritual welfare of the free population was cared for by a structure of parishes, and the religious orthodoxy of the population was scrutinised by occasional visits from agents of the Inquisition. This social control was now to be extended over the slave population as well.

The first royal orders for the baptism of all slaves had been issued as early as 1514 (Carreira 2000: 261), but presumably these had little effect and it was only when the Catholic missionary orders began to become more active in the early seventeenth century that the baptism of slaves sent to Brazil became a serious issue and one that was to be strongly contested. The Church, through the missionary priests, maintained that all slaves should be catechised and baptised before being sent to Brazil. Baptising slaves involved a minimum of instruction in Christianity, and the missionary orders demanded that this should be undertaken by the owners of the properties where the slaves were kept prior to sailing for the New World. The plantation owners protested that it was impossible to instruct Africans who could not speak Portuguese, complained about the shortage of priests, and pointed out that keeping slaves in numbers on the plantations while they were catechised invited violence, slave protests and insurrections.

The slave traders were intent on shipping their slave cargoes as soon as possible, and maintained that the slaves should be formally baptised at the port of departure in Guinea. This was frequently done through a process of mass baptism and without any instruction at all, but the Crown preferred that all slaves should be brought to the islands, ostensibly for instruction and baptism to take place but also to enable the payment of taxes to be enforced. Landing slaves in the islands had the additional advantage that the slaves would acquire a knowledge of the creole language or even Portuguese, along with their baptism, and this process of *ladinização* (literally, latinisation) would greatly increase their value. This process, by which slaves in Cabo Verde were catechised and baptised, and thereby brought nominally into the Christian community, helped to spread the use of the creole language in the islands, thereby promoting the emergence of a distinct Cabo Verdean creole identity.

The Crown also continued to be concerned with the issue of manumission and in 1607 ordered that all slaves should be freed after a certain number of years and that slaves who wished to marry free blacks (Carreira 2000: 263, 279–80) should be allowed to purchase their freedom. By the end of the seventeenth century the Crown was trying to extend its authority still further through a raft of decrees which aspired to regulate the trade, specifying the numbers that each ship could carry, ordering that there should be a priest on board every ship, and laying down feeding standards (Carreira 2000: 268–72).

The debate over the baptism of slaves and the decrees purporting to regulate the trade can be represented as a prolonged duel between Crown, settlers and contractors, but it is also an indication that the morality of the trade was beginning to be seriously questioned. Even if no one was yet actually advocating abolition, at least some concern was being shown at the highest level.

The result of this conflict was that fewer and fewer slaves were brought to the islands, and more and more slave ships leaving the African coast bypassed the islands entirely. Throughout the seventeenth century there were endless debates about how to revive the commercial fortunes of Santiago. As the Crown was unwilling to allow the islanders to trade freely with foreign ships, the only proposal under consideration was to try to restore Santiago's position in the slave trade by requiring all slaving ships to call to pay dues. But this was never likely to succeed, as the direct routes between West Africa and the New World markets were now well established and in any case the vast majority of slaves were now leaving Angola for the New World (Pereira 1964: 42–4).

Without the profits of the slave trade, commerce between the islands and West Africa went into decline. The import trade in rice and millet and the export of woven cloths and rum were not enough to sustain the Cabo Verde islands' mercantile prosperity.

Creole Influence and the Slave Trade in the West African Kingdoms

The first records that exist of Portuguese trade with the Senegambia region describe Portuguese caravels sailing up the tidal reaches of the Senegal and Gambia rivers to trading towns fifty miles or more into the interior. There they would soon have been aware that other traders, especially Muslim Mandinka, were coming to these fairs and that the presence of foreign merchants was not only accepted by the local African communities but was even institutionalised. The merchants would give presents to the rulers and would settle in the community for a greater or lesser length of time. They would take wives (and no doubt beget children), and in many cases these would be from locally important lineages.

It was not long before Portuguese *lançados* were following the example of Mandinka merchants and settling more or less permanently in and around the trading towns. At first it seems it was the *degredados*, convicts sent to the islands to serve their sentences, who saw settlement on the mainland as a kind of freedom. Later their number was swollen by New Christians who saw the African mainland as a place where Judaism could be practised safely. However, it is clear that settlement among the peoples of the land involved adopting not only the trading practices of their hosts but many of their religious ideas and practices. Toby Green has suggested that New Christians had been accustomed in Portugal to living with dual identities and adopting the religious practices of the majority population in order to survive. This tolerance of religious syncretism served them well in Africa, where the wearing of amulets and the honouring of spirit shrines no doubt did not compromise their beliefs too much. For trade to succeed there had to be trust between partners, and "bonds of trust were easier to create in an environment where people belonged to the same religion, practised the same rituals and believed in the same divine powers" (Green 2012: 145, 223).

The Cabo Verdean trader André Donelha tells a story which gives some idea of the complexities of the relationships that surrounded trade in the Guinea rivers and the multiple identities that participants assumed in order to be successful.

> I met a black Mandinga youth, by name Gaspar Vaz, who was a slave on this island of a neighbour of mine in São Pedro, a tailor called Francisco Vaz. The black was a good tailor and buttonmaker. As soon as he knew that I was in the port he came to see me ... He embraced me, saying that he could not believe it was me he saw, and that God had brought me there so that he could do me some service. For this I gave him thanks, saying I was very pleased to see him too, so that I could give him news of his master and mistress and acquaintances, but that I was distressed to see him dressed in a Mandinga smock, with amulets of his fetishes (gods) around his neck, to which he replied: Sir, I wear this dress because I am nephew of Sandequil, lord of this town,

whom the *tangomaos* [*lançados*] call duke because he is the person (who commands) after the king. On the death of Sandequil, my uncle, I will be inheritor of all his goods, and for this reason I dress in the clothes that Your Honour sees, but I do not believe in the Law of Mohammed. (Donelha 1977: 149)

This story of a slave being freed and returning to his country of origin, preparing to inherit power and status, maintaining good relations with his former master and willing to juggle with different religious identities, tells us a lot about slavery, the slave trade and the flexible semi-creolised identities in the trading communities of Guinea.

By the mid-sixteenth century, a hundred years of *lançado* activity on the mainland had given rise to Afro-Portuguese families that spoke the creole tongue, bore the Portuguese names of their fathers or grandfathers, but otherwise resembled the rest of the local population and largely followed their customs and way of life. However, there were a few cultural markers that continued to distinguish them from the local population—among these were the custom of building rectangular houses after the Portuguese fashion (Mark 2002) and the wearing of European-style clothes. However, it is perhaps significant that the *lançados* did not introduce any European technologies to Africa nor did they organise plantations, possibly because the domestic economy of the region was dominated by the women and their lineages, to whose "way of doing things" the *lançados* had to adapt.

For their part the rulers and merchant elite of the coastal states welcomed the strangers, through whom exotic imports—cloth, metalware and horses in particular—could be obtained. Increasingly there were also visits from Portuguese ships bound for the New World or returning from the East. Rare and valuable Indian textiles and other Eastern luxuries were added to the items of trade. André Donelha records: "I once found myself in the port of Guinala [on the Rio Grande] with eight ships from this island, and more than ten belonging to *tangomaos* [*lançados*], and two ships registered for the Indies; and each year there were taken from this river to (Santiago) and to the Indies, nearly three thousand blacks" (1977: 177).

To maintain the flow of imported goods, the supply of slaves had to continue. Few African rulers were able to stand aside from this gradual incorporation of themselves and their people into the Atlantic commercial world. The small lineage-based political units of the forest regions, with their varied dialects and shifting ethnic identities (Green and Chabal 2016: 19–36), were constantly in conflict with each other, and the Portuguese found that their presence was welcomed as it provided the rulers of these small units with valuable imported wares and with equally valuable assistance in their conflicts. The price for these alliances was the continued supply of slaves.

As African societies became partners in a rapidly growing transatlantic economic exchange, they struggled to maintain their autonomy and to control the market forces that soon exerted major pressures on the small-scale economies and social and political organisations of the forest regions. These societies had, for centuries, been vulnerable to their Muslim neighbours in the interior and to the north. Now they sought allies in the new strangers who arrived by sea with important goods to trade, but these allies brought with them demands that were hard to meet. The small lineage-based societies were trapped between the demands of traditional enemies and treacherous new friends.

Although gold and ivory were in high demand by the Europeans, the forest regions of Guinea could not supply these commodities in large quantities, and the manufacture of local cloth and ironware took place on too small a scale. Trade meant the slave trade or nothing. It is here that can be seen the unequal terms of trade between the relatively technologically advanced Europeans and small African communities without the resources to trade with the Europeans in any other commodity than slaves.

On the Gold Coast things were different. The trade in gold for a long time prevented the slave trade from gaining a large hold in the region, though it appears that, even though slaves were not exported, the African states of this stretch of the West African coast imported slaves for their own use, and these were supplied by obliging Portuguese traders.

António Carreira, in his major work on the formation of the slave society of Cabo Verde, examined the question of how the supply of slaves was maintained. He emphasised the way in which African individuals "were entirely 'tied' to the social structures and, within them, to a whole complex set of subjections to the practices of each class, to the ceremonies and the rites of passage, all of which imposed on him a total subordination to tradition and obedience to rituals with a stamp of authentic passivity" (Carreira 2000: 85). And they were also subject to supernatural sanctions "far more serious to him than slavery itself".

Carreira went on to list the ways in which Africans were enslaved, basing his analysis on contemporary accounts. Among these were kidnapping by force or fraud; seizing women, children and relatives because a member of the family was guilty of some offence; being captured in war; the sale of children by their parents; communities contacting the spirit of a dead man to identify the family of his killer; enslaving women for offences committed by men already slaves; compensation for the loss of something; adultery; and committing some ritual offence (Carreira 2000: 85–9).

What contemporaries emphasised was that slaves were obtained primarily through judicial processes (Green 2012: 244). This suggests ancient practice, which the growing demand for slaves made increasingly fraudulent. Fraudulent or not, enslavement continued to maintain the forms of judicial procedure. The Portuguese, of course, tended to downplay their own participation in the acquisition of slaves, but nevertheless it is clear that it was the structures, institutions and judicial processes of African society, stretched and distorted as they were, which remained the principal means by which slaves were obtained.

Technology and the Slave Trade

Although most European, North African and Middle Eastern countries bought slaves and employed slave labour, there was an increasing tendency, especially noticeable from the twelfth century onwards, towards the development of machine-based technology that contributed to reducing the reliance on slave labour within the economy. This was not reflected in developments south of the

Sahara, and by 1500 a considerable gap had opened up between the technologies employed in Eurasia and those in sub-Saharan Africa.

By 1500, when parts of sub-Saharan Africa were about to become partially integrated into the global economy, societies in Europe and Asia had already acquired quite sophisticated machine-based technologies. Waterwheels powered saws, hammers, fulling machines and the milling of grain; windmills pumped water and ground wheat; gears and cranks had been invented; and there were rotary wine presses operated by animal power. Spinning wheels had eliminated the "bottleneck" in the production of yarn for weaving; pottery was made using mechanised wheels; wheeled vehicles of all kinds supplemented human porters and pack animals in transport, and wheeled ploughs were widely used in cultivation; cranes and pulleys were employed in construction; shipbuilding had become more elaborate and produced vessels that had already crossed the Atlantic, while models of ship design, originating in the Indian Ocean, had produced the caravel, which was opening up sea navigation to the New World and to Asia. Deep sea navigators employed the compass and instruments for determining latitude; elaborate mechanical clocks were beginning to be used; and the printing press was poised to make mass literacy a possibility. The manufacture of firearms was transforming warfare and, with it, the whole political configuration of Eurasia and the New World.

None of this technology was in use in sub-Saharan Africa. There has been very little study of the way this technological difference impacted on relations between Africa and the non-African world, but as sub-Saharan Africa's relations with the Atlantic world were for some centuries primarily economic, the disparities in the technologies that underpinned the different economies would inevitably work to Africa's disadvantage.

The significance of the technological gap that had opened up between Eurasia and sub-Saharan Africa is a complex topic. It can be argued convincingly that African societies had developed the know-how and the technologies that they required to meet their own needs. Their expert woodworkers, metalworkers, goldsmiths, weavers and potters produced the goods that their societies wanted. They therefore had no need of different technologies. Technology is not just a catalogue of tools or techniques; it has to be seen as a whole system that involves ideas, social institutions and complex economic interactions. New technologies, if adopted, would have had profound implications at every level of society.

However, if African societies were not to be torn apart, social and political organisations would have to adapt to the new world of Atlantic commerce. There was a need for new technologies of production, exchange and defence. As Toby Green points out, the small polities did adapt by increasing their agricultural productivity "and the labour systems used for cultivation" (2012: 109). However, this increased food production was achieved through traditional agricultural methods and did not lead to "broader growth" in their economy comparable to the impact which increased agricultural yields had in preparing the way for industrialisation in Europe.

Although the Atlantic trade involved a wide range of products, Africa's dependence on the export of slaves in order to participate in the Atlantic economy was in part the result of its inability in the first 400 years of contact with the Atlantic world to produce any other commodity in sufficient quantity to meet the demands of the market. African weaving and metallurgy, although often of high quality, could not compete in the market because it could not produce goods in large enough quantities. Nor did any African society at this period develop a plantation economy to supply the growing world market with tobacco, cotton and sugar. There was no "technological revolution", and as sub-Saharan peoples were exposed more and more to trade with the Atlantic world, so they became ever more dependent on the export of slaves.

The Kongo Kingdom

The story of the Kongo kingdom and its relations with Portugal is the story of what happened to a large African kingdom that was gradually drawn into the expanding Atlantic economy and that experienced the deep penetration of Atlantic creole culture. In the 1480s São Tomé and Cabo Verde were struggling communities whose captains were finding difficulty in attracting permanent settlers, but in that decade the Portuguese Crown made important moves to take direct control of the developing trade of the African coast. In 1482, following the Treaty of Alcaçovas, they had built the royal fort and trading factory at Elmina, which was to secure a monopoly of the gold trade. Then an official expedition was sent out under Diogo Cão to explore the African coast beyond the point reached by Fernão Gomes's captains in the 1470s. Cão reached the mouth of the Zaire river and established contact with the Kongo kingdom, sending a delegation to the capital. He took hostages to secure their safe return, and in 1484 he was sent out again by the Portuguese king. This time he explored a hundred miles up the Zaire river and went in person to the Kongo capital. Sailing further down the coast, he died without having found the route round the end of Africa, which he had rashly proclaimed in 1484.

In 1487 D. João II dispatched another exploratory voyage down the African coast under Bartolomeu Dias, and, while waiting for Dias to return, he sent a large embassy to Kongo to make an alliance that would establish the king of Portugal's primacy in that part of the West African coast. The Kongo kingdom was probably the largest that the Portuguese had yet had contact with in Africa, and D. João was determined to open up trade and build an alliance, keeping the whole operation firmly in royal hands.

In 1491 a large embassy was sent to the Kongo with soldiers, mission priests and a royal trading factor. The embassy was more successful than the king could have imagined. First, the ruler of the Soyo province and then the Kongo king himself and a large section of the ruling lineages of the kingdom welcomed the Portuguese and saw in Christianity a way of strengthening royal control over the other religious cults of the kingdom. The result was the adoption of Christianity as the official royal cult. The backing of the Portuguese enabled the new cult to take root, as it brought wealth and prestige through trade and the lavish gifts of European luxuries that accompanied baptism. The Kongo king and the heads of the Mwissicongo elites took European names and titles, and began to wear European clothes. Younger members of the elite families were sent to Portugal for education.

The Christianity that was adopted in Kongo was, from the start, deeply influenced by African ideas of the spirit world, but as the cult was supported by Portuguese priests and the entourage of the Portuguese ambassadorial mission, it took on a hybrid cultural form—a unique creole identity, distinct from that evolving in São Tomé and Cabo Verde and tied closely to royal policy administered from Lisbon. Early in the relationship the Portuguese were able to intervene when the succession to the throne was contested. Portuguese backing given to the Christian claimant, Afonso, proved to be decisive, and the whole episode was recorded as a reiteration of the conversion of the Roman emperor Constantine.

The price that the king of Kongo had to pay for this support was set in terms of trade with the Portuguese. The Portuguese were anxious to obtain the bark cloth for which the region was famous, as well as the *cori* beads and *nzimbu* shells which were used as currency in much of West Africa, and, of course, they were looking to purchase slaves. The Kongolese found that they had to provide increasing numbers of slaves in order to secure continuing Portuguese support.

By the 1520s, when large numbers of slaves were leaving the Kongo, the king protested against this to the king of Portugal. The latter replied at length, refusing to accept that the slave trade was depopulating the kingdom and stating that the alternative was to end all commerce between Portugal and the Kongo kingdom (Newitt 2010: 151–3). The Portuguese in Kongo had meanwhile settled inside their own walled quarter in the capital. Large stone buildings had been constructed, including a cathedral, and many Portuguese were to be found in the kingdom trading and carrying out various official functions.

The process of creolisation proceeded rapidly among the Kongo elite, but it was very different from that in Guinea or the islands. The political structure of the kingdom remained in African hands, in marked contrast to the European-dominated plantation societies of the islands. Nor was there anything comparable in Guinea to the wholesale adoption in Kongo of Christianity as a royal cult. At best in Guinea, some individuals adopted Christianity but there were no whole kingdoms where it became the official religion.

There was a certain tension between the Kongo Portuguese and the settlers in São Tomé, who were officially excluded from trade with the kingdom. Many of the islanders started a contraband trade with outlying areas of the Kongo kingdom where royal control was weak enough to allow it to develop. Moreover, there were occasions of outright confrontation when São Tomé islanders detained Kongolese on their way to Portugal. When the diocese of São Tomé was established in 1534, its jurisdiction included that of the Kongo kingdom, creating another area of tension and conflict between the island and the mainland.

In Portugal great importance continued to be attached to the alliance with the Christian king of Kongo. Members of the Kongolese leading families were to be found receiving education in Portugal. Some acquired entry to the orders of knights, and the Portuguese king persuaded the Vatican to appoint one of the sons of the Kongo king as a bishop *in partibus*. Later there were to be embassies sent by the Kongo kings not only to Portugal but also to the Vatican.

Then, in 1568, the Kongo kingdom was invaded by outsiders described by the Portuguese as Jaga, who defeated the Kongo king's army and forced him and his nobles into exile in the island of São Tomé, while the Jaga plundered the kingdom. In São Tomé the Portuguese assembled an army and in 1571 were able to restore the king to his throne, though very much on Portuguese terms. Portuguese influence now became dominant in the kingdom, which continued as a major supplier of slaves for the transatlantic trade (Newitt 2010: 162–5).

Yet, although the Kongolese elite adopted many aspects of Portuguese culture, including the Christian cult, it does not seem that this "creolisation" penetrated very far into the rest of the population, and no Portuguese-Kongolese creole language developed. Although the kingdom was very large and comparatively well organised, the kings were not able to control the slave trade, presumably because there were too many interests, both Portuguese and African, determined that it should continue, and the kings had become too dependent on Portuguese support to do anything to limit its destructive effects.

The Kingdom of Angola

At first, spreading Christianity does not appear to have been of paramount importance for the Portuguese who settled on the mainland. Many of them were New Christians or Jews, and there is no record of any priests or missionary friars accompanying the *lançados*. However, missionary priests did form part of the embassy to the Kongo, and concern for religion showed itself in the moves made by the Crown to reassert royal authority in the islands—notably measures against New Christians and the establishment of bishoprics in Cabo Verde and São Tomé. However, it was the founding of the Jesuits in 1540 that was to stimulate a much more active Christianising policy in all areas of Portuguese activity. Not only did the Jesuits pursue their own energetic mission but this activity stimulated a response from the orders of friars, the Franciscans, Dominicans and Augustinians.

Following the death of D. João III in 1557, the Jesuits became the dominant influence at the Portuguese court during the minority of the new king, D. Sebastião. Following the deaths of their charismatic leaders, Ignatius Loyola in 1556 and Francis Xavier in 1552, the Jesuits planned missions to both East and West Africa. The missions of Gonçalo da Silveira to East Africa and of Francisco Gouveia to the region south of the Kongo kingdom departed in 1561. Silveira was martyred in 1563 and Gouveia was detained as a prisoner in Ndongo. This prompted the decision to send military expeditions to conquer African territory for the Portuguese Crown, something that hitherto the kings of Portugal had never done.

There were, of course, economic considerations too. As the Spanish began to exploit the silver mines in Potosí and New Spain, the Portuguese came to believe that Africa also had its gold and silver mines which were there for the taking. It was an illusion but nonetheless powerful for that. An army set off for East Africa in 1569 under a former viceroy of India. By 1571 it was poised to enter the Zambezi valley and conquer the gold and silver mines believed to lie in the interior. The same year the Crown decided on the conquest of the Ndongo kingdom and, to achieve this end, turned to the old practice of granting the right of conquest and settlement to a donatary captain. The contract was an elaborate one binding the captain to build forts, establish settlements and invest in establishing a local economy. The grantee was Paulo Dias de Novais, the grandson of Bartolomeu Dias, who had been the first navigator to round the end of Africa but had been the victim of the Crown's displeasure for his failure to reach India. His family now restored to favour, Paulo Dias set off to claim his captaincy in 1575.

Paulo Dias' first move was to found the city of Luanda on the coast south of the Cuanza river, where there was already a well-established *nzimbu* shell fishery. It was an area claimed by the kings of Kongo, and from the start there was potential for conflict between the king with his Portuguese backers and the new captain with the settlers he was contracted to bring. Dias also began the conquest of the Cuanza valley but had made little progress towards achieving his objective by the time of his death in 1589. However, in the long history of western Africa, Dias' captaincy was of great significance. As a result of his efforts a Portuguese city had been founded on the coast of West Africa defended by a fort like Elmina. However, while Elmina had remained merely a trading post, Luanda was to be the capital of a new kingdom of the Portuguese Crown, the kingdom of Angola.

Gradually soldiers, settlers, traders and missionaries arrived and the peopling of the city began. Although some white female *degredadas* were among the early settlers, for the most part the settlement was made up of single males, as had been the case in Cabo Verde and São Tomé, and, like the settlers in the islands, the Portuguese in Luanda formed partnerships with African women. Within a short time a mixed-race population began to be formed and, as had happened in the islands, this population tended to become more African in appearance as the generations proceeded. A creole population, comparable to the islanders and the *lançado* populations of the Guinea rivers, became the main operators in the expansion of the Angolan slave trade.

Outside the city and in the lower reaches of the Cuanza valley, the African population came under permanent Portuguese control, their *sobas* (chiefs) paying an annual tribute to Luanda. They provided labour services and became part of the semi-creolised community that was forming in the city.

By the time of Dias' death little progress had been made in finding, let alone conquering, any silver mines. The trade in *nzimbu* shells hardly proved an adequate economic base, but the trade in slaves was rapidly expanding and proving extremely profitable. The wars waged by Dias with his African enemies began to generate large numbers of captives, and this commodity greatly expanded after his death when the Crown appointed a captain to run the colony on a three-year contract. Angola rapidly turned into a slave-trading kingdom complementary to the sugar economy that was emerging on the other side of the world in Brazil.

Unlike Cabo Verde and São Tomé, where the creole society was formed from a coming together of people of African, New Christian and Portuguese origin, there was another factor at play in the formation of the Angolan creole society. From the start the settlement had close ties with Brazil, to which its slaves were sent. By the early seventeenth century ships were arriving directly from Brazil and, with them, Brazilian soldiers and traders. Later there would be captains appointed who were Brazilian. The Angolan creole culture was from the start largely an extension of Brazil, rather than Portugal, into Africa.

As Marianna Candido has emphasised, the creolisation process in Angola affected not only Africans and people of mixed race but also the Portuguese and Brazilians who came to Africa. This new Angolan polity, which in 1617 extended its reach south to Benguela, from where it could penetrate the southern highlands, soon became not only a major military power in the region, reducing many African societies to client status, but the most important base for the expanding commerce with the Atlantic world. Through the creole-controlled ports of Angola, imports from Europe, India and the Americas were taken by creole *pombeiros* to inland fairs, where they were exchanged for slaves. The importance of this trade attracted a wide range of African participants and opened trade routes deep into the interior. It helped to determine the evolution of African kingdoms extending as far as the upper Zambezi, whose social and economic structure became organised to serve the Atlantic trade (Candido 2013: 139).

The elites of some African societies in the region adopted aspects of creole culture, importing European weapons and consumer goods and even adopting Christianity, European dress and European names. If the most striking example of this partial creolisation had been the kingdom of Kongo, there were also examples among the minor rulers in Angola, where, for example, Queen Njinga, famous for her resistance to the Portuguese, was a baptised Christian and had a Portuguese as well as an African name (Heywood and Thornton 2007: ch. 4).

Conclusion: Africa and the Atlantic Trade

Atlantic trade profoundly affected African societies, but in different ways: imported firearms and horses influenced warfare, state formation and the acquisition of slaves for export; the bronze casters of Benin and the ivory carvers of Sierra Leone responded artistically to new ideas and new markets; while traditional honey hunters turned to the large-scale production of beeswax for the Atlantic market (Mark 2014; Gemery and Hogendorn 1978; Tuck 2012). New World food crops were widely adopted in Africa, contributing to population growth, which to some extent mitigated the losses due to the slave trade. In central Angola, "daily activities and the lifestyle of populations located far from the coast changed, reflecting the widespread consumption of imported goods" (Candido 2013: 190). Yet creolisation did not result in any significant transfer of technology. The wheel-based technologies of contemporary Europe were not adopted (Law 1980), possibly owing to the importance African elites attached to wealth in people, including slaves, which tended to delay or even prevent the adoption of new technologies. As a result the economic gap between Africa and the rest of the world inexorably widened—and over the *longue durée* this became the story of Africa's underdevelopment.

4

THE CREOLE ISLANDS: THE UNCERTAIN YEARS

Overview

In 1580 the creole islands, Santiago and Fogo in the Cabo Verde group and São Tomé and Príncipe in the Guinea islands, were still relatively prosperous. From Cabo Verde slaves were shipped in considerable numbers to the New World, while the customs revenues from trade with Guinea provided the Crown with a significant revenue stream, whether they were collected by an *almoxarife* appointed by the Crown or farmed out to a contractor—a way of handling the royal monopolies that was becoming increasingly common throughout the Portuguese maritime empire. Meanwhile, the other eight islands of the Cabo Verde archipelago were granted to persons close to the king, like the count of Portalegre, to draw from them what profit they could—mostly through the exploitation of wild cattle and goats.

São Tomé and Príncipe were still exporting large quantities of sugar from plantations (known as *roças*) worked by slave labour. This was the basis for a considerable trade with the countries of the Gulf of Guinea and the regions south of the Zaire.

By 1620 all this had changed. During these years, the king of Spain had successfully established himself as king of Portugal, and the Portuguese Atlantic islands had increasingly become the target of attacks by Spain's enemies. The most memorable of these was Drake's plundering of Ribeira Grande in 1585, but there were many others. While English, French and Dutch traders and corsairs were diverting much of the trade of the Guinea regions away from Portugal, the Portuguese settlements in Brazil were rapidly expanding. The hesitant early days when the Brazilian coast had been divided between twelve donatary captaincies, only four of which had succeeded in planting settlements, were now over. Large plantations were being laid out along the tropical northern coast and slaves were being imported by the thousand. These slaves were mostly coming from Angola and Kongo, and not any longer from the creole islands, and it was to Brazil and Angola, not the islands, that merchants from Portugal headed to trade within the Portuguese Atlantic economy.

The decline of São Tomé was even more marked than that of Cabo Verde. The islands had suffered attacks from the Dutch and the devastation of the maroon uprising of Rei Amador in the 1590s. Most of the sugar planters had moved to Brazil to benefit from the expanses of virgin sugar-growing land and more secure conditions. As the sugar economy of São Tomé experienced rapid decline, a new creole community of planters and slaves began to be formed on the other side of the Atlantic.

For two centuries the creole islands largely disappeared from the radar of history. The Cabo Verde islands continued to be visited by some long-distance sailing ships and increasingly by English traders seeking cargoes of salt for the Newfoundland fisheries, but the monopolistic regulations of the Portuguese Crown curtailed the trade that could be legally conducted in the islands. São Tomé briefly passed under Dutch control. The Dutch West India Company captured the sugar-growing regions of Brazil in 1630 and followed this with the seizure of Angola and São Tomé in 1641. Although the Portuguese rapidly re-established control, the economy of the islands, which did not lie along the main shipping routes, never recovered its old prosperity.

Unwilling to relinquish the islands but finding that their economies brought little reward, the Portuguese Crown transferred Cabo Verde and the control of what was left of the Guinea trade to a commercial company in 1676, the Company of Cacheu, Rivers and Commerce of Guinea, which held it until 1690, when it was replaced by the Company of Cabo Verde and Cacheu. The Crown eventually resumed direct control of the islands but tried again to experiment with a monopoly company in 1755 when the newly formed Maranhão and Pará Company was allowed to collect what revenues it could extract from the small island economies (Amaral 1964: 183).

This long period of two centuries, when the two groups of creole islands ceased to have any importance in the world economy and were almost totally forgotten, was nevertheless a period when the creole identity of their inhabitants strengthened and matured. Largely cut off from influences from Europe and separated by the sea from mainland Africa, the islands developed a kind of cultural independence which protected them from many forms of colonial exploitation and from the conflicts within Africa. This was also the period when all the islands of the Cabo Verde archipelago were at last settled on a permanent basis and when the legacy of plantation slavery gradually gave way to the establishment of communities of free people.

The period of economic decline lasted until at least 1830, when Portugal and the Portuguese maritime empire underwent revolutionary change leading to the establishment of what has been described as the Third Portuguese Empire. Arising out of this period of turmoil, both groups of creole islands experienced an unexpected economic revival.

Although during these two centuries the importance of the islands in Atlantic commerce declined almost to the point of vanishing, there is a surprising amount of information about them to be gathered from the records of those ships that did call. These accounts of the islands and the way of life of their inhabitants are those of foreigners for whom the islands were strange and exotic, but they represent one version of reality. Through these descriptions, the islands and their inhabitants became in some ways better known than they had been in their sixteenth-century heyday.

The Cabo Verde Islands Subject to Piratical Attacks

As already described, the Cabo Verde islands had, by the end of the seventeenth century, ceased to have much importance in the transatlantic slave trade, partly because the English, Dutch and French dominated trade with West Africa and partly because Portuguese and Spanish slave ships now departed directly from ports on the Guinea rivers. However, there was another reason behind the decline in the trade of the islands which is not at first apparent.

The islands had been raided again and again during the long period between 1580 and 1640, when the Portuguese and Spanish crowns were united, and thereafter while conflicts between the Portuguese and the Dutch continued in the Atlantic. These only came to an end in 1654, when the Dutch finally surrendered the last of their conquests in Brazil. A final episode of this conflict occurred in 1655 when, over a period of four days, the crew of a Dutch warship plundered the town of São Filipe in Fogo, sacking the churches, taking numerous hostages and demanding ransoms for their release (Carreira 2000: 327). On this occasion an English warship helped the islanders drive out the Dutch and even contributed to the restoration of the town.

This long period of warfare had shown how vulnerable the islands were to attack from the sea, a lesson not lost on the pirates who began to frequent Caribbean and Indian Ocean waters during the final years of the seventeenth and the beginning of the eighteenth centuries. As well as plundering the coastal settlements, which often yielded little of value, the pirates would seize cattle, though their preferred tactic was to take hostages and demand ransoms. Even when ransoms were paid, the hostages were often abducted. William Dampier, who was in Maio island in 1683, records that "for about a Week before our Arrival there came an *English* Ship, the Men of which came ashore, pretending Friendship, and seized on the Governour with some others, and carrying them aboard, made them send ashore for Cattle to ransom their Liberties. And yet after this set sail, and carried them away, and they had not heard of them since" (Dampier 1937: 59). So frequent were pirate attacks that George Roberts recorded that many of the Cabo Verdeans thought that pirates came from a nation of that name (Green 1745–7: I, 620).

During the War of the Spanish Succession (1701–14) Portugal had joined the Grand Alliance against Louis XIV, with the result that French ships joined the pirates in raids on the Cabo Verde islands. In 1712 Jacques Cassard captured and plundered Ribeira Grande, finally bringing about the demise of this once prosperous city. Raids continued after the war was over, and pirates often lay in wait near the salt islands of Maio, Sal and Boa Vista in order to plunder the ships that came in search of cargoes of salt.

In 1718 the pirate Christopher Condent sailed to Maio, where

> he took the whole Salt Fleet, consisting of about 20 Sail; he wanting a Boom, took out the Main-Mast of one of these Ships to supply the Want: Here he took upon him the Administration of Justice, enquiring into the Manner of the Commanders' Behaviour to their Men, and those, against whom Complaint was made, he whipp'd and pickled. He took what Provisions and other Necessaries he wanted, and having augmented his Company, by Voluntiers and forced Men, he left the Ships and sailed to St *Jago,* where he took a *Dutch* Ship ... from hence he stood away for the Coast of *Brazil,* and in his Cruise, took several *Portuguese* Ships, which he plundered and let go. (Defoe 1972: 582)

The same year the Welsh pirate Howel Davis attacked shipping off Maio and then went on to Santiago to obtain water. There he fell out with the governor and at night attacked the fort, which he occupied long enough to dismount all the guns before retreating to his ship (Defoe 1972: 72).

Pirates found the little settlements on the coasts of the Cabo Verde islands easy targets to plunder. Some of these were so often attacked that what had once been relatively prosperous settlements had to be abandoned, their populations retreating inland, where it was much more difficult for the pirates to reach them. The pirate attacks, however, had one unforeseen consequence for the islanders. When raids took place, the opportunity was often taken by slaves to leave the plantations where they were kept and find refuge with the rural populations in the mountainous interiors. In this way piracy struck a blow not only at the commercial prosperity of the islands but also at the institution of plantation slavery.

Early in the eighteenth century England began to take the problem of piracy seriously. Royal Navy ships were sent to areas known to be haunts of pirates and were often deployed to the Cabo Verde islands, where they offered some protection to the vessels coming for cargoes of salt (Soares 2011: 138). However, although in this way the damaging effects of piracy were limited, pirates were still a problem in the early nineteenth century. As late as 1818 corsairs from Baltimore attacked the island of Santiago, and the last recorded attack was by a pirate from South America in 1827.

The Decline of Agriculture: Drought and Famine

During the sixteenth century, the system of entailed estates (*morgadios* and *capelas*) had led to the growth of a modestly successful plantation economy dependent on slave labour. Sugar and cotton had been produced, the sugar largely being used for the manufacture of rum. However, the decline of the slave trade and the increasing frequency of pirate attacks gradually destroyed the plantation economy. With its *raison d'être* gone, the entails remained a juridical skeleton without a living body.

The collapse of the system of plantation agriculture was also caused in part by the increasing frequency of drought and famine. There is little specific information about droughts in the islands until 1580–3, when conditions were severe enough for some of the population of Santiago to flee to the mainland of Guinea. Then in 1609–11 there were reports of famine accompanied by outbreaks of smallpox. In 1680 the eruption of the Fogo volcano caused the flight of many of the island's population, and this was followed by prolonged droughts and famines in the years 1685–90 and again in 1704–12, when for three years there was no rain at all. There is little doubt that the effect of drought on the islands was made considerably worse by the destruction of the vegetation caused by the wild cattle and goats that roamed the islands (Pereira 1964: 59–60, 390; Patterson 1988).

Englishmen who visited the islands during these years described the effects of the failure of the rains. The case of Fogo provides an example. As a result of the years of drought which followed the 1680 eruption, most of the cotton bushes died and the making of cotton cloth ceased. Cattle also died, and it was reported that the French, who used to buy mules to take to the West Indies, no longer came, as most of the mules had died as well (Green 1745–7: I, 660; Defoe 1726: 420).

The effects of drought conditions on Sal are graphically described in George Roberts' account. "The Island formerly was well stocked with Goats, Cows and Asses: But about the year 1705 ... it was intirely deserted for want of Rain, by all the Inhabitants, except one old Man, who resolved to die on it, as he did the same year. The Drought had been so extreme for some time that most of the Cows and Goats died for want of Sustenance" (Defoe 1726: 390; Green 1745–7: I, 633).

Drought, followed inevitably by famine, continued relentlessly through the eighteenth century and was often accompanied by epidemics. Famine years were recorded in 1719–23, 1738–40, 1742, 1748–50, 1754–5, 1764, 1773–5, 1788–9 and 1790–1. The only recourse that the population had was to emigrate, a response which became deeply embedded in the islanders' experience (Patterson 1988). Faced with starvation and the lack of any government action, the populations were forced to move when they were able to do so—from island to island, from the islands to the fertile and better-watered mainland of Guinea, and ultimately to the New World and Europe; but for most people emigration was not a possibility and large numbers simply died of starvation.

There was apparently no attempt by any authority to deal with the recurrent problems of famine. In 1792 John Barrow, who accompanied Lord Macartney's embassy to China and later was to mastermind Britain's exploration of the Arctic, gave an account of the fleet's visit to Santiago. His description of what he saw was bleak, but most of his comments were echoed by contemporary Portuguese writers.

> In expressing my surprise to the secretary that the mother country so far from employing precautions had taken no steps to procure succours against a calamity so dreadful and of such long continuance, he observed that the Court of Lisbon considered these poor islands, and the few black subjects scattered over them, of too little importance to demand any part of its care or attention; that they produced very little revenue to the Crown,

which arose chiefly from a monopoly of the slave trade on the coast, and from the sale of an exclusive privilege of supplying the Brazils with salt. (Barrow 1806: 67–8)

Already by the end of the seventeenth century, commercial decline, coupled with the increasingly serious droughts and famines, was having a profound effect on the island population and its institutions. The holders of the entails for the most part left and became absentees. The estates were rented out in small lots to the free black population under short-term contracts or share-cropping arrangements. The departure of the holders of the *morgadios* more or less wiped out the upper social stratum of European Portuguese settlers. Emigrants who left the islands during this period apparently took any wealth they possessed with them in the form of coin, leaving the islands with almost no money in circulation. The surviving population, now more than ever before, became a people of mixed cultural origin imprisoned in what were rapidly becoming desert islands. Most of the slaves, meanwhile, deserted the plantations and established their freedom in remote mountainous districts in the island interiors. During his stay in the islands George Roberts records being asked to go ashore near Tarrafal in the north of Santiago. "I did not care much for trusting myself ashore … for that Part of St Jago consists mostly of Banditti, who frequently fly thither from Justice, and sometimes make Incursions among the more civilized Parts of the Island where, if they are catched, they suffer, but if they escape thither, they are secure, for no Officer of Justice dare follow them there" (Defoe 1726: 309–10).

Guinea Islands in Decline

With the departure of most of the owners of the *roças* to Brazil at the end of the sixteenth century, São Tomé experienced some of the same economic and social changes that marked Cabo Verde. The economy of São Tomé went into sharp decline, though its role in the export of slaves continued at about the same level as that of Cabo Verde through the contacts the islanders had with the Kongo kingdom on the mainland.

THE CREOLE ISLANDS: THE UNCERTAIN YEARS

However, in the 1640s São Tomé became caught up in the struggle between the Dutch and Spain. The Dutch West India Company, which had been founded in 1619, aimed to take over Portugal's Atlantic maritime empire. In 1624 the company launched an attack on northern Brazil which failed, but in 1630 it took control of most of the sugar-producing regions of the north. It then turned its attention to West Africa. Dutch ships had already effectively placed the Portuguese at Elmina under blockade, and in 1612 and again in 1626 had attacked the island of São Tomé. In 1637 Elmina finally surrendered, and in 1641 a large Dutch fleet captured Luanda and occupied the Guinea islands. For eight years the Dutch were masters of the Portuguese South Atlantic empire, but, although their ships often made free use of harbours in the less populated Cabo Verde islands, they did not try to capture them, and they also left the Portuguese in control of southern Brazil.

Meanwhile, in Luanda and São Tomé, groups of Portuguese held out in the interior against the Dutch occupation. São Tomé experienced a small commercial revival under Dutch occupation, but in 1648 the Portuguese took back possession of the island and the following year a fleet organised in southern Brazil regained Luanda. The struggle in Brazil continued until the Dutch finally agreed to leave in 1654. The creole world of the South Atlantic was once again restored to Portuguese control.

Only Elmina was never recovered by the Portuguese, and Brazilian traders who wanted access to West African markets for their tobacco had henceforward to make use of the minor port of Whydah, which was founded in 1721. Brazilian traders also used São Tomé as a clearing house where they were able to supply Dutch and English buyers. São Tomé, now largely ignored by Lisbon, became in effect an appendage of Bahia, an outpost of the burgeoning economy of Brazil.

The withdrawal of the Dutch left São Tomé very isolated. With the decline of the sugar plantations, its population had dwindled, though the formal institutions that had been established a century earlier, in the days of its prosperity, continued. São Tomé retained its status as a bishopric, the town had its *senado da câmara*, and the island recruited its own militia regiment; even a seminary for the training of priests was set up—the first in tropical Africa (Boxer 1978: 6). Its high-ranking citizens were now all black-skinned freemen (*forros*), who occupied all the official positions. Only the governors and bishops (who, however, were often absentees) came from Europe. The *roças* were now in the hands of the small group of landowning *forro* families and continued to produce food crops and small amounts of sugar and rum. The Guinea islands also exported some cotton, and there was even a small industry producing soap.

São Tomé and Príncipe continued to provide services to the slave ships of different nations that now visited the West African coast and came to take on water and food. One such ship was captained by Thomas Philips, who in 1693 was given leave to "supply himself with Wood, Water and Provisions". Philips commented that "the most convenient Time to fill Water here is in the Night, by Reason the Women of the Town are washing their Cloaths, and otherwise muddling the Water all Day". He also recommended keeping a strong guard "else the Portuguese (who are the greatest Thieves in the World) would have stolen all their Iron-Hoops off " (Newitt 1988: 24–5). William Smith, writing in 1745, also comments on the soapy water: "'tis nothing but Sudds enough to poison our Men" (1745: 241).

Like Cabo Verde, São Tomé attracted the attentions of pirates. In June 1719 the pirate Howel Davis anchored off Príncipe. What followed was an incident similar to many others that could be related during this period, and it turns a vivid spotlight onto creole society and its relations with the outside world in the early part of the eighteenth century.

Davis entered the harbour of Príncipe and anchored near the small fortress. He informed the governor that his was a Royal Navy ship in search of pirates. When a French ship also entered the harbour, Davis boarded it and claimed to have found pirate booty, receiving the congratulations of the governor. Then, "Davis, with fourteen more, went privately ashore, and walk'd up the Country towards a Village, where the Governor and other chief Men of the Island kept their Wives, intending, as we may suppose, to supply their Husbands' Places with them." The women took fright and escaped into the woods. Apparently Davis had not been recognised and went ahead with his plan to capture the governor and hold him to ransom. The plan was to give the governor a gift of ten slaves and then invite him on board the ship "to an Entertainment". However, the plan was betrayed by a "Portuguese negro" who swam ashore with the information. When Davis and his men landed the next day to go to the governor's house, they were ambushed and all were killed. This was not the end of the matter, for the pirates took their revenge by seizing the fort and throwing its guns into the sea and then bombarding the town and destroying a number of houses (Defoe 1972: 192–3).

The Creole World of São Tomé and Príncipe

Although the great days of sugar production were long gone, the Guinea islands retained more of the character of a plantation society than Cabo Verde. The small number of *forro* families all had slaves who cultivated their estates and performed domestic services. Someone who had been involved with Howel Davis later gave an account of the islands to the author of the *General History of the Pyrates*, which was published in London in 1724. This was incorporated into the narrative of Davis' exploits. It is a surprisingly detailed and even intimate portrait of the creole world of the *forro* population, a picture of what might almost be described as a world of tropical contentment. "St *Thome* is the principal [island] of the three. Whose Governor is stiled Captain General of the Islands ... It is a Bishoprick with a great many secular Clergy who appear to have neither Learning nor Devotion." The account goes on to record that "these Clergy are the chief Traders", and they and the Governor are in competition to "monopolize what strangers have to offer for Sale, whether Toys or Cloaths, which of all sorts are ever [in demand] with the *Portuguese*, in all parts of the World". "The Town is of mean Building but large and populous, the Residence of the greater Part of the Natives, who thro' the whole Island are computed at 10000, the Militia at 3000, and are in general, a rascally thievish Generation" (Defoe 1972: 178).

Portuguese and foreign ships called for water and provisions, and the Portuguese had to pay customs dues for their slaves, "which is always in Gold ... this being a constant Bank to pay off the civil and military Charges of the Government, prevents the Inconveniency of Remittances, and keeps both it and *Princes* Isle rich enough to pay ready Money for every Thing they want of *Europeans*." The island lies on the equator, and the informant mentioned that there was a "wooden Bridge just without the Town" which lay exactly on the line. The islanders, he thought, were very healthy, "imputed by those disposed to be merry ... to the Want of even so much as one Surgeon or Physician amongst them" (Defoe 1972: 179, 180).

The unknown informant had a very high opinion of Príncipe. He described it as "a pleasant and delightful Spot to the grave and thoughtful Disposition of the *Portuguese*, an Improvement to Country Retirement in that, this may be a happy and uninterrupted Retreat from the whole World". There were plenty of whales to be found in the island waters, but this fishery was not exploited. "All therefore that the Islanders do, is now and then to go out with two or three Canoes and set on one for Diversion" (Defoe 1972: 180, 182).

The main town, Santo António, "consists of two or three regular Streets, of wooden built Houses where the Governor and chief Men of the Island reside" (Defoe 1972: 183). William Smith, writing two decades later, described how "the Houses here are two Story high neatly built of Wood and surrounded with handsome Balconies after the *Portuguese Fashion*" (Smith 1745: 241).

Across the bay weirs had been created, and at low tide 500 people would come with baskets and sticks to collect the fish. There was a mission with two Venetian priests. The informant describes the vegetation of the islands at length, then says that there are cinnamon trees that grow well at the approach to the governor's villa, and speculates that the main reason why they are not more cultivated is that this would make foreigners want to seize the islands (Defoe 1972: 188).

"The manner of living among the *Portuguese* here, is with the utmost Frugality and Temperance, even to Penury and Starvation." The only recreations were to go round to each other's houses "and sit down at each other's Doors, in the Street, every Evening ... Their talk is mostly how Affairs went with their Negroes, or their

Ground." The Portuguese pilot writing in the 1540s had described creole society in a very similar way.

The Africans, the informant continues, "are rather happy in Slavery" (Defoe 1972: 190). The hardest work they have is carrying their "Patroons or their Wives, to and from the Plantation" in covered hammocks. The Africans are Christian "at least nominal but ... they adhere still to many silly Pagan Customs in their Mournings and Rejoycings". The Portuguese, he says, "tho' eminently abstemious and temperate in all other things are unbounded in their Lusts", and he speculates that their abstemiousness acts "as a Counterpoison to the Mischief of a promiscuous Salacity" (Defoe 1972: 190).

He concludes with a reference to Ano Bom, where "there are Plenty of Fruits and Provisions exchanged to Ships for old Cloaths and Trifles of any Sort; they have a Governor nominated from St *Thome* and two or three Priests, neither of which are minded, every one living at Discretion, and fill'd with Ignorance and Lust" (Defoe 1972: 191).

São Tomé did not suffer from drought and famine like Cabo Verde, but the island was extremely unhealthy and mortality was high among any Portuguese sent by the Crown to the island. As a result the decision was taken in 1753 to move the seat of government to the town of Santo António on Príncipe, as this island was considered to be more healthy than São Tomé. However, the move was also an attempt to neutralise the fractious opposition of the São Tomé town council, which had a long tradition of obstructing the island's governors. The seat of government continued in Príncipe until 1852, when it returned to São Tomé.

During these years Brazil became the Guinea islands' principal trading partner, supplying the tobacco which was in much demand on the coast as well as buying slaves. As the links with Brazil grew, Portugal played almost no role in the life of the islands beyond supplying a governor or occasionally some other official. The islands cost Portugal nothing, and the contribution made by the customs revenues of the islands to the Portuguese treasury was minimal as most of the trade there was clandestine smuggling. Islanders looked to Brazil for commercial partners, and the wealthier islanders were as likely to go to Brazil for education or health reasons as to Portugal.

The *forro* population, which provided personnel for the municipal offices, priests for the church and officers for the militia, numbered only a few thousand. In 1758 in São Tomé they numbered 2,797 and in 1807 3,849. At the same dates the slave population numbered 5,023 and 3,102 respectively. Most of the slaves appear to have been domestic servants. There were only 21 people described as white in 1758 and 47 in 1807, though in Príncipe, where the capital was located, there were 80 Europeans in 1807. There were very few people described as of mixed race in either island, which suggests that most of the white population were officials of one sort or another and were not permanently resident (Lucas 2015: 64). It is also possible that people of mixed race were classified as "white".

An account of the islands was written in the early nineteenth century by Raimundo José da Cunha Matos, a Portuguese military engineer who had originally been sent in 1797 to command the fort of São Sebastião in São Tomé and who had served briefly as governor from 1816 to 1817. His description of the islands' inhabitants, like those written at this time about Cabo Verde, is moralistic in tone but nevertheless describes what was to him the strange in-between world of the creole islands. The free inhabitants of Príncipe are "black and endowed with a seditious spirit. They do not work and love the good life and libertinage. As a result they roam like bands of slaves among the houses of rich colonists who they rob without pity ... The persons of quality are very polished, affable, courteous and lovers of hospitality towards strangers. The plebeians are cowardly, faithless, lazy and lovers of revolt and mutiny." As for the military presence in the island, "there are in this island two companies of creole women. However, as the women here share in the same spirit of sedition which animates the men, the aforementioned creole women are of no use to their sovereign" (Cunha Matos 1916: 62, 67).

Cunha Matos is also one of the first writers to mention the Angolares, the descendants of maroons from earlier centuries. "On a mountain in the north-east is built the town of Santa Cuz dos Angolares. Here and in the surrounding forest is the residence of these people who live by working the timber which they prepare and export to the city ... and here a lot of pigs are bred and bananas are grown" (1916: 49).

Like Cabo Verde, São Tomé and Príncipe were described in José Joaquim Lopes de Lima's multi-volume account of the Portuguese colonies, which began publication in 1844. By that time coffee and cacao had both been introduced into the islands, and already the cry had been raised, which was to be echoed in every book and article written about the islands for the next hundred years, about the shortage of labourers (*falta de mão d'obra*). Lopes de Lima suggested that *degredados* should be sent and employed on the twenty-two Crown estates (*fazendas*), which were at that time simply rented out "to tenants who don't enjoy much benefit from them and do them no good, growing crops on only a portion of the lands and leaving the greater part uncultivated or breeding wild cattle on their natural pastures".

Among the *degredados* there should be carpenters and woodworkers because the use of the saw had been quite forgotten. However, although *degredados* were regularly sent to the islands, these usually took the first opportunity to escape on board Brazilian trading ships (Caldeira 1999: 39–42). Like Cunha Matos before him, Lopes de Lima complained that the *forros* would not work and "only active force would succeed in getting a small amount of rural labour from a *negro forro*". He thought that the islands needed to be repopulated with people who were less lazy (Lopes de Lima 1844b: I, 21, 23; II, 20). This negative view of the *forro* population was to influence Portuguese policy-makers for the next hundred years and was partly responsible for the catastrophic events of 1953.

The Death of Ribeira Grande

When William Dampier visited the Cabo Verde islands in 1683, he was able to describe Ribeira Grande as a functioning port, still supplying refreshment to the few ships that called there on their longer voyages to South America or round Africa. But by 1727, when the judge Bravo Botelho wrote a report on the islands to the king, Ribeira Grande was in effect a ruin and largely abandoned.

What had once been described as among the richest cities of the Portuguese world had long been in decline, as the slave trade inexorably moved away from the islands. In 1643 Portuguese slave ships were no longer required to call at Ribeira Grande to pay duties on their slaves, and with the loss of this trade, the commerce of the port drained away. By the end of the century virtually all the Portuguese had left, and public offices in the islands were now in the hands of creoles, including the post of governor (Pereira 1964: 47).

In 1711 a French fleet commanded by René Duguay-Trouin had captured and plundered Rio de Janeiro. The following year twelve ships commanded by Jacques Cassard attacked Santiago, captured the two towns of Praia and Ribeira Grande, and plundered them, removing everything of value, including slaves. The attack is described by Cabo Verde's leading historian, António Carreira.

> They captured the *capitão-mor* and spread throughout the island robbing what they could, burning houses and plantations and destroying what they could not carry away. They took women and children as hostages for the men ... After burning houses and their contents including valuable documentation, they sacked the churches and in particular the rich houses. They removed the bells of the Cathedral and of the other churches in the city and all the powder and shot from the fortress; more than 110 people, both slaves and freemen, boys and girls, all the silver from the Misericórdia, amounting to more than 8000 *cruzados*; all the silver and sacred vessels from the Cathedral ... and all the goods which they found in the houses, tables, desks, counters, beds and everything made of metal or bronze ... According to Senna Barcellos the total value of this sack amounted to three million pounds. (Carreira 2000: 328)

Although Ribeira Grande's cathedral still stood after the departure of the French, the city was never reoccupied. Bravo Botelho, describing it in 1727, saw nothing but desolation.

> The greater part of the houses are in ruins and even those that were still habitable had no inhabitants because their owners in their poverty and misery live inland seeing to the cultivation of their properties and do not come to the city except for official functions and even then all do not come ... So, it is deserted except for the canons and some clergy and their slaves. The

seat of the *câmara* is destroyed and the prison in ruins so that justice cannot be performed ... The weakest town which your Majesty has in his kingdom is more populous than this so-called city in which there is no preacher except the Bishop, no doctor, no surgeon, no pharmacist, which is destitute of everything and where most people die without any remedy from the evils arising from the malignity of the climate. (Pereira 1964: 45)

The old town still had a few gaunt structures surviving from the earlier days. The town had a *camâra* which had no funds and no functions. There was a Misericórdia which had a church but no hospital and no funds to dispense. The cathedral stood grand and empty, served only by three or four canons. The ancient church of Our Lady of the Rosary stood, as it still does today, one of the relics of a grander past. There was a convent of Franciscans with three or four friars (Santos 2017: 142). In this one religious house, George Roberts, also visiting Ribeira Grande in the 1720s, found something to praise: "Here also is a religious House of Cordelier Friers [Franciscans], who are the only Men on these Islands who constantly eat fresh-baked, as well as fermented wheaten Bread, Flower etc. being sent them yearly from *Portugal*. They have very fine Gardens, stored with Salad, and the best Fruit on the Island, and have brought a Part of the running Brook of *Ribeira Grande*, not only to run through their Gardens, but also, in a manner, to every part of their House, which, except the Cathedral, makes the best Prospect in or about the City" (Defoe 1726: 405). By 1755 the bishop had moved to São Nicolau, which was thought to be a more healthy location, but the Misericórdia was only moved to Praia in 1834 (Lopes de Lima 1844a: 57).

The death agonies of Ribeira Grande lingered on, and it was only in 1770 that the capital of the islands and the seat of government was formally moved to Praia. The anonymous account of Cabo Verde written in 1784 pointed out that Ribeira Grande had not been built in the best place. It had been sited where two streams met before entering the sea. The result was " a lake which could not help but become harmful and prejudicial to health, for the fresh flood water was full of slime" (Carreira 1985: 23). At one time there had been a public fountain where ships could replenish their water supplies.

When it rained there were floods. In 1763 whole houses had been swept out to sea and nine people had died.

In January 1832 Ribeira Grande, now a romantic ruin, was visited by Charles Darwin in the company of two officers from the *Beagle*. He described the visit in his journal. "The little town, before its harbour was filled up, was the principal place in the island: it now presents a melancholy, but very picturesque appearance ... Having procured a Black Padre for a guide, and a Spaniard, who had served in the Peninsular War, as an interpreter, we visited a collection of buildings of which an ancient church formed the principal part." This was Our Lady of the Rosary. "The church or chapel formed one side of a quadrangle, in the middle of which a large clump of bananas were growing. On one side was a hospital, containing about a dozen miserable-looking inmates." There was an inn where they were served with a meal, and the party then visited the cathedral, which was still functioning in a manner of speaking. "It does not appear so rich as the smaller church, but boasts of a little organ, which sent forth most singularly inharmonious cries. We presented the black priest with a few shillings" (Darwin 1989: 42–3).

The lingering death of Ribeira Grande marked the final end of the grandiose plans of Portugal's monarchs to found a new Portugal in the South Atlantic and to transplant there Portugal's Renaissance Christian culture.

Settlement of the other Cabo Verde Islands

At the beginning of the seventeenth century the only islands with permanent populations were still Santiago and Fogo. On the other islands small seasonal camps were set up to slaughter the wild cattle and tan their hides, work which was performed by slaves or convicts. There was a convict settlement on Boa Vista, and small settlements were made on Maio and Sal in order to gather salt from the salt lakes (*salinas*) and sell it to visiting ships.

With the decline of the slave trade, the only products of the islands that attracted foreign traders were salt and, to a lesser extent, woven cotton cloth (*panos*), horses and mules, and turtles, whose meat was salted. Much of this trade was "small retail trading", with the islanders bartering their produce for old clothes or simple utensils (Soares 2011: 136). As there was no effective administration outside Santiago and Fogo, the way was open for illicit commerce and smuggling of all kinds. The collection of the orchilla lichen, used in the dyeing industry, which grew naturally on many of the islands, remained a royal monopoly throughout this period (Ribeiro 1997: 99). The Cabo Verdean product was of high quality, and in the eighteenth century it became one of the principal exports of the islands to Europe.

Well into the eighteenth century the Crown continued to make grants of the islands to important figures in Portugal. These *senhores* (comparable in some respects to the lords proprietors in the early English settlements in the New World) were able to claim all kinds of rights over the land, the wild cattle and even the vestigial trade conducted by the islanders, but as the settlements expanded and a rudimentary structure of government was introduced, there were endless opportunities for conflict between the islanders, Crown officials and the agents of these island *senhores*.

During the seventeenth century, permanent settlements had gradually begun to be made on all the islands except São Vicente, and during the following hundred years their population grew. There was no organised programme of settlement, but with the decline and eventual abandonment of Ribeira Grande and the *morgadio* plantations, many people began to move to the other islands in search of new opportunities. A notable feature of this internal migratory movement was that the societies formed on the newly settled islands were almost exclusively made up of freemen. George Roberts (perhaps through the pen of Daniel Defoe) described how this came about.

> As it was a usual thing with them [the Portuguese] ... when a Man or Woman died, to set one or more of the Slaves free, which they do as a meritorious Act of Atonement for their Sins, and the Climate being more agreeable to the Constitutions of those Blacks, than to the *European Portuguese* they increased much faster, and found Means to get themselves transported to the neighbouring Ilands, where they could live more free from the

> Oppressions of the Whites ... The Blacks all the Time increasing more than the *Portuguese*, they claimed an equal Degree of Liberty and Freedom with their Masters who thereupon mostly returned either to St *Jago*, or to *Portugal*. (Defoe 1726: 387)

Slavery, which had been so important in the make-up of society in Santiago and Fogo, was never firmly established in the other islands, and this became of significance as creole identity took shape in the coming years. Even though some slaves accompanied their masters to the new settlements, these soon merged with and became indistinguishable from the small subsistence farmers who populated the fertile valleys of the island interiors.

One major problem had to be overcome if the other islands were to be settled. The Cabo Verdeans had little or no shipping of their own. There was no timber to build boats, and the islanders came to depend on visiting ships to find opportunities to move from one island to another. As Maria João Soares put it, "with significant Portuguese navigation missing and no funds to buy ships, local merchants relied upon the only maritime assets available: English ships. When Lisbon royal officials came to or returned from Cape Verde and when bishops or *ouvidores* (justice officials) inspected other islands within the archipelago, all were compelled to use English vessels" (Soares 2011: 135).

In order to provide some government structure for these new settlements, the governor appointed a *capitão-mor* in each island, who had overall responsibility for its defence and for the protection of the fiscal rights of the Crown. The *capitães-mores* were also responsible for the appointment of any other officials that were considered necessary. This rudimentary administration was much criticised at the end of the century by writers who saw the system as highly corrupt.

There are a number of accounts written by English seamen who visited the Cabo Verde islands in the late seventeenth and early eighteenth centuries. Some of these, like those by Dampier and George Roberts, were separately published, but a collection was made by John Green in the first volume of his *New General Collection of Voyages and Travels*, which was published between 1745 and 1747. These accounts, and those of Dutch and French authors, give a detailed description of the creole world of the islands and provide much of the information about how the new island settlements were developing and the setbacks they were experiencing from the recurrent droughts and famine.

Brava, lying very close to the west coast of Fogo, had often been visited by ships attracted by its green appearance and good fresh water. However, permanent settlement of the island appears only to have been made as a result of the eruption of the Fogo volcano in 1680, when people took refuge from the devastation on the nearby island. Originally building houses in Furna on the bay facing Fogo, the settlers moved inland after experiencing attacks from pirates in 1686. There they built the town which later became known as Nova Sintra in a location that was more secure. Early in the eighteenth century the English cleared the island of pirate ships and Brava's population then began to grow, partly as a result of its favourable geographical environment and partly due to profitable trade in the orchilla lichen. Nevertheless the island suffered from the failure of the rains, and the anonymous author of the *Notícia corográfica e chronológica* wrote in 1784 that the population "was so poor that they could not support another priest apart from the parish priest" (Carreira 1985: 31). Brava also suffered, like all the islands, from being virtually undefended. It was attacked by a French warship during the Revolutionary Wars in January 1798, when a trading ship was captured and eleven houses burnt and some people killed (Carreira 2000: 330).

In the second half of the eighteenth century the anchorages at Brava began to attract American whalers which needed access to a shore base to maintain and resupply the ships. The whalers brought new opportunities to the island. Men were recruited as crew, and in time this led to new openings for permanent emigration to the United States.

Boa Vista, one of the barren and low-lying islands in the east of the archipelago, had been granted to private individuals, who made a profit from the wild goats that lived on the island; these were occasionally rounded up and slaughtered by the poor colony of *degredados* that eked out an existence there. At one time the island had been divided up into estates, as can be seen by the survival of stone boundary walls that still criss-cross the island. Boa Vista was occasionally visited by English ships in search of a cargo of salt, but the *salina* was not close to the coast and transporting the salt was difficult. Nevertheless the island's first settlement, now known as Povoação Velha, was established in 1620 near the biggest of the salt pans in the south of the island. A second settlement named Porto Ingles, and later renamed Sal Rei, was eventually established at the end of the eighteenth century and became the main town.

In the early eighteenth century, increasing numbers of English ships were visiting Boa Vista, and George Roberts described how the salt was obtained.

> They went ashore to agree with the Inhabitants for the Assistance to bring Salt from the Salt-Pans down to the Water-Side; as also to settle the Prizes of Goods of the Island—Horses and Asses which they were to take in after the Salt. This done they set all Hands to work making Salt. The Custom is for the Ship's Crew to make it, and wheel it out a little Way from the Ponds to a dry Place and there heap it up in large Heaps to drain and dry. From thence the Natives bring it down upon Asses, a Negro Driver being allowed to every fifteen. (Green 1745–7: I, 599)

According to Roberts, "the People of *Bona Vist* naturally love the *English* Nation and most of them can speak a little of the *English Tongue*, and even some of the Women make shift to understand one in it" (Defoe 1726: 400). He also writes at length about the wild cotton and the cloths, dyed with indigo, which were manufactured there.

The author of the *Notícia corográfica e chronológica* said the island had two parishes and that when there was rain, crops of maize and pumpkin could be sown, but if there was a lack of rain the islanders lived on meat and milk. He adds that "in this island the people are more civilised than in other of the Barlavento islands because of the communication they have with people from the ships which come to buy goats and *bestas* [other animals]" (Carreira 1985: 33).

Early in the nineteenth century, the salt industry became concentrated in Sal, but Boa Vista was chosen as the location for the so-called Mixed Commission. This was established by Britain and Portugal after the signing of the 1842 treaty which finally outlawed the slave trade. The Mixed Commission adjudicated cases of ships arrested on suspicion of being slavers. John Rendall was appointed the first British consul and member of the commission. Rendall eventually moved his consulate to Mindelo and became an enthusiastic advocate for the newly established international port of Mindelo, publishing *A Guide to the Cap de Verd Islands* in 1856. The name Rendall became quite common among the Cabo Verdean population, but whether this had anything to do with any extracurricular activities of the consul or was just in recognition of his self-evident virtues is not clear.

Boa Vista had briefly enjoyed a "place in the sun", but with the rise in importance of Mindelo, shipping ceased to call at the island. The Reverend Charles Thomas, chaplain to the American anti-slave trade squadron, described the island in 1855: "Boavista (literally good view) is said to have been productive at one time; at present it is almost a desert. Its people, of whom there are four thousand, are always hungry, and the lean cattle, with sad faces and tears in their eyes, walk solemnly in endless rumination over grassless fields. In the valleys there is some vegetation. Fishing, salt-making and going to funerals, are the chief employments and amusements of the people" (Thomas 1860: 330).

Maio, like Boa Vista, had been granted as a range for wild cattle, and in 1606 was said to have ten or twelve people living on it (Filho 1996: 34). According to Jean Barbot (Green 1745–7: I, 640), "the Inhabitants salt the Flesh of goats, and export it in Casks; dressing the Skins very neatly in the Nature of Turkey Leather". Five thousand skins were said to be exported yearly, but Maio's principal resource was salt rather than cattle. At one time eighty English ships a year came to Maio and extracted 11,000 tons of salt, paying for the cargo with old clothes. Dampier visited Maio in 1683 and left a brief account of the island.

> This Isle of *Mayo* is but small, but invironed with Sholes, yet a Place much frequented by Shipping for its great plenty of Salt: and though there is but bad landing, yet many Ships lade here every Year. Here are plenty of Bulls, Cows, and Goats; and at a certain Season of the Year … a sort of small Sea-Tortoise come

> hither to lay their Eggs; but these Turtles are not so sweet as those in the *West Indies*. The Inhabitants plant Corn, Yams, Potatoes, and some Plantains and breed a few Fowls; living very poor yet much better than the Inhabitants of any other of these Islands, *St Jago* excepted. (Dampier 1937: 60)

Although Maio, like the other islands, was wide open to attacks by pirates who waylaid the salt ships that visited the island, there was a great trade with the English, who took the salt to Newfoundland to supply the fishing industry there, another manifestation of the triangular Atlantic trade.

> The English drive here a great trade for Salt, and have commonly a Man of War stationed for the Guard of their Ships and Barks that come to take it in of which ... there have been not fewer sometimes than an hundred in a Year. It costs nothing but the Labour of raking it together, and wheeling it out of the Pond, except the Carriage: and that also is very cheap, the Inhabitants having plenty of Asses for which they have little to do besides conveying the Salt from the Ponds to the Sea-side at the Season the Ships are here. They lade and drive their Asses themselves, being very glad to being employed. (Green 1745–7: I, 640)

In the second half of the eighteenth century the trade in salt declined sharply. The English ceased to call during the period when the Company of Grão-Pará and Maranhão was granted the monopoly of trade with the Cabo Verde islands (1755–78). The company had apparently demanded that payments for the salt be made in coin and not in old clothing, as had been the custom (Carreira 1985: 32). And drought affected Maio as it did the other islands. According to the *Notícia corográfica e chronológica*, most of the animals died during the drought of 1773–5, and the islanders depended on food brought in small boats from Santiago in exchange for wild cotton and salt.

Sal island was not permanently settled until the eighteenth century. Although it had rich salt deposits, the salt was difficult to access as the main salt lake lay inland at Pedra Lume within an old volcanic crater, fed with seawater from underground. There were problems transporting the salt to the beaches, and this discouraged the use of Sal by traders. Eventually Sal was to become one of the most prosperous of the islands, though this is difficult to imagine from the accounts of visitors who saw it in the eighteenth century.

Dampier visited Sal in 1683 and saw little there to recommend the island. "This Island of *Sall* is ... not above a League and an half or two Leagues wide. It hath its name from the abundance of Salt that is naturally congealed there, the whole Island being full of large Salt-ponds. The Land is very barren, producing no Tree that I could see, but some small shrubby Bushes by the Sea-side. Neither could I discern any Grass; yet there are some poor Goats on it. I know not whether there are any other Beasts on the Island."

Dampier then described the flocks of flamingos which frequented the salt lakes and which are still to be found in the islands. He thought they were not good to eat, with the exception of their tongues: "a Dish of *Flamingo's* tongues being fit for a Prince's Table". He added that "when many of them are standing together by a Pond's Side ... they appear to him like a Brick Wall; their Feathers being of the Colour of new red Brick ... There are not above 5 or 6 Men on this Island of *Sall*, and a poor Governor, as they called him, who came aboard in our Boat, and about 3 or 4 poor lean Goats for a Present to our Captain, telling him they were the best that the Island did afford." The captain rewarded him with the gift of a coat to clothe him and an old hat, "for he had nothing but a few Rags on his Back ... We bought of him about 20 Bushels of Salt for a few old Cloaths: And he begged a little Powder and Shot" (Dampier 1937: 57).

An English description of the island in the eighteenth century paints another rather desperate picture of drought and its consequences for people brought to the island to slaughter turtles. "A French Ship coming to fish for Turtle ... by Stress of Weather, or some other Means, left behind here thirty Blacks which she had brought from St Antonio [Santo Antão] to carry on the Fishing. These People finding nothing else fed mostly on wild Goat, till they destroyed them all but one old He-goat which was then on the Island ... They also killed most of the Cows, so that they were at last forced to eat Asses" (Green 1745–7: I, 633). Sal and its poor population had to wait until the nineteenth century before its fortunes began to change.

São Nicolau was to have a very special place in the development of Cabo Verdean culture. The background to this lies in the relatively prosperous settlements that grew up in the eighteenth century. At first it was known principally for its wild cattle, but its high mountains and rocky valleys were comparatively well-watered and fertile—as well as inaccessible to pirates. Already in the sixteenth century there were reports of fruit trees being planted there, as well as the famous dragon's blood trees. While it was still in the hands of private grantees, the best known being the count and countess of Portalegre and the marquess of Minas, a number of settlements were established.

The most detailed accounts of São Nicolau at the beginning of the eighteenth century come from English visitors to the island. Most were favourably impressed by the contrast with the barrenness and poverty of the salt islands. Dampier stayed for some days off São Nicolau in 1683.

> This is a pretty large Island; it is one of the biggest of all the *Cape-Verd,* and lieth in a triangular form ... It is a mountainous barren Island, and rocky all round towards the Sea; yet in the Heart of it are Valleys, where the *Portuguese,* which inhabit here, have Vineyards and Plantations, and Wood for fewel. Here are many Goats, which are but poor in Comparison with those in other Places, yet much better than those at *Sall.* There are likewise many Asses. The Governour of this Island came aboard us, with three or four Gentlemen more in his Company who were all indifferently well cloathed, and accoutred with Swords and Pistols; but the rest that accompanied him to the Sea-side, which were about twenty or thirty Men more were but in a ragged Garb. The Governour brought aboard some Wine made in the Island which tasted much like *Madeira* wine: It was of a pale Colour, and lookt thick. He told us the chief Town was in the Valley fourteen Mile from the Bay where we rode; that he had there under him above one hundred Families, beside other Inhabitants that lived scattering in Valleys more remote. They were all very swarthy; the Governour was the clearest of them, yet of a dark tawny Complexion. At this Island we scrubb'd the

bottom of our Ship, and here also we dug Wells ashore on the Bay, and filled all our Water. (Dampier 1937: 59)

It is clear that the island was now attracting settlers, and the reference to vineyards shows that an effort was being made to develop its agriculture. According to George Roberts, "they have Vineyards, of which they make a tartish Wine, and, in a good Vintage, commonly 60 or 70 Pipes" (Defoe 1726: 436); and, as John Green wrote, "there is always good water in a valley about half a Mile from the Sea, when the Natives will bring it down on Asses for a Trifle" (Green 1745–7: I, 668).

In 1719 the pirate Howel Davis anchored off São Nicolau. The inhabitants, we are told, "both treated him very civilly, and also traded with him. He remained five Weeks, in which Time, he and half his crew, for their Pleasure, took a journey to the chief Town of the Island which was 19 miles up the Country: Davis making a good Appearance, was caressed by the Governor and the Inhabitants, and no Diversion was wanting which the *Portuguese* could show or Money could purchase." When he eventually left, five of his men deserted; they were "so charm'd with the Luxuries of the Place, and the free Conversation of some Women, that they stayed behind" (Defoe 1972: 169).

As the island did not produce salt, few ships visited and, according to George Roberts, the islanders were very isolated. "They sometimes have not had a Ship once in two Years" (Defoe 1726: 436–7). As a result they had become "more industrious than any of the Neighbours", and he goes on: "they can, and do make Cotton Cloths as fashionable as our common Country Tailors, and will make Buttons to imitate almost any Pattern you show them. They knit Cotton Stockings, tan Goat and Cow Hides, and make tolerable Shoes, and their Women by far are the most Housewifely and ingenious with their Needles of any of the Islands ... They make the best Cloths and Cotton Quilts of all the Islands, but they are too good for the *Guinea* Trade, but do well for that of *Brasil*, for which the *Portuguese* were wont to touch there" (Defoe 1726: 437).

In 1731 the main settlement, Ribeira Brava, was formally made into a town and allowed to elect a *senado da câmara*. At that time the town had 270 households and it is described in Green's *New General Collection of Voyages and Travels*. "The Town belonging to St Nicholas is the most populous, as well as compactest, of any of all the Islands; and although not built so large, nor the Walls cemented with Lime-Mortar, as the Houses at the City of St Jago are, nor covered, not even the Church with anything but Grass Thatch; yet for Number of Houses, as well as regular Streets, it exceeds that City" (Green 1745–7: I, 668–9; Defoe 1726: 439). The inhabitants "are all black or copper-coloured with frizzled Hair: except a few of the French Race, left there by the Pirate Marengbwin and three old Portuguese, and two or three old Portuguese women ... The best Portuguese is spoken here in all the Cape de Verde Islands" (Green 1745–7: I, 664).

São Nicolau suffered from the recurrent droughts along with the other islands. The anonymous author of the 1784 *Notícia corográfica e chronológica* records that as a result of the 1773–5 drought and famine, almost all the population of the parish of Queimadas on São Nicolau, one of two parishes in the island, "died of hunger" (Carreira 1985: 33). Nevertheless, over the course of the century the island had achieved a level of prosperity not least because of its relatively healthy climate. In 1764 the suggestion was made for the first time that the capital of the islands should be moved there. The suggestion was revived in the 1790s when the bishop decided to relocate his residence permanently to São Nicolau, and in 1802 the Cabo Verde governor also moved his residence there. However, the suggestion that it become the capital was again rejected in Lisbon.

Santo Antão and São Vicente lie so close to each other that their history is intertwined rather in the same way as that of Brava and Fogo. Administratively, São Vicente was a dependency of Santo Antão, but in 1752 it was transferred to São Nicolau. In 1818 it once again became a dependency of Santo Antão, a relationship which remained until 1852.

São Vicente had no water source, and although it had the finest sheltered harbour in the archipelago, no one settled there until the very end of the eighteenth century, though John Green records that "the inhabitants of Saint Anthony come hither a Turtling every year" (1745–7: 673). During the seventeenth century, partly because there were no inhabitants and no official Portuguese presence, the fine harbour, later known as Porto Grande, was frequented by foreign ships, especially by the French and by the Dutch, who needed a waystation before their fleets headed for the South Atlantic during the mid-years of the century. In 1629 the Dutch fleet, on its way to the capture of Olinda in Brazil, stayed at São Vicente for four months (Correia e Silva 1998: 28). In 1724 the government of D. João V at last decided to construct a fort there to secure Portugal's possession of the island. An engineer was sent to make a survey and the so-called Forte Velho was built.

Until the 1780s the island "was used by fishermen as a shelter where they could salt their catch to preserve it with the salt existing there. It was still used by the inhabitants of the nearby islands to collect orchilla and the ambergris left by whales. Certain illicit activities also went on, as the island was frequented by smugglers and pirates who felt safe there because of its abandoned state" (Medina 2009: 44).

Nearby Santo Antão was rather different. Like São Vicente, it had very little rain and the coastal lowlands were barren and desolate, no doubt discouraging any idea of settlement. Instead wild cattle were allowed to roam and survive as best they could. However, the interior of what was the second-largest island of the archipelago had very high mountains, and these habitually trapped the clouds. The tops of the mountains were shrouded in mist, and the water vapour allowed forests to grow and condense into mountain streams which made their way down deep valleys (*ribeiras*) to the coast.

In the eighteenth century, Santo Antão was still subject to a Portuguese aristocrat, the marquess of Gouvea, who had been granted the island to exploit in whatever way he could. John Green mentions "several large Plantations [that] are walled in and cultivated for the Use of the Marquis; being managed by a European Portugueze. There are also cotton Plantations cultivated and Cloths for the Marquis." The lord of the island also took the hides and tallow of the wild goats which were killed, and sent a ship from Portugal every year to collect them (Carreira 1985: 35).

Mysteriously, and without explanation, the author of the *Notícia corográfica e chronológica* said that "the inhabitants of this island were almost like rebels. However, the assistance that the bishop gave for nearly twenty years left them quite tamed and disciplined with good education" (Carreira 1985: 35).

Once discovered, the green uplands of the island attracted settlers, and the first town, also called Ribeira Grande like that of Santiago, was established in 1732. Estimates of population numbers show the extent of the settlement and something of its character. In 1727, the colonial judge Bravo Botelho recorded that 4,000 "believers" lived in Santo Antão, of which 502 were slaves. Another population count at the time estimated that there were 4,302 inhabitants: 10 whites, 1,746 mulattos, 1,900 *forros* or free blacks and 646 slaves (Ferreira 1999: 11).

The inhabitants of Santo Antão were later to acquire a reputation for being refractory, difficult and unmanageable. It is quite possible that these internal conflicts can be traced back to the eighteenth century when the interests of the Crown, the local *câmara* and the agents of the marquess of Gouveia frequently clashed. In 1753 the *ouvidor-geral* (chief justice) of the islands received a report from the officers of the *câmara* about the clashes of interest. He was told of the fines levied on the owners of goats and pigs that ran wild and caused damage; of the improper interventions of judges appointed by the marquess in cases at all levels; of the "despotic and unjustified custom practised by the agents of the marquess of making themselves the heirs of those who died without children even if there were other relatives". This abuse extended not only to freemen (*forros*) but also to slaves who had been allowed to build their own houses. The marquess had also demanded that the *forros* should come to work in his vineyards alongside his slaves, which had not been the custom previously. The *donatário* had prevented people from owning boats for fishing and fetching salt on the grounds they were used for smuggling, and he had had them burnt. The *câmara* maintained it should have the right to distribute vacant lands to the needy with only a fee paid to the *donatário* (Senna Barcellos 2003: II, part 3, 11–14).

In these disputes the rights of slaves and freemen are given some kind of equivalence. This underlines the extent to which, in the settlement of the islands, the distinctions between slaves and freemen had begun to disappear.

5

THE NINETEENTH AND EARLY TWENTIETH CENTURIES

Overview

During the nineteenth century, the creole islands briefly enjoyed a period of great economic growth, their economies flourishing as favourable conditions in the world economy opened up new opportunities for the Atlantic islands in general. However, this burst of prosperity was relatively short-lived as Portugal proved unable to make the most of the islands' assets in the global marketplace.

During the long nineteenth century, the problems caused by the periodic failure of rain appeared to become worse, with droughts and the resultant famines occurring ever more frequently. However, in spite of the heavy mortality that resulted from famine, the population of the islands grew steadily. A possible explanation for this may lie with the changes that began to be made in the government and economy of the islands, which resulted in a transformation of Cabo Verdean society. One result of the political turmoil in Portugal during the first half of the nineteenth century was that the government in Lisbon began to take more interest in the islands, while there was some significant foreign and private investment. On Sal the salt lake of Pedra Lume was brought into production with some investment in infrastructure. Then in the middle years of the century British coaling companies began to make use of the sheltered bay of Porto Grande on São Vicente for supplying coal to the growing number of steamships plying the South Atlantic. The coaling companies employed local labour, and the port town of Mindelo soon grew into the largest town in the archipelago. In the 1860s the coaling companies were joined by the companies managing the long-distance submarine cables, which created the first networks of international telegraphic communication.

The liberal and constitutional regimes which ruled in Lisbon after 1834 brought about important legislative changes, in part motivated by the independence of Brazil and Portugal's concern that it might lose its African colonies as well (Correia e Silva 2004: 153). In the years immediately following the liberal victory in 1834, a slew of decrees reorganised the government of the Cabo Verde islands, creating for the first time a modern administration. Although some slaves continued to be imported for agricultural labour up to the 1840s, slavery was eventually abolished, and this was followed by the abolition of the system of entails, allowing the emergence of a new class of landed entrepreneurs. In 1865 the Banco Nacional Ultramarino (National Overseas Bank) opened in Praia and began to lend on the security of mortgages on the estates. Foreclosing on properties led to the transfer of landownership away from the traditional owners (the *morgados*) and to the appearance of a new class of bourgeois property owners.

The other major socio-economic development was the growth of emigration, especially to the United States. Emigration not only helped to relieve the islands' problems during years of drought but led to an income flow in remittances, which supported families still resident in the islands and the island economy more broadly. Emigration opened up the world to the islanders, who hitherto had been imprisoned in their sterile rocky environment. For António Correia e Silva, the influence of the United States, felt indirectly through the growth of emigration, literally created the modern Cabo Verde—"Cabo Verde is the fruit of Cabo Verdeans from North America". Why did drought and famine cease to be seen simply as a scourge from God and become an example of misgovernment, and why did the lack of schools cease to be just the norm and become a problem that could be tackled? The answer was the experience of emigration (Correia e Silva 2004: 152–3).

Perhaps the most important innovation of all, in its long-term influence on the future of the islands, was the beginnings of an education system in the 1840s, especially the founding of a secondary school on Brava and the seminary on São Nicolau. These, together with the rapid growth of the city of Mindelo on São Vicente, were to result in considerable social change. Although the capital of the islands remained in Praia, Santiago and Fogo were no longer the sole focus of the economic and cultural life of the islands.

In the wider creole world in western Africa there were also major changes under way. In Angola the creole elites of Luanda and Benguela continued to dominate the slave trade, and their trading activities extended ever further inland, with important creole settlements at Ambaca and on the central plateau of Angola. From there trading caravans penetrated the interior, reaching as far as the upper Zambezi and the Barotse kingdom. With the caravans came a flow of firearms and European consumer goods. Although governors were appointed from Lisbon, Luanda and Benguela were largely self-governing creole cities with municipal and ecclesiastical offices held by members of the leading creole families. Further south, in 1840 another coastal city was founded in the bay of Moçâmedes, from where traders began to penetrate the southern interior.

On the West African coast the influence of the old Afro-Portuguese trading families was in decline, their place being taken by Brazilian, Dutch, English and French traders, all of whom attracted a community of African servants who absorbed cultural influences other than those of Portugal. Portuguese influence increasingly became confined to the region of Casamance and the coast of what was later to become Guinea-Bissau. The populations of the creole port towns of Cacheu, Farim and Bissau retained their strong creole culture, including the creole language, and their close connections with the islands, on which they depended for military support.

The most significant developments of all occurred in the Guinea islands. Here the establishment of cocoa and coffee plantations proved highly profitable. The population of the islands grew rapidly with the import of slaves and, later, contract labourers and the personnel to run the plantations. From being remote and largely forgotten island communities, São Tomé and Príncipe now became the jewels in the crown of the Portuguese overseas empire.

As Cabo Verde and the Guinea islands, each in their own way, moved into the orbit of the expanding global capitalist economy, so their orientation moved away from Africa and towards the wider Atlantic world, especially Brazil, Europe and the United States. With the development of education and the spread of literacy among the population of the Cabo Verde islands, a cultural gap opened up between them and the African peoples of the mainland, where similar developments had not yet begun.

A Word of Caution on Nineteenth-Century Writing

In 2017 Danilo Santos published a detailed analysis of Portuguese writing on the Cabo Verde islands, entitled *A imagem do cabo-verdiano nos textos portugueses, 1784–1844* [The image of Cabo Verdeans in Portuguese texts, 1784–1844]. He pointed out that almost all the authors came from Portugal and viewed the islands with a sceptical European gaze. Their emphasis, without exception, was on the backwardness, neglect and lack of civilisation that they saw. Their prejudices, he warned, need to be treated with caution. The same warning needs to be made about the long and detailed account of the islands published in two volumes in 1861 by Francisco Travassos Valdez, entitled *Six Years of a Traveller's Life in Western Africa*. The author was the son of the count of Bonfim, a Portuguese political figure of some importance. In 1852 he had obtained an official appointment as the Portuguese member of the Mixed Commission in Luanda, and determined to use his position to write an account of the Portuguese territories in western Africa. Although it is clear that he made use of published sources, like Lopes de Lima's *Ensaio sobre a statistica*, he also visited the Cabo Verde and Guinea islands. However, the unacknowledged purpose of the book, which was published in English, was exactly the opposite of that of the writers considered by Danilo Santos. He was determined to paint a glowing picture of prosperity and progress. Although he first visited the islands in the early 1850s when there was a series of severe droughts, these are scarcely mentioned and the islands are described as green and fertile—in Fogo, for example, "the eye is gratified by numerous gardens and farms in a flourishing condition. From on board the ship the scene presented is most beautiful" (Travassos Valdez 1861: I, 143), and this is a constant theme throughout the book. So, although his account of the islands is full of rare and colourful detail, the author's judgements need to be treated with extreme caution.

Drought, Famine and Population Increase

Though not all the islands were equally badly affected, the historical record shows that the Cabo Verde islands suffered famine conditions in 1790–1, 1804–6, 1810–14, 1826–7, 1830–4, 1845–6, 1850–1, 1853–5, 1856–60, 1863–6, 1875–6, 1883–6, 1889–90, 1896–7 and 1899–1900 (Patterson 1988: 305; Carreira 1982: 16). The northern *barlavento* group suffered in particular from the failure of the rains, and the eastern islands from effects of the climate of the Sahara. The droughts were made worse by the long history of exploitation of the land in the islands. For centuries most of the islands had been in effect ranges for wild cattle and goats, and the destruction of vegetation due to unregulated grazing had been severe. Soil erosion had stripped mountain slopes of topsoil, while the system of share-cropping and renting of tiny plots of land, coupled with the effects of the monoculture of crops like sugar on larger estates, had effectively prevented the development of farming practices that would have preserved the fertility of the land.

During the periods of drought there was little the inhabitants could do. Some were able to escape to mainland Africa to find a living, and Cabo Verdeans were increasingly to be found cultivating tracts of land (known as *pontas*) around Guinea villages. Emigration to the United States was also gradually becoming an option, but emigration was never cost-free and depended on networks of support for would-be migrants. By the 1860s Cabo Verdeans were being forced to work on the cocoa plantations of São Tomé—a kind of solution to the problems caused by famine that was to be repeated from time to time until independence in 1975 (Patterson

1988: 305). However, none of this prevented massive increases in mortality due to malnutrition, disease and starvation.

According to David Patterson's calculations, the total population of the islands fell from 88,000 in 1831 to 56,000 in 1834, a decline of 15 per cent each year over this period. A similar decline in population was registered between 1864 and 1867. Starvation and early death became the life experience of large sections of the population. Most were trapped in their barren islands, with what little communication between the islands that existed being dependent on the movement of the occasional sailing ship.

However, this story cannot be written in the figures of mortality alone because the statistics also show an extraordinary resilience in the population and a marked growth overall in the course of the century. Between 1800 and 1900 the total population of the islands grew from 56,000 to 147,000, and there were periods of growth as exceptional as the intervening periods of high mortality. Between 1867 and 1874, for example, the population rose from 57,000 to 91,000, peaking with annual increases of 5.9 per cent. And population growth was particularly marked between 1874 and the end of the century, when the total rose from 91,000 to 147,000 and annual growth rates ranged between 2 and 3.3 per cent (Patterson 1988: 297). By the end of the century the growth of the Cabo Verde population had already far exceeded the capacity of the islands to feed themselves, and the twentieth century was to see a great Cabo Verdean diaspora throughout Europe and the Atlantic world and the birth of a nation whose strong sense of identity was not confined within any national boundaries.

It is difficult to account for this extraordinary resilience of the population. In the previous century and up to the 1840s, some of the population loss had always been made up for by importing slaves to fill gaps in the labour force. Convicts also continued to be sent to serve their sentences in the islands. John Barrow, visiting in 1792, thought that this had become a major element in the islanders' ethnic make-up.

> The only Europeans we saw were the Governor, his secretary, the officer commanding of the troops, a raw-boned Scottish sergeant six feet high, and his wife ... The clergy were people of colour,

and some of them perfectly black. The officers of justice, of the customs and other departments in the civil and military services, the troops, the peasantry, and the traders, were all blacks, or at least so very dark that they could scarcely be supposed to have any mixture of European blood in their veins. Yet most of them aspire to the honour of Portuguese extraction and are proud of tracing their origin to a race of heroes who, disdaining the restraints of laws at home, contrived to get themselves transported abroad, where their free and ungovernable spirits could exert themselves without control. The Cap de Verd islands were to Portugal what Botany Bay is to England, an asylum for convicted criminals. (Barrow 1806)

However, the numbers of convicts were never great. Between 1800 and 1880, 2,570 convicts (*degredados*) were sent to Cabo Verde (2,487 men and 83 women), an average of 32 per year, and only 307 of these were sentenced to perpetual exile (Carreira 2000: 340).

Some commentators attributed population growth to the unrestricted sexual promiscuity of Cabo Verdeans, an explanation still being advanced by Orlando Ribeiro in his study of Fogo Island in the 1990s (Ribeiro 1997: 160). Few demographers would subscribe to such an explanation, expressed in terms of morality, though the comparative rarity of formal marriage and the early age at which girls became pregnant may have been a factor, the age of marriage (or first pregnancy) often being considered of particular importance in explaining demographic profiles. This explanation apart, a Malthusian explanation for both the decline and subsequent overall growth of the population is all that is possible. In spite of regular droughts and famines, there must have been some overall improvement in nutrition and general living standards in the course of the century.

Protest and Civil Disorder

Following the liberal revolution in Lisbon in 1820 and the independence of Brazil in 1822, Portugal suffered a prolonged period of unrest which, in 1832, became a full-scale civil war. The Atlantic islands and the mainland colonies did not escape involvement in these conflicts. While the Azores became the centre of opposition to the absolutist regime of Dom Miguel and declared for Queen Maria II and her liberal backers, in Mozambique, Angola and Madeira there were movements to break with Portugal altogether. These creole communities had by the early nineteenth century formed strong ties with Brazil, with which most of their trade was conducted, to which wealthy creoles often went for education, and with which cultural ties were strong. In the end these separatist movements collapsed, partly at least because Britain was prepared to recognise Portugal's sovereign rights to these African territories in order to pursue its own agenda of suppressing the slave trade.

Cabo Verde was also to experience a prolonged period of social unrest, linked to metropolitan politics but also reflecting the tensions of a slave-owning society in an age when the winds of liberal reform had already begun to blow. One such incident which occurred in Boa Vista was described by Travassos Valdez. "On the day of Vera Cruz, the third of May … all the slaves are allowed to be free for twenty-four hours, and to enjoy all sorts of amusements during that time, without any restraint from their masters. The indulgence granted on such occasions was sometimes carried to great excess, and serious results often followed. On one occasion in 1811 they entered into a conspiracy to rebel and free themselves from servitude, first murdering their masters. But fortunately their design was discovered" (Travassos Valdez 1861: 80).

In 1822, shortly after the adoption of the liberal constitution in 1821, there was an attempted rebellion of the 300 *degredados* in Santiago, and in January 1824 there was an uprising among the slaves, who had heard about the new civil liberties enshrined in the Portuguese constitution and claimed that this meant they were free men. The newly appointed governor reported the incident: "The slaves, considering themselves freed by the Constitution and hoping that by my arrival they would have their manumission; the *degredados* tried a general uprising and flight. And the good and honourable citizens fearing how this whole scene might develop, armed themselves and prepared to defend their houses at all cost" (Carreira 2000: 339).

In March 1835 (shortly after the final victory of the liberals in Portugal and the exile of D.Miguel), the battalion of troops in Santiago, described by Lopes de Lima as "criminal elements from the army of Dom Miguel" (Lopes de Lima 1844a: 61–2), mutinied, plundered the town of Praia, and declared for D.Miguel, murdering all of their officers except two. On this occasion the rural population "took up arms for the Queen and the Charter". Some months later, in December, an uprising broke out among the slaves on the Santiago estates who had noted that the mutinous soldiers had not been punished. The plot was hatched on an estate four kilometres from the capital, and the plan was for the slaves, aided by free blacks, to murder all the "whites". The plot was betrayed, and although a party of armed slaves attacked the capital, the town was defended by its inhabitants and the slaves dispersed. Two of the ringleaders were subsequently shot.

A few years later there was a revolt by poor peasants who rented land on one of the *fazendas* near Praia. They refused to pay their rents and declared that the land they worked was theirs. António Carreira had no doubt that these and other disturbances were in part stirred up by the presence of dissident convicts and by the relative powerlessness of the authorities to maintain control, as well as by the political turmoil of the times (Carreira 2000: 345). As a result of the political conflagrations in Portugal, the numbers of *degredados* sent to Cabo Verde had increased, and many of them were political dissidents. According to Carreira, thirty-three of these were sentenced for "*conjuração contra a realeza ou ofensas ao rei*" (conspiracy against royalty or offences against the king) and nineteen for sedition or rebellion (2000: 340).

Although these revolts had a specific and local context, they took place "at the turning of a great page in the social and economic history of the slaveocracies of the whole world" (Carreira 2000: 345–6).

The Beginning of the Modern State

A number of descriptions of the Cabo Verde islands were produced by Portuguese writers towards the end of the eighteenth and in the early nineteenth centuries, culminating in the work of José Joaquim

Lopes de Lima, who worked on a factual and statistical survey of all Portugal's overseas possessions. These writers were mostly officials who served in the islands and were appalled at the backwardness and primitiveness of what they found. One of the problems on which all commented was the isolation of the communities within the islands and the isolation of the islands themselves in relation to each other. There was no regular contact between one island and another, and it often took months before a communication issued by the authorities in Praia was received by communities in the other islands. The lack of inter-island shipping was only partially made good by the presence of American ships in the ports of some of the islands.

Francisco Travassos Valdez records that even in mid-century, travel between the islands was by no means easy. One feature that struck him was the difficulty of going ashore when a ship made landfall at one of the islands. In spite of major improvements to the government of the islands in the previous fifty years, few of them had any quays or harbour works. Having commented with approval on the investment of Manuel António Martins, who had constructed wharves at Sal and Boa Vista to aid the loading of salt, he noted that, in order to take on water at Santo Antão, "it has to be brought by men swimming with the casks to the beach and returning in the same manner". At Praia, there were two possible landing places. At one, passengers were "compelled to jump on the rocks, against which the waves were furiously beating", while at Praya Grande "a strong surf is always breaking, through which passengers and goods must be conveyed to and from ships on the shoulders of men". The same was true at Fogo, where passengers had to be carried to shore on the shoulders of the "blacks" (Travassos Valdez 1861: 96–7, 142).

Even within the islands the isolation of small communities was extreme. A large part of the population had settled inland away from pirate raids, and there were few roads—at best a rough network of paths linked the settlements. One consequence of this was the almost total absence of wheeled vehicles (Santos 2017: 98, 104–5, 109). Worst affected was Santo Antão. The fertile cloud forest on the high mountains and the deep mountain valleys were almost inaccessible, and a visiting priest recorded having to be hoisted up the cliffs with ropes (Santos 2017: 108). A. B. Ellis, in his unpleasant and prejudiced book *West African Islands*, recorded a story (which sounds rather improbable) about a bishop who wanted to travel overland to visit the community at Ribeira Grande on Santo Antão. He had to be hoisted up the cliffs, but when he got halfway through his journey, he refused to go on or turn back. As a result he camped where he was, and his companions began work on a road to rescue him. The bishop apparently died before he could be rescued, but work on the road continued and Ellis claimed that he himself had travelled along it in the 1870s (Ellis 1885: 153–4).

The isolation in which many inland communities lived meant that they had little contact with the outside world—with "civilization", as it was described by contemporary writers. Ironically it was the three desert islands of Sal, Maio and Boa Vista that had the most regular contact with foreign ships coming to collect salt, and their few inhabitants were more in touch with "civilisation" than those of the other islands. In contrast, few foreign ships now called at Santiago or Fogo, which had been the earliest islands of settlement. Brava and São Nicolau were already on a wholly different trajectory, as they were the islands most visited by American whalers.

In 1834 the Portuguese liberals, having triumphed in the civil war, began the overhaul of the whole administration. The Cabo Verde islands were now to be referred to as a *provincia*—beginning the use of names by which successive Portuguese regimes tried to redefine what was the reality: that the islands were just a colony. As well as the islands, this province included five garrisoned settlements (*presídios*) on the Guinea coast, which were subject to the island government. The Cabo Verde bishopric covered the same area as the civil administration. The province was administered by a governor general, a post originally created in 1587, and each island constituted a *concelho* and had an administrator in overall charge of its affairs—these included the organisation of local militias, the supervision of the Crown's revenues, and the administration of justice. The governors had overall control of the military and civil government, and financial matters were handled by a Finance Board presided over by the governor. There was a Government Council made up of the heads of the military, judicial, fiscal and ecclesiastical departments.

Although Praia remained the capital of the province, the disorders and maladministration of Cabo Verde had often given rise to the idea that the capital should be located elsewhere, not least because Praia was deemed to be unhealthy. Various projects were advanced to move the capital to São Nicolau, where the bishop resided, Fogo or even São Vicente—though in the end none of these were adopted (Santos 2017: 130–4). Praia, meanwhile, had been partly rebuilt and made into a presentable town between 1823 and 1826 by Governor João de Mata Chapuzet, a military architect. Streets and squares were laid out, good stone houses built and, according to Travassos Valdez, "a beautiful embowered garden planted for public accommodation ... Near the hospital is a windmill which was erected by order of Governor Chapuzet, and which I believe is the only one in the Cabo Verdes." Ever keen to promote the commercial potential of the islands, he added: "there are also a number of good shops which sell every description of European and American produce" (Travassos Valdez 1861: I, 97, 99).

A Board for Agricultural Improvements had been established in 1811 to oversee "the distribution of uncultivated waste lands as *sesmarias*". *Sesmarias* were a type of tenure created in Portugal in the fourteenth century by which the holder had to show he had cultivated his land within the number of years specified in the grant. Improving agriculture was a priority, according to Lopes de Lima, writing in 1844: "I never tire of repeating that the first necessity to improve the agriculture of the islands of Cabo Verde is the planting of trees", but he says this was actively opposed by the landowners, who claimed that trees made the desiccation of the land worse (1844a: 8, 33).

The first printing press was brought to the islands in 1842, and the *Boletim Official* began publication the same year. For thirty years this was the only regular publication in the islands and it became an outlet not only for official government announcements but for early examples of Cabo Verdean literature. In 1877 the *Independente* began publication in Praia, and there followed a whole series of non-official publications, mostly published in Mindelo or in the capital (ISCSP 1966: 295–301).

The situation of the Church was rather confused. The bishop had oversight of all ecclesiastical matters in the islands and on the mainland, but since the late eighteenth century he was usually resident in São Nicolau, while the official centre of the diocese remained the ruined cathedral of Ribeira Grande. In 1844 there were in all 33 parishes, 11 of them being in Santiago (Santos 2017: 118). Lopes de Lima was emphatic that the bishop and his cathedral should be located in a single place, which should be the effective centre of church administration.

Contemporary commentators blamed the poverty and backwardness of the islands on the lack of education and religion, the two being closely connected as the Church was the only institution able to offer education of any kind (Santos 2017: 170–2). The need to provide education in the islands had first been recognised during the rule of the marques de Pombal in Portugal. While he was carrying out the first major reforms in education in Portugal, the Overseas Council issued instructions for creating an education system in the Cabo Verde islands and initiated a scheme whereby boys would be sent to Lisbon to receive an education. A school was opened in Praia in 1817, and after this twelve elementary schools were opened in Fogo, Brava, Maio, Boa Vista, São Nicolau and Santo Antão. A scheme was proposed for each parish to have its school, and the budget of 1842–3 made provision for a total of thirty-eight island schools.

What was striking was the way that the islanders, accused by so many contemporaries of being ignorant and barbarous, responded to educational opportunities. In 1841 José Chelmicki could write that "it was rare to find anyone in the islands of Cabo Verde who did not know how to read and write" (Santos 2017: 175). Although proposals for secondary education had been put forward as early as 1841 and a secondary school had briefly functioned in Praia in 1860, it was not until 1866 that a seminary, dedicated to São José, was set up in São Nicolau, which in 1892 added a secondary school and became a *seminário-liceu*, with a curriculum that included mathematics, science, classical languages and literature. This centre of secondary education continued until 1917 and was responsible for the education of generations of Cabo Verdeans, who became prominent in creating the literate and political culture in the islands. This set them apart from most of mainland Africa and even from rural Portugal, where levels of literacy remained stubbornly low throughout the same period. By the First World War a system of primary education was in place throughout the archipelago, and it became the boast of Cabo Verdeans that there was a higher level of education in the islands than in Portugal itself. The creation of an education system, limited at first but of great long-term significance, was one of the principal achievements of the nineteenth century.

While these administrative changes were taking place, the whaling industry had led to the growth of new ports and urban centres with some basic industrial installations. This, and the increase of emigration, forced the Portuguese to extend effective bureaucratic control over all the islands. Just as the slave trade in the early sixteenth century had given birth to a governmental structure, which was needed so that it could be regulated and taxed, so emigration in the nineteenth century was to prompt the creation and extension of new bureaucratic structures.

As droughts and subsequent famines and epidemics were so frequent, it might have been supposed that the government would organise programmes of relief and make provision for future emergencies. However, it appears that each outbreak of famine was treated as an isolated emergency, with some relief being organised locally or sent from Lisbon but with no prior development of contingency plans. During the famine of 1830–4, "The captain of an American ship who was trading in Cabo Verde, in sympathy with so much misery made representations to his country's Congress which generously sent eleven ships with food to aid the starving while a merchant benefactor ordered a cargo of maize to be sent at his cost from the Gambia" (Ribeiro 1997: 185).

Measures were seldom taken by the authorities until famine had already begun. The government then tried to obtain emergency loans and public works were initiated, though there was often no food to be bought with the wages and the people were too weak to work anyway. Moreover, the government often responded to the famine emergency by trying to prevent people moving from island to island in search of food or charitable relief—a bureaucratic response which continued from time to time until the end of Portuguese rule. The famines of the 1890s gave rise for the first time to a programme of government-funded public works (Filho 1996: 230), but the finances of the government were too stretched to pay for this and provision was made instead for "vagrants" to be contracted for São Tomé. It would not be until the twentieth century that any serious thought was given to anticipating the crises caused by recurrent droughts and to making preparations in advance.

The Portuguese government, so often criticised for its inaction when faced by famine in Cabo Verde, was not alone in its failures. Between 1845 and 1852 the British government had failed to intervene when famine killed at least one million people in Ireland, and as late as 1943 the British government in India did little to mitigate the disastrous Bengal famine, which saw between one and four million deaths.

Cabo Verde Islands and the Global Economy: The Salt Trade

With the decline in the slave trade, salt had remained the one commodity that the Cabo Verde islands produced for a worldwide market. The salt had always been exploited in a rather haphazard manner. It was produced by a natural process of evaporation in salt lakes, and when ships called, the few inhabitants of the salt-producing islands (Boa Vista, Maio and Sal) made money hiring out donkeys to carry the salt down to the ships. There was little attempt by the Portuguese Crown, or the captains to whom the islands had been granted, to develop or even derive much profit from the commodity.

However, in the early nineteenth century, a Portuguese named Manuel António Martins began the large-scale exploitation of the salt lake on Sal known as Pedra Lume. This was located in the crater of an extinct volcano, and the problem of moving the salt was overcome by digging a tunnel through the side of the volcano to provide access for pack animals. Later a cable was run on pylons through the tunnel and a narrow-gauge railway constructed, which José Lopes de Lima proudly declared to be the first railway in the Portuguese dominions (the first railway in Portugal itself was constructed in 1856) (Lopes de Lima 1844a: 42). Along this railway wagons pulled by donkeys brought the salt to a quay at Santa Maria; the empty wagons then hoisted sails and apparently "sailed" back along the tracks (Massa and Massa 2001: 43, 138). Francisco Travassos Valdez's description in 1852 reverses this procedure. According to his account, in order to operate this "tramway", "to save the expense of steam, sails are attached to each carriage, by which it is propelled from the salt pits to the south ports, where a wharf has been erected ... the empty waggons being then drawn up to the salt pits by donkeys" (Travassos Valdez 1861: I, 45).

Martins also invested heavily in Boa Vista, where he financed the building of a quay at Sal Rei, the main port. According to Travassos Valdez, he also laid the first iron pipes to channel drinking water to the town of Praia (1861: I, 72, 102).

On Sal island the town of Santa Maria was officially founded in 1830 by Martins. The original small wooden houses were all built with timber sent from America. Slave labour was imported from West Africa and was used to extract the sand and soil until bedrock was exposed, upon which the "salt pans" would be constructed. Slaves built the original wooden windmill pumps which fed the saltwater into the *salinas*. The original dock at Santa Maria was constructed by this same labour force. At the peak of its production, up to 30,000 tons of salt were exported each year, particularly to Brazil and mainland Africa. For a brief period the Cabo Verde islands played a significant part in this sector of international commerce. In the 1880s, however, Brazil raised tariffs against Cabo Verdean salt and the export went into decline.

A novel entitled *O senhor das ilhas* [The lord of the islands] was written about the career of Manuel António Martins by his great-granddaughter, the distinguished Portuguese writer Maria Isabel Barreno, one of the three authors of *Novas cartas portugesas* (*New Portuguese Letters*), which was published in 1972 and which became a major challenge to literary culture in the era of the Salazar dictatorship.

Cabo Verde Islands and the Global Economy: Porto Grande

Meanwhile, Porto Grande on the island of São Vicente was to enjoy a hundred years as one of the major ports of Atlantic navigation before also facing decline, as the salt trade had done (Newitt 2019). Porto Grande is by far the best natural harbour in the archipelago.

A British Foreign Office handbook, produced during the First World War, neatly summarised its advantages: "The bay has an entrance two miles wide and penetrates inland for one and a half miles. Between the points of entrance there is an even bottom of 22 fathoms, shoaling on the west side to nine fathoms at three-quarters of a cable from the shore. There is ample anchorage on hard sand and the harbour is sheltered by lofty hills, though when a north-east wind is blowing there are often sudden squalls. In the centre of the bay the depth of water is 10 fathoms, but alongside the wharves 8 feet only" (British Foreign Office 1920: 14).

However, in spite of these advantages, the island of São Vicente had attracted no permanent settlement because of its exceptionally dry, almost desert-like, conditions, and for 400 years Porto Grande had been almost totally neglected by the Portuguese. It was, in fact, Dutch and English Indiamen and American whalers, vessels which had need of a safe anchorage but had good reason to avoid the Portuguese authorities, that made most use of the bay. In 1784 the anonymous author of the *Notícia corográfica e chronológica* listed São Vicente among the "*ilhas desertas*", commenting that it was "almost totally arid, produced no food at all, and only cotton and orchilla" (Carreira 1985: 36). As late as the 1820s sailing ships bound for the Cape of Good Hope or South America still avoided São Vicente and stopped at Praia, occasionally at Brava or Fogo, or at Maio to take on a cargo of salt.

São Vicente had usually been linked with Santo Antão when grants for the exploitation of the islands were made, but in 1786 the island was given, along with the title of *capitão-mor*, to João Carlos da Fonseca from Fogo. In 1795 twenty married couples and thirty African slaves from Guinea were sent to found a settlement. A church was built and a priest appointed. A further attempt to plant a settlement was made in 1819 by the governor of Cabo Verde, António Pusich. He brought in some peasants from Santo Antão and renamed the settlement Leopoldina after the Austrian bride of the Infante Dom Pedro. This settlement failed during the drought of 1824–6 (Almeida 1925: 67; Correia e Silva 1998: 30).

It was the changing commercial and political world of the South Atlantic that turned the arid and deserted bay on São Vicente into a thriving seaport and a vital strategic link in two interlocking imperial systems. During the 1820s, Brazil and Argentina, now independent countries, had opened their ports to European, principally British, commerce. At the same time the campaign against the slave trade was gathering momentum, and squadrons of warships from Britain, France, the United States and Portugal operated against the trade. Although the forced emigration of African slaves to the New World eventually began to decline under this international pressure, it was replaced by a steadily increasing flow of emigration from Europe and the Atlantic islands. These factors all pointed to the need for a major international port to service transatlantic flows of people and goods.

However, these factors alone would not have created the city of Mindelo, had steam navigation not begun the slow but inexorable process of replacing sail. Steamers moving between Europe, South America and the East could not carry enough fuel for their whole voyage and needed to take on more coal at some port en route. For bunkering purposes, steamers needed large, sheltered, deep-water ports, and Porto Grande offered exactly the right conditions.

The first attempts to set up a coaling depot were made by the East India Company in 1838, and in the same year the Septembrist government in Portugal officially established the town of Mindelo and declared that it would be the future capital of the archipelago (República de Cabo Verde 1984: 13). However, it was after 1850 that the development of Porto Grande really took off. In that year the Royal Mail Steam Packet Company obtained a concession for a coaling station and made Porto Grande a regular stop on the voyage to the Cape and India. That year the British consul, John Rendall, decided to move the British consulate to the new town of Mindelo. Rendall was an enthusiastic advocate of Porto Grande and founded one of the earliest coaling companies. As described in his book *A Guide to the Cap de Verd Islands*, which he published in 1856, with the official approval of the Foreign Office, the arid, desert island of São Vicente seems hardly recognisable. "The salubrity of St Vincent is very superior", he wrote. Water is in "great abundance" six to ten feet from the surface; a road has been completed to Green Mountain (Monte Verde); and "at present a good deal of cultivation is going on". The harbour, he optimistically declared, can shelter 300 ships

(Rendall 2004: 2, 3, 27). When Francisco Travassos Valdez visited the island in 1852, he saw 47 ships in the port and thought that 6 or 7 ships arrived daily to take on coal (1861: I, 34).

The American anti-slave trade squadron also needed a base for its operations and began to use Porto Grande. A vice-consul was installed and an American cemetery was walled off a little way from the beach (Thomas 1860: 332). A number of British steamship lines now visited Porto Grande to resupply their vessels with coal, and by 1860 there were eight British coaling companies established in Mindelo. Travassos Valdez described how "The captains of vessels find it a great convenience to obtain coals and secure anchorage in [São Vicente], and a plentiful supply of good water and refreshment at [Santo Antão] ... There is a great influx of passengers from Europe, Africa and America; these, together with the crews of the numerous vessels, contribute much to the increase of the wealth of the islanders" (Travassos Valdez 1861: I, 35).

Coal bunkering required large amounts of labour. Cabo Verdeans began to come from the other islands to work for the coaling companies, which built them small stone houses near the coal depots. The Portuguese administration followed. In 1852 a small fort, Fortim del Rey, was constructed; in 1858 a customs house was built; and in 1860 a Municipal Committee was established, marking the separation of the island administration from that of neighbouring Santo Antão (Correia e Silva 1998: 36). Later a residence was built for the governor of Cabo Verde, who began to spend some time in the island because of its growing international importance. However, the official capital of Cabo Verde was never transferred from Praia, as the Septembrists had intended.

Mindelo suffered a catastrophe early on when, following severe drought in 1850, the population was devastated by an epidemic of yellow fever. People fled the town and there was not enough labour to load the ships. Francisco Travassos Valdez, unwarily going ashore, found most of the inmates in the English hotel confined to bed. "Most of the houses we passed were deserted and shut up, the former occupants either being dead, or having escaped from the contagion of the city to a more salubrious part of the island" (1861: I, 37–8).

The embryo town administration was in no condition to deal with such a problem, and the disease was left to run its course.

The prosperity of Porto Grande fluctuated as the coaling companies vied with each other to establish a monopoly over the supply of coal. As a consequence of their monopolistic practices, coal prices remained generally high. When, in 1875, another large coaling company entered the market, the immediate consequence was the lowering of the price of coal and the doubling of the number of ships calling at the port. The Portuguese took advantage of this situation to raise the tax on coal, and state revenues increased five times by 1885 and nine times by 1890. In 1884 two new coaling companies appeared, but this was followed by another round of mergers and the new company, holding a near monopoly, once again raised the price of coal until, in 1891, it was twice as expensive as the coal sold in Gran Canaria. In 1891 an experiment was made of granting a licence to a Portuguese coaling company, and this resulted once again in the lowering of the price of coal and a boom in the numbers of ships arriving in Porto Grande. However, within three years this company had been bought up by British interests as well (Prata 2014: 49–69; Newitt 2019).

In 1894, the year when Porto Grande reached the height of its importance, 2,464 ships used the port—1,881 being long-haul steamers and 34 non-Portuguese warships—while 194,793 passengers passed through the port in transit. Altogether 156 coaling ships delivered 657,634 tons of coal, a figure exceeded only by Port Said, Singapore and Malta (Machado 1891: 34–5). Between 1890 and the First World War, Porto Grande saw a gradually declining level of activity as rivals in Gran Canaria and Dakar ate into its business. In 1910, 301,400 tons of coal were imported; in 1913, 1,414 steamships cleared the port at a rate of about three a day. Before the First World War, on average, goods imported by British firms in São Vicente accounted for two-thirds of all the imports into the Cabo Verde islands, providing the government with a substantial part of its revenue (Newitt 2019).

However, Porto Grande was not just a coaling station. With the laying of the transatlantic cables, São Vicente became a major link in the network connecting Europe with South America and Africa. The first cables reached São Vicente in 1874 and from there lines ran to the Azores, Portugal and England and to Cape Town and South America. By the end of the century lines also ran to Bathurst and Freetown in West Africa. The Western Telegraph Company maintained offices and staff in São Vicente, and in 1916 a wireless relay station was also in operation.

In 1914 the city of Mindelo had a population of 8,500, twice the size of any other town in the archipelago, including Praia (British Foreign Office 1920: 7). The character of the city was in the process of being forged by the rivalries and interactions of the British commercial community and the Portuguese administration, while ordinary Cabo Verdeans, subjected to the harsh conditions of drought, famine and a ruthless proletarianisation, were increasingly using Porto Grande as a staging post for emigration to the United States.

The Rise of Mindelo and Cabo Verde's Links with the Wider World

In 1836, when the town of Mindelo was officially created, São Vicente had almost no native population. The few inhabitants of the island, it was reported, went round in a state of *"nudez absoluta"* (República de Cabo Verde 1984: 13). The city was entirely the creation of transatlantic commerce. From the date of its foundation, it was part of two competing colonial empires. The British provided all the economic activity of the city, and the port developed entirely to meet the various needs of the British empire. In 1879 there were 157 businesses established in the town, virtually all of them British, and British companies owned most of the waterfront of the port (Prata 2014: 55, 58). At the same time, Mindelo was politically and administratively controlled by Portugal. This dual relationship, so important in shaping São Vicente society, was not unique. Parallels can be found in Madeira and, more clearly, in the Mozambican port city of Lourenço Marques (Maputo), which, nominally ruled by Portugal, became a port of great strategic and economic importance for Britain in the last years of the nineteenth century.

Seen from the long perspective on Cabo Verdean history, the rise of Mindelo replicated the rapid rise of Ribeira Grande during the first century of Portuguese settlement, when it became a port of call for international shipping. It also helped to rescue the islands from the remorseless poverty that had become their lot. A steady income stream enabled proper government buildings to be erected and for the infrastructure of a modern state to be put in place, not only in São Vicente but also in the other islands. Moreover, the cosmopolitan atmosphere of Mindelo, where people from all over the world intermingled, created the conditions for a flourishing cultural life, which was to prove crucial for the emergence of a modern Cabo Verdean identity.

Mindelo also contributed to the racial diversity of the islands' population. While Santiago, with its dispersed peasant population inhabiting the remote island interior, retained strong elements of African culture and the population a distinctly African physiognomy, Mindelo from its inception was outward-looking, culturally aligned with the Atlantic world and much influenced by the large resident English population. The make-up of its population from the first reflected the passage through the port of peoples from every part of the world. The only other island to experience a similar turn to the outside world was Brava, with its strong connections with the United States

Abolition of Morgadios and Slavery

The regime of land tenure introduced in the earliest days of settlement had continued to shape landholding in the islands. The *morgadios* and *capelas* were entailed estates secured in the ownership of certain families, but from the start these large estates had been worked by slaves imported from West Africa. In the course of the seventeenth and eighteenth centuries most of the owners of the *morgadios* were absentees living in Portugal, and the estates were managed by agents. Frequently no attempt was made to cultivate plantations or to produce exports crops, and the estates were divided up into smallholdings and either rented out or let on the basis of share-cropping. There was common agreement that this system of land management was highly inefficient and in part responsible for the deterioration of the land and the widespread poverty among the peasantry.

THE NINETEENTH AND EARLY TWENTIETH CENTURIES

Meanwhile, the slave population was on the decline. Pirate raids often provided an opportunity for slaves to desert, and the frequent famines were particularly severe on the slave population. Slaves continued to escape and rob the properties, and in 1835 there was a slave revolt in Santiago. As António Carreira summarised the situation: "everyone—government and *senhores* [slave owners]—had lost control of the slaves" (2000: 383). Yet still the institution did not entirely die. New slaves continued to be purchased whenever possible and brought across from Portuguese settlements on the Guinea coast.

The abolition of the slave trade, and of slavery in the Portuguese Atlantic world, was drawn out over a hundred or more years, beginning with the abolition of slavery in Portugal itself in 1761. In 1817 Portugal had agreed to end the slave trade north of the equator, though the trade between Portugal's colonies was allowed to continue. In 1836 the Septembrist government in Portugal formally abolished the slave trade, though Portuguese settled in Guinea could still bring up to ten slaves with them when travelling to the islands. It was only in 1842 that another treaty, forced on Portugal by Britain, declared the slave trade to be piracy, thereby allowing British warships to arrest Portuguese slavers.

The first moves to end slavery in the African territories were taken soon after Brazil banned the import of slaves in 1851. In August 1852 the governor of Cabo Verde addressed a memorandum on the topic to Lisbon. He pointed out that the treaties with Britain made it impossible for slaves to be moved from one island to another. As slave owners could not now employ slaves productively, he said, the only option was to end slavery altogether (*acabar com a escravidão*). This would best be done in stages, first banning all imports and granting freedom to any slaves brought in against this law; then to declare all children of slaves to be free; and, finally, to allow slaves to buy freedom by working for their *senhores* until their value had been paid off. Freeing the children of slaves would, he maintained, "put an end to the scandalous scenes of prostitution which many *senhores* facilitated in order to possess a greater number of miserable slaves" (Carreira 2000: 382).

Between 1853 and 1856 a detailed census of slaves and their owners was carried out in Cabo Verde, a fact which by itself demonstrates how far a working bureaucracy had established itself in the islands. The census included details of the slaves' ethnicity, their physical characteristics and state of health. In 1858 it was announced that slavery would finally come to an end in twenty years' time. In 1869 the end of slavery was declared but with the proviso that the slaves would continue to work for their masters in the meantime. Even this provision was finally ended in 1875, which should be considered the definitive date for the ending of slavery as such in all the Portuguese colonies. However, forced contracted labour continued in the Guinea islands and a compulsory labour obligation was introduced in the mainland colonies in 1899—though this obligation did not apply in the Cabo Verde islands. The last count of slaves in Cabo Verde was made in 1868, when there were 4,020 still officially registered.

Figures from the slavery census of 1856 are quite revealing. Two-thirds of the slaves came from the region that would eventually be the Portuguese colony of Guinea-Bissau, and most of them appear to have been domestic servants. There was a total of 1,358 registered owners of slaves, and the average slave holding was 3.49 slaves. Not surprisingly, in Santiago, the home of the old slave plantations, the average holding was 4.41, but in Brava, where emigration to the United States was already well established, it was only 1.95. Figures seem to show that on Sal slaves were still employed in the salt-works (Lobban 1995: 31–5). Of a total of 5,182 registered slaves, 2,422 were located in the island of Santiago, and a quarter of all slaves were under the age of 10 (Carreira 2000: 396).

The decline of the *morgadios* or great estates of Santiago and Fogo had been the theme of numerous reports on the islands (Santos 2017). In 1844 Lopes de Lima had written of Santiago, "this island has 54 *vinculos* [entails]—between *morgadios* and *capelas* ... and this is without doubt one of the reasons why two-thirds of the land is uncultivated" (1844a: II, 22). The victory of the liberals in the civil wars in 1834 had been followed by acts abolishing the various entails, life leases and feudal dues that entangled the market for land in Portugal, but it was only in 1865 that the *morgadios* and *capelas* were finally brought to an end in Cabo Verde. The indebted and encumbered estates could now be mortgaged or sold, and the same year the Banco Nacional Ultramarino was established in Praia. Access to credit and the freeing up of the market in land made possible the emergence of new entrepreneurs who sought to acquire landed estates. A solid landowning bourgeoisie began to be formed, particularly in Fogo and Santiago. In the town of São Filipe in Fogo, the large *sobrados* or townhouses that were built were a sign of the wealth and high social status now acquired by those with the resources to buy landed estates. These changes, however, did little to benefit the vast majority of the landless population.

Emigration to the United States

Although failure of the rains and frequent famines were conditions peculiar to the Cabo Verde islands, the other Atlantic islands (the Azores and Madeira) were also experiencing conditions that would drive their inhabitants to emigrate. Both the Azores and Madeira suffered from the concentration of land in the hands of absentee landowners, with the resulting poverty of the small-scale tenant farmers. These conditions became ever more severe as the population grew. In Madeira disease hit the vines which provided the island with its main export crop, and in the Azores earthquakes and eruptions proved highly damaging. In the seventeenth century there had been seven occasions when the islands were hit by earthquakes. Azorean emigration to Brazil began in the eighteenth century, but the population continued to grow and by the middle of the nineteenth century had reached an unsustainable 250,000. The story in Madeira was similar, as the population grew to 67,000 by 1800 and doubled again during the following century (Newitt 2015a).

Starting in the eighteenth century, emigration became the only relief available to the poor of the Atlantic islands, and this gave rise to one of the great ironies of history. Through four centuries the Portuguese had shipped more African slaves than any other European country, first to Europe, then to settle their Atlantic islands, and finally to provide labour for the sugar and coffee estates and mines of Brazil. However, as the slave trade was eventually brought to an end during the nineteenth century, the demand for labour on Brazilian plantations was increasingly met by the contract labour of poor Portuguese, many of whom went under contracts that bound them to a kind of serfdom. During the nineteenth century Azoreans and Madeirans also emigrated under contract to the British Caribbean, Brazil and distant Hawaii, where they worked in conditions that had been established to exploit slave labour (Newitt 2015a).

In the Cabo Verde islands, emigration was at first linked to the whaling industry. Brava and São Nicolau were the islands favoured by the whalers, as there was less likelihood of interference by Portuguese officialdom in these remote islands. Throughout the nineteenth century the American whalers maintained establishments on shore and set up the first semi-mechanised industrial plant. This provided employment for some of the islanders, while the Portuguese administration looked on without the ability to intervene or regulate. The importance of Cabo Verde for the American whaling fleet resulted in the United States opening a consulate in Praia in 1818.

It was in this context that the whalers, and other foreign ships that from time to time still visited the islands, gave the population an opportunity to emigrate. Service on board whalers proved a major boon for the isolated island communities. Young men were able to earn a wage to supplement the meagre subsistence of their families, and whaling opened up opportunities for them to see the world and make their fortunes. Cabo Verdeans were to become expert at whale hunting and some even became captains of whaling ships.

The whaling industry reached its peak around 1840 and continued on a plateau for twenty years before going into decline. One reason for the decline in the number of whalers coming to the islands was that the killing of so many whales did not prove sustainable and the sea around Cabo Verde emptied of whales to hunt.

Frank Bullen describes the Cabo Verdean whalemen in his book *The Cruise of the Cachalot*, published in 1875, which shows how central to the success of the whaling industry the recruitment of Cabo Verdeans had become. "More than half of the total crews of the American whaling fleet are composed of these islanders. Many of them have risen to the position of captain, and still more are officers and harpooners; but though undoubtedly brave and enterprising, they are cruel and treacherous, and in positions of authority over men of Teutonic or Anglo-Saxon origin, are apt to treat their subordinates with great cruelty" (Bullen 1953: 32; Newitt 2015a: 198).

This was a world where the hierarchies of race were frequently reversed, the skilled "black" Portuguese from Cabo Verde lording it over the inexperienced "white" American crews shipped in the New England ports. When the ships returned to their home ports of New Bedford and Nantucket, sometimes after as long as two years at sea, members of the Cabo Verdean crew were able to settle ashore in New England. In the early days most of these immigrants came from Brava, and in the United States the islanders were often referred to generically as "Bravas" rather than "Portuguese".

James Farr described the dying days of the whaling industry in America. "As the whaling industry declined, the babel of tongues that characterized life aboard a whaleship in the prosperous antebellum years increasingly gave way to the Portuguese of men from the Azores and Cabo Verde Islands. These whalemen had gravitated to New Bedford to work the nation's whaling fleet and stayed long after the industry lost its luster."

He went on to quote a historian of the whaling industry describing the men who stayed in the industry. "The whalemen who ship on the few whaling vessels that sail from New Bedford today are mainly men of a different sort—Portuguese from the Azores or the Cape Verde Islands—many of them nearly full-blooded negroes [sic] and black as ebony, but hardworking, industrious, and good whalers … The Portuguese skippers are skillful whalers, good businessmen, strict disciplinarians and secure catches which would make the old-time whalemen turn green with envy." Farr continues:

> These men came to own much of what remained of the whaling fleet, paying the purchase price in installments with the profit from each voyage; some shipowners even gave away vessels to these men who kept afloat the tattered traditions of the industry. Many of the Portuguese-Africans became naturalized Americans and put down roots along the New England seaboard. Maritime historian Samuel Eliott Morison called the Cape Verde Bravas and the Azorian Portuguese "the most numerous alien element

in the Old Colony". Alien or not, the Bravas were among the few Americans of African descent who came as free men to live and work in the New World. (Farr, 1983: 49–50)

In the early twentieth century, as the whaling industry went into terminal decline, the skilled island whalemen no longer found employment.

> The industry of the Bravas and Azorians counted for little, however, as the fate of the whale fishery had been decided long ago in Titusville, Pennsylvania with the discovery of oil. The end might be forestalled, but not denied; no amount of skill or hard work could resist the dynamics of economic change. As the industry died Cape Verdean whalemen shipped out in the American coastal trade or abandoned the life at sea for the mixed blessings of life ashore. By 1924 the American whaling industry was dead and the last wooden whaleship would soon lie entombed as a museum in Mystic, Connecticut. (Farr 1983: 168)

Whales had largely disappeared from the seas round Cabo Verde when in 1914 the Portuguese government at last introduced regulations covering territorial waters, the right to hunt whales, and the payment of taxes on whale products. Once whaling effectively ceased, many of the old sailing vessels associated with the industry were scrapped (or superseded by modern vessels). Cabo Verdeans often took over the wooden ships which were otherwise earmarked for scrap, and continued to operate them on the Atlantic routes, carrying migrants as well as miscellaneous cargoes. As Marilyn Halter expressed it, "Cape Verdeans came to have control over their own means of a passage to the US" (Halter 2008: 36). In this way the first small Cabo Verdean shipping businesses grew on the back of the old whaling industry.

In the last decades of the nineteenth century, the hundreds of islanders from Brava who had signed on as crews in American ships created a striking imbalance in the island population, and the number of women came greatly to exceed that of men. Figures for 1875 show that the island population had 2,480 men but 4,104 women (Carreira 1982: 51). This gender imbalance was to be reflected in the story of migrations from the Azores and from Portugal itself—male exodus, more or less permanent, with women left behind to manage any family property, to bring up children, and to be the main cultural resource for the island. By the end of the century, some women were also finding ways to ship on board whalers or other vessels bound for America. However, emigration to the United States was not always permanent, for already in the 1870s some seamen were returning to the islands, bringing hitherto unimagined wealth with them. It was not to be long before returning migrants, known as Americanos, became a factor in the marked social change that was then taking place (Carreira 1982: 50).

Once a Cabo Verdean community had been established in the United States, a chain of migration began, with islanders leaving to join family members on the other side of the Atlantic, where they obtained work in textile factories and farms or picking berries in the cranberry bogs. Many clandestine migrants also travelled in open boats to reach America. Meanwhile, the growth of Porto Grande in São Vicente and the arrival of large numbers of steamers to take on coal provided other opportunities for Cabo Verdeans to enlist as crew or otherwise obtain passages to the New World. In 1916, for example, São Vicente registered the second-largest official emigration of all the islands, only two people short of Fogo.

There are no statistics for emigration to the United States in the nineteenth century, and when figures are available in the early twentieth century, they suggest that numbers may have amounted to around 1,000 per year. Between 1901 and 1920 there were 18,629 emigrants recorded. Of these 11,000 came from the islands of Brava and nearby Fogo. These are the official statistics of migrants who departed legally, equipped with passports. At the same time there was an unknown clandestine emigration, often fired up by the attempt to conscript soldiers for the Portuguese army. The total numbers of those who departed was, therefore, very much larger than the official figures suggest.

The attitude of the Portuguese administration towards emigration was two-faced, as it was in Portugal, where, in the same period, emigration was also rising steeply. Against the loss of young men and the gender imbalance this caused in communities were the strong incentives provided by the wealth of returning Brasileiros and Americanos, and the steady flow of remittances, which helped sustain the economy. Emigration also took the pressures off rural poverty and suppressed demands for serious land reform or for more active intervention by the government in economic and social affairs. In the islands, emigration was seen as the most effective form of famine relief and one that benefited the population and the government as the flow of remittances became an important factor in the island economy. At first the Portuguese tried to control or, at least, monitor emigration, using old regulations that demanded passports for those travelling between the islands, passports which had to be paid for, but gradually these demands were relaxed until in 1914 the requirement to possess a passport was waived altogether.

The numbers of emigrants began to decline after the First World War. This was in large part due to measures taken in the United States to control immigration, in particular literacy requirements, which were first introduced in 1915. Many at the time interpreted these measures as being specifically aimed at Cabo Verdeans, who were registered as Portuguese but many of whom had the appearance of black Africans. These measures had their effect, and between 1927 and 1952 only 1,946 official emigrants are recorded (Carreira 1982: 80; Newitt 2015a: 189–210).

Most the Cabo Verdeans who settled in the United States were to be found in Massachusetts, Rhode Island and Connecticut, eastern seaboard states that maintained the connection of the Cabo Verdean population with the sea. At the same time there was even larger migration from the Azores, so that two parallel Portuguese island communities came into existence in New England alongside each other.

Although emigration from Cabo Verde had very specific causes in the geography, climate and land tenure system of the islands, it was also part of a wider phenomenon affecting much of western Europe and almost all the other island groups in the Atlantic. While a few hundred Cabo Verdeans were enlisting on American whalers and putting down tentative roots in New England, large numbers of emigrants were fleeing famine and the life of poverty on great landed estates in Ireland, Scotland, Italy and eastern Europe. Cabo

Verdeans were a mere cupful added to this tide of migration that began to flow around the world.

However, the importance of Cabo Verdean emigration to the United States does not lie in numbers alone but in the strong ties that were created between the communities in the United States and the islands. This led not only to a flow of financial remittances but also to cultural exchange and a knowledge of the English language. Hitherto the islands had been part of a Portuguese South Atlantic creole culture. Now there was to be an Anglo-Saxon, North American element added to the mix, as emigrants began to return with wealth acquired in the United States. Emigration enabled the islanders to break out of the relentless cycle of poverty and famine. It offered hope of a better life and widened horizons, which, in turn, had a profound impact on the identity of the islanders and how they viewed themselves and their islands. Cabo Verdeans now became citizens of the world as well as denizens of their own small island communities. This was to be the experience of the inhabitants of many other islands once the waves of globalisation reached their shores, and was to give birth to the idea of the worldwide nation, strong in its own identity and cultural loyalties but not confined within the frontiers of any small state.

São Tomé: The Rise and Decline of a Creole Capitalist Powerhouse

In Cabo Verde the old plantations had ceased to be productive during the seventeenth century. Fewer and fewer produced any significant amount of sugar, cotton or other saleable crops, and their owners, tied to the land through the system of *morgadios*, sank into debt or became absentees. When the fortunes of Cabo Verde began to revive, it was not through plantation agriculture but through investment in the salt trade, the growth of services to shipping and the telegraph, and emigration and the remittances sent home by migrants.

The story of the Guinea islands was to be quite different. The settlement of these islands had started in much the same way as Cabo Verde, with plantations producing sugar, and trade with the mainland African states. In São Tomé the plantations went into decline when sugar production was relocated to Brazil, but through the seventeenth and eighteenth centuries the Guinea islands continued to provide services for visiting slavers, especially those trading on the coast of Gabon and the region north of the Zaire estuary.

During the Napoleonic Wars, São Tomé once again became of great importance in the slave trade, and between 1809 and 1815 33,000 slaves were shipped to Brazil through the islands. Brazilian ships regularly visited and Brazilian money circulated. The smuggling of slaves continued during the early days of Britain's campaign against the slave trade, and when international treaties banned the trade north of the equator, São Tomé was placed in an ambiguous position, as it lay exactly on the line and slaves shipped from there could be represented not as exports but as labour being moved within the slave-owning economies of the creole world.

After 1842 the ambiguities were resolved when Portugal banned the slave trade altogether, and Brazil ceased all slave imports in 1851. The end of the Atlantic slave trade was the end of the commerce that had been so profitable for the creole society on São Tomé, but the Brazilian connection had already begun to offer the islanders an alternative. In the first half of the nineteenth century there was rapid growth in the consumption of cocoa, coffee, palm oil and sugar within the global economy, and the Guinea islands were well placed to profit from these commodities. São Tomé had three great natural advantages: its fertile volcanic soils and plentiful rainfall were ideal for the growth of tropical products, while access by sea facilitated transport, and the relative isolation of the islands offered security for capital invested in plantations, which the exposed mainland areas of Africa did not enjoy. So, as the last vestiges of the plantation economy died away in Cabo Verde, the Guinea islands were about to experience a revival of tropical plantation agriculture that was to become truly spectacular—and Cabo Verdeans were to find themselves caught up in the revival of what was in effect a new form of slavery.

Coffee was first planted in Príncipe in 1800 and cacao plants were brought from Brazil in 1822. These crops were produced on the estates of local *forro* landowners, and from the start the new plantation economy was a cooperative effort between local creole entrepreneurs and their Brazilian counterparts. Charles Thomas, chaplain to the American Africa Squadron, visited Príncipe in 1855 and declared that the island produced "coffee and cocoa, both of superior quality". "The only remarkable person of the island, and the largest slave and land-owner on it, is Madam Fereira, a lady of eccentric but strong and cultivated mind, who, like Lady Hester Stanhope, prefers the associations of half savage life to the restraints of civilized and enlightened society" (Thomas 1860: 256–7).

However, it was not until the late 1850s that plantation production really took off. As prices for coffee and cacao increased, there developed a scramble for land in São Tomé and Príncipe and a search for supplies of labour. Although the early entrepreneurs had mostly been local landowners, the free creole population was unwilling to undertake plantation work, and in 1875 slavery finally came to an end, as it had in Cabo Verde. Carlos Espirito Santo describes the final end of 400 years of enslavement: "On the 19 October 1875 some slaves from the *roça* Conde dos Frades headed for the administration of the *concelho* to complain about the bad treatment they received on the *roça*. Many others followed the example of the *serviçais* who gathered in the city of São Tomé on 4 November. Thousands and thousands descended on the city and gathered en masse peacefully before the palace of the governor Gregorio José Ribeiro, calling for the abolition of slavery. From a window of the palace, José Ribeiro declared slavery abolished in São Tomé" (Espirito Santo 1979: 53).

Some migrants from Cabo Verde had been forced to sign labour contracts as a relief from famine, but from at least the 1870s the plantation owners began to contract for workers in Angola and the notorious system of *serviçal* labour began. Africans, captured or traded in the interior, were sold to plantation owners who made them work under contract. The workers were supposed to be paid and the contracts were time-limited, but the practice arose of automatically renewing contracts once their time had expired. Similar to the *engagé* system which supplied labour to the French Indian Ocean islands, *serviçal* labour was in effect a continuation of slavery, as there was very heavy mortality on the plantations and no contracted labourers ever returned home.

Large estates (*roças*), some amounting to as much as 24,000 acres, were marked out in the south and west of the islands, away from the areas that had been settled by the creole population for centuries. The higher land was used for coffee, the lower reaches near the coast for cacao and palm oil. Each estate had quays so that it could be served by boats, as there was no internal road system. As the *serviçal* system began to supply forced labour, cocoa production rose. In 1890 some 1,519 tons of cocoa were exported, and this rose dramatically, so that between 1908 and 1919 an average of 30,000 tons a year was being exported. Between 1893 and 1923, São Tomé and Príncipe produced between 10 and 15 per cent of the world's cacao. So prosperous were the *roças* at this time that some of the largest built narrow-gauge railways to provide a transport system on their land.

Some of the early creole entrepreneurs became very rich, buying titles for themselves in Lisbon, like the Baron Agua Izé, but, as in Cabo Verde, the arrival of the Banco Nacional Ultramarino in the 1860s encouraged estate owners to obtain mortgages. Many of these ended in foreclosures and bankruptcies, and there was a gradual transfer of *roças* into the hands of large metropolitan companies and away from creole ownership. This, of course, had an impact on São Tomé society, as the managers of the *roças*, mostly from Europe, had no local roots and had no intention of becoming permanent settlers. They and the *serviçal* workforce they administered became largely isolated from creole society and culture. However, the *roça* system produced one remarkable cultural legacy—lavish expenditure on great plantation houses. Nowhere in the world did exotic tropical architecture flourish as it did on São Tomé and Príncipe, where splendid, even palatial plantation houses surrounded by tropical gardens were built to grace the island *roças* (Newitt and Hodges 1988).

While these palaces were being built on the *roças*, the rest of the island, including the capital, where the *forros* population lived, was notoriously neglected. A British consular report for the year 1915 spelt out the problem: "The existing town is in a lamentable condition. A decent house is scarcely to be found, and the tumble down, evil smelling huts of the natives are everywhere in close proximity to the houses inhabited by Europeans. A proper drainage system does not exist, rank grass grows in each vacant space which are used as dumping grounds for bottles, tins and rubbish of all kinds. The woods on the outskirts of the town are the latrines of the natives and the stench is over powering. To all this the Portuguese inhabitants seem to be absolutely indifferent" (BPP 1914).

During the first decade of the twentieth century, São Tomé and Príncipe found themselves the centre of unwelcome publicity as hostile critics of colonialism focused on labour conditions in the islands. There had been international outrage as details began to emerge of conditions in the Congo Free State, and eventually in 1908 the Belgian government took over the administration of the Congo from King Leopold. However, already, as a spin-off from the campaign against King Leopold's rule, concern had switched to São Tomé. The British journalist Henry Nevinson published a series of articles on the conditions of slavery under which labour for São Tomé was recruited in Angola. These articles were published in 1906 as a book entitled, uncompromisingly, *A Modern Slavery*. The furore caused in liberal circles by Nevinson's revelations prompted William Cadbury, a Quaker and head of the chocolate firm, to visit São Tomé in person. His account of labour conditions, published in 1910 as a book entitled *Labour in Portuguese West Africa*, did little to allay suspicions that the cocoa was being produced in São Tomé by slave labour. The Portuguese launched a vigorous counter-propaganda, and the spate of publications that resulted makes São Tomé one of the best documented of all Portuguese colonies. However, not all the Portuguese rallied to the defence of the cocoa-growing regime. In 1912 a former *curador* (inspector of labour) from Príncipe wrote one of the most damning descriptions of life on the *roças*, entitled *Alma negra!* (Black soul!), in which he gave graphic accounts of the punishment meted out to workers, and declared unequivocally, "the existence of slavery in the islands is a fact, although it is presented to public opinion as a regime of free labour" (Paiva de Carvalho 1912: 5).

Portugal was lucky not to suffer the fate that had overtaken King Leopold, and as a consequence labour conditions in São Tomé gradually improved, especially with respect to the repatriation of workers whose contracts had finished (Newitt and Hodges 1988: 38–9, 63–4; Duffy 1967; Higgs 2012).

The large numbers of workers imported under contracts radically changed the make-up of the island populations. The *serviçais* and their children, known as Tongas, formed a large population, without citizenship, property or rights of any kind. Until 1920 they were numerically the largest part of the population. Their living standards were very low and they suffered from a range of diseases, especially from sleeping sickness, which became a major epidemic in Príncipe in the first decade of the twentieth century (Bruto da Costa et al. 1916). One method used to eradicate the tsetse fly was to dress *serviçais* in clothing covered with a sticky substance and to send them out into the forest as human flypapers. The process by which slaves had merged with the free black population in Cabo Verde was not repeated in São Tomé, where the *forros* kept themselves aloof from the taint of working on the *roças*.

Into this world of new plantation slavery, hundreds of destitute Cabo Verdeans were thrust by a Portuguese state which wanted to solve two problems at once—to provide the booming cocoa estates with labour and at the same time to relieve the destitution of the poor in the Cabo Verde islands. The first major exodus of Cabo Verdeans to the plantations of São Tomé and Príncipe seems to have been the result of the serious famine of the years 1863–4, when there was widespread starvation in the islands. There was another major exodus in the 1890s and in 1903, again as the result of severe famine. This was actively aided by the governor, who is even alleged to have prevented islanders from leaving for mainland Africa in order to force them to contract for São Tomé. According to António Carreira (1982), between 1904 and 1922 17,948 Cabo Verdeans left as contract labourers. It is not known how many ever returned. This is approximately the same number as the legal emigration to the United States.

Emigration under contract to the cocoa plantations brought with it none of the benefits associated with emigration to the United States, as the workers were poorly paid, suffered high rates of mortality, and were not able either to improve their own situation or to remit money home to their families. Nor were the Cabo Verde contract workers treated noticeably better than the workers contracted under conditions of virtual slavery from Mozambique or Angola.

In the twentieth century, whenever there were famines in Cabo Verde, large numbers were forced to seek relief by going to São Tomé, where they remained a distinct and separate part of the population. The Cabo Verdeans did not integrate with the *forros* or with the other contract workers. Alexander Keese found that "relations between the migrants from the island and other African workers in the cocoa plantations of São Tomé and Príncipe were tense and that repatriated Cape Verdeans brought a number of reinforced negative stereotypes towards Angolans and Mozambicans with them, such as their alleged violence, their 'primitive' culture, and their unfamiliar food habits" (Keese 2020: 87).

At independence many of the Cabo Verdeans remained stranded like refugees when the Portuguese eventually left the island. In 1975, there were some 15,500 Cabo Verdeans in the archipelago, including 6,500 children. When multi-party elections in São Tomé were held for the first time in 1990, the Cabo Verdeans were not given the right to vote (Nascimento 2008: 59).

However, just as the great days of Porto Grande as an international port were over by the 1920s and the port city of Mindelo began a period of steep decline, so the great days of the *roças* of São Tomé and Príncipe also peaked in the early 1920s and a spiral of decline set in. Disease affected the cocoa trees and São Tomé cacao lost market share and declined. As the profitability of the *roças* fell, investment dried up, and the plantations and their equipment became antiquated and out of date. The rhythms of prosperity and decline in the creole islands were in some crude way synchronised, the decline reaching its lowest point during the middle years of the Salazar dictatorship when both groups of islands once again became the neglected, forgotten outliers of Portugal's New State, as they had been of the post-Philippine monarchy of the seventeenth and eighteenth centuries.

Conclusion

Looking back over the history of the long nineteenth century, there are many similarities in the experience of the two creole archipelagos, not least in the rise and decline of their economic fortunes; but in terms of the development of their societies the contrasts were glaring. While Cabo Verde eventually saw the end of slavery, the population achieving its emancipation even from the forced labour laws of the twentieth century, and at the same time opening itself to the outside world through emigration to the United States and the experience of the international port of Porto Grande, the Guinea islands became a closed society. There was little emigration, while the immigration of contracted labourers maintained in effect a society and economy based on slavery until at least the 1950s. Nor was there any opening of the country to outside influences, and São Tomé narrowed its horizons, as its experience approximated to that of Portugal's mainland African colonies rather than that of Cabo Verde.

6

THE CABO VERDE NATION COMES OF AGE

Mindelo and the British

Three developments in the nineteenth century had transformed life for the people of Cabo Verde—the establishment of an organised structure of government, emigration to the United States, and the development of Porto Grande and the city of Mindelo. Although the problems caused by drought and famine remained and may even have grown worse, this no longer held back Cabo Verde's transition during the twentieth century from a scattering of barren islands, barely supporting a poverty-stricken population, to a modern state and a modern nation.

With the development of Porto Grande and Atlantic steam navigation, the Cabo Verde islands were once more at the heart of a cosmopolitan trading network, as they had been in the early sixteenth century. The modern world had arrived in the islands and its impact was to transform them not only in the eyes of foreigners but in the eyes of Cabo Verdeans themselves. Important in this transition was the presence of a large population of Portuguese and English expatriates and a fluctuating number of transient foreigners (Newitt 2019a).

In 1910, the British employees of the telegraph and coaling companies numbered 170. They formed a distinct colonial elite, reproducing the social relations typical of British colonies throughout the world. The British were a transient community but even so, until at least the end of the nineteenth century, they outnumbered the European Portuguese. Few if any of them settled permanently in São Vicente, which they referred to as the "cinder heap", nor did many of them visit the other islands of the archipelago. They were there to make money and felt no commitment to the local population or to the welfare of the islands. At the head of the community was the British vice-consul and the managers of the different companies. Below them was a bachelor community whose members lived separately from the local population in large, purpose-built residences. Life revolved around drinking and sport. Within three years of establishing themselves in Porto Grande, the British had petitioned for a grant of land for a golf course. Later, tennis and football were introduced and a cricket club was formed. A small commercial community of Gibraltarian Jews also existed, running hotels and shops and linked inevitably to the British.

The Portuguese community in Mindelo was made up, for the most part, of the officials in charge of the police, the military, customs and administration. This community aspired to a certain cultural elegance. Francisco Travassos Valdez in 1861 had described the municipal balls, society marriages and formal parades in the presence of the governor and, according to João de Sousa Machado writing in 1891, "the dances of the upper classes are perfectly comparable to those of second-ranked cities of Europe" (1891: 16–17).

As in so many other parts of the Portuguese world, British and Portuguese found themselves locked into a loveless marriage, each needing the other but each resentful of the attitudes and behaviour of their partner. There was continual tension between the Portuguese administrators, the economically dominant and culturally exclusive British community, and the constantly changing population of foreigners in transit whose presence exacerbated the problems of smuggling and prostitution.

Both the captains of the ships that came to load coal and the personnel of the British coaling companies looked in vain to the

Portuguese authorities to provide port services. Quarantine facilities and a customs house had duly been built, but proper harbour works were never constructed. In the last quarter of the century almost the entire waterfront of Mindelo was owned by British coaling companies, but the simple wooden jetties compared unfavourably with the facilities available at Spanish ports like Gran Canaria. Archibald Lyall, visiting São Vicente in 1936, described how "the passenger reaches the little jetty pied with black stains where he has been splashed by the coal-dust laden water ... he has to clamber up a rusty iron companion-way and pick his way carefully along the broken wooden jetty to avoid falling through the holes into the sea". This, he comments, "was once the fourth greatest coaling station in the world" (Lyall 1938: 76–7). Not only were there no harbour works, but there was no proper water supply and no ice plant. "If the town ... were made more attractive by the installation of electric light, better buildings, shops, amusements etc. there would be inducement for passengers from ships calling to land and spend money", wrote the British vice-consul in 1912 (British Foreign Office 1912: 4).

While the British complained that the Portuguese did nothing to improve the port in spite of high levels of local taxation, the Portuguese complained that the British companies were unwilling to invest any of the excessive profits they made from over-priced coal. Each side blamed the other for the slow but inexorable decline of the port.

The single greatest complaint of the British community was the lack of adequate policing. Shortly after the declaration of the Portuguese Republic in 1910, the workers in Porto Grande went on strike for more pay. The acting vice-consul sent a panic-stricken telegram to London: "British merchants property in hands of mob and business suspended authorities powerless". In fact the Portuguese police managed to protect the transatlantic cable from interference and, when the strike was over, it was admitted by Captain B. Miller of HMS *Aeolus* that "the Authorities ashore seemed determined that order should be kept and except for the presence of large numbers of unemployed labourers in town, I saw nothing to cause apprehension to the white community" (Newitt 2019a: 173).

The Portuguese blamed the British for much of the disorder in the town, for the rampant contraband trade carried on from the ships, and for the drunken and disorderly behaviour of the British community. In 1920 the British minister in Lisbon told Lord Curzon, the foreign secretary, that "all the trouble has been caused by Mr Butler [the vice-consul] and his particular friends ... he was often drunk and he and his companions when in that condition had made scandalous scenes in the street at night and had defied the authorities for whom they perpetually created every sort of annoyance and difficulty" (Newitt 2019a: 174–5). Archibald Lyall, writing a decade later, commented that "one would gather from the few survivors of the good old days that half the colony spent Saturday night bailing the other half out of gaol" (1938: 78).

The Cabo Verdean Working Class

In the nineteenth century, the working population of Mindelo was entirely made up of migrants from the other islands. Used to migrating in search of work, Cabo Verdeans now found a foreign colony installed on one of their own islands where work of a kind was available. At first the migrant workers retained their roots in the agricultural communities of their islands of origin. It was reported that, whenever it rained, the city would be emptied as the workers returned home to help with planting or travelled inland to cultivate small plots of land on Monte Verde, the only part of São Vicente that received sufficient moisture to allow any agriculture. João de Sousa Machado echoed this report in 1890: "When the first rains fell, almost the whole able-bodied population of the city ran off to the fields for the work of sowing, to the great prejudice of the port and at times placing the [coaling] companies in great difficulties" (1891: 3–4).

The bunkering of ships was very labour-intensive. Porto Grande had no quays, and all ships rode at anchor in the bay and had to be supplied by lighters. The coal, stored in sacks, was manhandled into the lighters, which were then taken out to the steamers in the bay. If the steamers had hoists fore and aft, 100 tons could be loaded in an hour and the average steamer could be turned round in a day. Labour costs were low, and much of the work of moving the coal was actually performed by women, "who carry great buckets of coal and *bidons* of water as large as their own torsos; and it is on their kerchiefed curls that the huge sacks of flour and maize and rice are carried up from the lighters" (Lyall 1938: 80). A report, dating from 1925, claimed that it took 17 women and 18 men to load 200 tons of coal. The men were paid 1s 4d a day and the women 7d—in 1911 the rates had been 1s 5d and 10d respectively (Newitt 2019a: 176).

In 1880 the Portuguese administrator had described the population of Mindelo as "peaceful, lazy, lacking any education and much given to the use and abuse of alcoholic beverages, friends of dancing and revelry and consuming in a day what they earned in a week". João de Sousa Machado, who carried out a study of the coal trade in 1890, also described the population of São Vicente as "peaceful, kind, humble and happy" (República de Cabo Verde 1984: 33; Machado 1891: 16). In fact, labour relations were poor and were exacerbated by the effects of the droughts that regularly struck the islands. Cabo Verdeans were not subject to Portuguese colonial labour laws and escaped the forced labour which, under various disguises, was imposed on the inhabitants of the mainland colonies. Instead labourers, who had been small peasant farmers in their islands of origin, were reduced by the monopolistic practices of free capitalist enterprise to becoming proletarians in the city without rights except those they could extort through collective action or subterfuge.

Labourers were employed by the coaling companies on a daily basis. If there were no ships, there was no work and no pay. The earliest strike took place in 1855, when famine conditions in the islands made the small wages earned by the workforce valueless as there was nothing to buy. The workers demanded that they be paid in food (República de Cabo Verde 1984: 20). After this the port labourers received part of their pay in kind, to be spent in the company stores—the notorious "truck" system so hated by industrial workers everywhere. Another major strike occurred in October 1910 soon after the declaration of the Republic. The numbers on strike were variously estimated at between 1,000 and 2,000, and the coal lighters were prevented from being towed out to the waiting ships. The strikers wanted a doubling of their wages and were, allegedly, supported by "the small shopkeepers of the place, to whose advantage it would be if they were to obtain an increase of pay" (Newitt 2019a: 177) . In the end the strikers settled for 15 per cent. Low as these wages were, they attracted ever-growing numbers of migrants to the city. Those who were not employed by the coaling companies worked as household servants. In 1879, out of 1,623 people employed in the city, 671 worked for the companies and 224 were household servants (República de Cabo Verde 1984: 33). The only alternative was to make a living by prostitution, petty crime or dealing in contraband goods.

Living conditions in the city were appalling. At first there was only one well supplying water. Visiting ships brought typhoid, yellow fever and bubonic plague. Yellow fever broke out in 1852 and cholera in 1858, carrying off half the population before subsiding. In 1911 the British vice-consul reported "there is no drainage, refuse being cast upon the waste lands near the towns or onto the sea-shore, with the consequence that during, and after, the rainy season outbreaks of malarial fever occur". There had been an outbreak of typhus and malaria among the British inhabitants, and four people had died (British Foreign Office 1912). As late as May 1921 the British vice-consul summed up the situation in an official report: "the Port of St Vincent (Porto Grande) itself is in a very poor state of development, with no running water, town sanitation, electric light, telephones, wireless station, ice-plant or good roads" (Newitt 2019a: 178) .

Disease not only arrived with the ships and bred in the appallingly insanitary conditions of the town but was exacerbated by the state of semi-starvation in which most of the population lived. Hunger lay at the root of much of the lawlessness of which the British complained, but for them it remained a police matter and the responsibility of the Portuguese authorities. This attitude, that destitution was primarily a question of law and order, was to remain the official response until the end of Portuguese rule.

Petty thieving increased during the periods of severe drought when desperate and starving people would steal from the houses and business premises of the Europeans. In September 1920, all 104 members of the British community in São Vicente signed a petition drawing the government's attention to "the present undesirable and indeed serious state of affairs in this island" and demanding "protection against the wanton aggression of the lower class native population". The petition went on to assert that "the unfriendly attitude of the Authorities towards British interests is the basic cause of the conduct of the natives towards us" and "shipmasters on whose opinion the whole life of the community depends are treated with the utmost discourtesy and abuse" (Newitt 2019a: 179).

The clash of interests between the coaling companies and the workers in Mindelo came to a head in 1925. For years small sailing boats had been used by men from São Vicente to dredge the harbour floor for coal that had fallen into the sea during loading. This practice, known as *rocega*, was resented by the coaling companies, which claimed that the dredgers stole coal directly from the lighters, that the coal on the seabed was theirs and that they should have the sole right to dredge. Although it was pointed out that the coal being loaded actually belonged to the ships which had paid for it, the Portuguese authorities sided with the coaling companies and dredging was banned (Newitt 2019a: 180).

When drought struck, the population of the city would be swollen with the destitute from other islands. The Portuguese government had no systematic relief policy, while the coaling companies considered that the poverty was none of their business. Lyall describes the famine riots of the early 1930s and the resulting *taxation populaire*—the political economy of riot, which has been described so often in early modern Europe.

> The storm broke one morning, when some men paraded the town demanding food, work or maintenance. Others joined them and in an hour or two there were ten thousand people marching through St Vincent with the black banner of hunger waving at their head. Then they began to loot the foodshops. Even then the fundamental decency of these miserable people showed itself. The police had refused to fire; the town was theirs; but the starving mob, which could easily have embarked on a wholesale *jacquerie*, preserved a sort of discipline and discriminated between friends and foes. They did not touch the merchants who had shown them charity … The others were looted. (Lyall 1938: 84)

If tension constantly existed between the working population of Mindelo and the British community, the same was also true of relations between the workers and the Portuguese authorities. Smuggling became Mindelo's greatest industry, second only to the bunkering trade. Each ship that docked presented an opportunity for evading the official customs regulations. In collusion with sailors from the ships, contraband of every sort was landed and retailed in the black market.

Mindelo also became the focus of another form of smuggling, that of people. Legal emigration was handled from Praia, but it was Mindelo that offered endless opportunities for illegal emigrants. Large numbers of the destitute collected in the port waiting for the opportunity to stow away on passing steamers or for a passage on the small sailing boats that brought cargoes of boots, shoes and timber from the United States. The United States and Brazil were the favoured destinations, and this emigration was eventually to generate the flow of remittances which sustained the economy of the city when the coaling trade, which had provided the escape route for so many migrants, ceased.

Mindelo Caught between Rival Imperial Powers

In the protectionist world of the late nineteenth century, Porto Grande was only able to survive by becoming another incarnation of the old Anglo-Portuguese alliance. Threats to its survival came not only from the Spanish Canaries where, by the end of the nineteenth century, the free port was thriving but, nearer to home, from the French decision to develop Dakar. This diverted French traffic from Porto Grande and, incidentally, cut deeply into the salt trade from Cabo Verde to Senegal. This made Porto Grande all the more dependent on the British, who maintained the coal trade as a British monopoly, largely closed to international competition.

Porto Grande remained of great strategic importance to British imperial commerce, as can be seen in the figures for 1913. In that year 870 British ships used the port, twice the number of Portuguese and four times the number of German vessels. That year, however, only 16 French ships used Porto Grande. When workers in the port struck for better pay in 1910, the British government sent a cruiser squadron to São Vicente, ostensibly to protect British lives and property but in practice to overawe the strikers and to force the Portuguese authorities to take appropriate action (Newitt 2019a: 182).

The Portuguese recognised the strategic importance of Porto Grande for the British and cooperated reluctantly as a member of the old alliance, aware that in practice they had little alternative. Porto Grande had been used by the British as a port of assembly during the Ashanti Wars, and the Portuguese regularly welcomed visits by British warships. During the First World War, Porto Grande was regularly used for refuelling British warships. At the peace conference, the British suggested that they should take over the port "as a set-off to financial claims of Great Britain on Portugal, or in exchange for territory captured from Germany", just as they also considered annexing Delagoa Bay (Newitt 2019a: 183).

However, important as it was for British interests, the British government did next to nothing to develop the port and even blocked Portuguese initiatives in this direction. Ever since the 1890s, when concern was being expressed about the future of Porto Grande, numerous plans for improving the port and reviving its fortunes were prepared—"the harbour scheme bacillus is very prevalent in Portugal", commented a Foreign Office minute (Newitt 2019a: 183). In 1925, among many plans for the rejuvenation of the port, a scheme to convert Porto Grande into a naval base was put forward by the head of the Public Works Department in the island. Like all other such schemes, this one fell on deaf ears in both London and Lisbon. Commenting on the scheme, Lancelot Carnegie, the British minister in Lisbon, did, however, agree that Porto Grande with all its advantages had fallen far behind its rivals. In 1889 Las Palmas and São Vicente had serviced the same number of ships, but in 1924 9,108 ships had called at Las Palmas compared with only 1,145 visiting Porto Grande. He summarised the British perspective on why this was so—excessive import duties on coal leading to higher prices, the exaggerated price of water, bad arrangements for loading and unloading, no prepaid facilities, lack of fresh provisions, customs difficulties, and the lack of attractions for tourists on shore—all by implication the fault of the Portuguese. In 1934, with the port now in steep decline, João Gomes da Fonseca, writing the official account of the port for the Portuguese Colonial Exhibition, stated unequivocally the Portuguese perspective: "Among the principal reasons for the low frequenting of the Porto Grande de São Vicente, the first, and more important than any other, is the high price of coal which is sold to shipping" (Fonseca 1934: 11).

Proposals to revive the port reappeared after the Second World War in the official Portuguese development plans. Funds allocated to modernise Porto Grande took up a third of all investment allocated in the 1959–64 economic plan (Agência-Geral do Ultramar 1961: 35), and the future of the port has remained high on the agenda of every government since.

Mindelo and Cabo Verdean Identity

Lia Medina has described Mindelo as "a city of two faces, one a city of opportunities", whether professional, academic or cultural; the other a "land of perdition where prostitution and venereal disease find a fertile soil and where nights and festivities never seemed to end" (2009: 1). As the story of the rise and decline of Porto Grande unfolded, the city—and with it the whole archipelago—was being transformed. In spite of all the troubles, the strikes, the riots, the petty crime and poverty, a modern city was emerging complete with government services, hotels, shops, eating places, sports clubs and, most important of all, schools and a press. An educated class of writers established themselves in the city, in touch with the wider world and reflecting on the experience of being Cabo Verdean in works of poetry and fiction. In 1936 the periodical *Claridade* was first published in Mindelo by writers who came mostly from Santiago and from São Nicolau, which had seen the founding of the first secondary school in Cabo Verde and had already educated three generations of islanders.

Claridade was launched during the period of the Portuguese dictatorship and was closely watched by the secret police, which probably accounts for its preoccupation with history and with cultural expression rather than current affairs. It called itself *Revista de arte e letras* (Review of art and literature), but in spite of avoiding controversial political issues, it was to prove hugely influential in creating a distinct Cabo Verdean consciousness rooted in the centuries-old experience of famine and peasant poverty. This could now be seen in the context of Cabo Verde's place in a wider world. Its first issues also appeared at a time of marked pessimism in São Vicente, when the fortunes of Porto Grande were in steep decline and emigration to the United States had been severely curtailed. It also gave prominence to Crioulu, the creole language, especially through publishing the creole texts of folk songs, which appeared on the covers of the early issues. The contributors to *Claridade* also engaged with questions that have been of fundamental importance to subsequent generations of Cabo Verdeans, exploring the contrasting inheritances which islanders have received from Europe and Africa (Sapega 2003). The most famous among the writers was Balthasar Lopes (1907–89), who came to be the leader of a generation of intellectuals and poets.

However, only three issues of *Claridade* appeared in 1936–7, and publication was not renewed until 1947, in circumstances that had radically changed. The final issues appeared in 1960.

The Estado Novo

The Portuguese Republic was replaced in 1926 by a military regime. This in turn gave way in 1930 to a dictatorship headed by António Salazar, which is always referred to as the Estado Novo (the New State). This regime lasted till 1974, and the forty-five years of the dictatorship brought major changes to the islands.

It was part of the ideology of the Estado Novo that Portugal and its colonies should be treated as a single state, a single Portuguese nation, with its inhabitants all Portuguese citizens. However, the majority of the African inhabitants of the mainland colonies were still classified as *indígenas* (natives), which made them liable to forced labour. The Cabo Verde islands were not subject to these rules and were treated like the inhabitants of Madeira, the Azores and the Indian territories, all of whom technically enjoyed full citizenship rights.

The Estado Novo was nothing if not systematic in its determination to establish control over this global Portuguese state. As a consequence there was an almost obsessive gathering of statistical information, following the bureaucratic axiom that control of information was the key to political control. In 1934 a vast statistical survey of the empire was published, covering every imaginable aspect of the life of the community. As well as key topics like imports and exports, navigation, finance and aspects of the macro-economy, the statistics gathered also included how many seats existed in the three venues in the islands that showed films, the nationality of missionaries, and the diseases from which people died. Almost anything that could be counted was counted—though, of course, the accuracy and the meaning of these statistics remained, and still remain, a wide-open question.

Given its importance in the formation of the modern Cabo Verdean nation, it is interesting to look at the statistics for education. Early in the twentieth century provision had finally been made for a primary school to be maintained in every parish, and in 1906 a decree established trade schools providing training in fishing, carpentry, seamanship, shipbuilding, ironwork, masonry, tailoring and shoemaking (British Foreign Office 1920: 12).

Government statistics showed that in the years 1932–3 there were a total of 7,856 pupils in school, Praia, Mindelo, Ribeira Grande (in Santo Antão) and São Nicolau each having more than 1,000. This number was down on 1928–9 when there had been 8,091. In 1932–3 boys had outnumbered girls by 5,144 to 2,712, and of these 366 were described as "white", 1,648 as "black" and 5,842 as "mixed", reminding one that racial classifications continued to be of importance in descriptions of society at that time. There were a total of 151 schools or *postos de ensino* (teaching posts), each one with a single teacher. The single *liceu*, located in Mindelo since 1921, the successor to the *seminário-liceu* of São Nicolau, and bearing the name Infante Dom Henrique, who was to become a sort of patron saint of the regime, had 15 teachers and a total of 264 pupils. Between 1928 and 1933, 1,305 pupils had matriculated (Exposição Colonial Portuguesa 1934: 194–207).

However, there was not much progress in this sector during the Estado Novo. In 1961 there were 11 primary schools and 109 *postos escolares* (school posts). Secondary education was now established in Praia as well as Mindelo, and there were technical schools: industrial and commercial in Mindelo, agricultural in Santiago, nursing in Praia, and arts and crafts in Mindelo (Agência-Geral do Ultramar 1961: 18–19). It was still common for the backwardness of the islands and the persistent poverty of much of the population to be attributed to lack of education, as it had been by writers in the early nineteenth century (Keese 2012). Although these figures for education are not high by modern standards, at least they show how important education had become in the life of the islands and why educated Cabo Verdeans were to be highly valued in the wider administration of the empire.

Movement within the Portuguese empire was largely without restrictions, and this was greatly to aid emigration. Figures for official emigration in 1933 show a total of 559 emigrants, of whom 305 were listed as going to destinations within the empire. Of those going to destinations outside, 113 went to Dakar and 75 to the United States (Exposição Colonial Portuguesa 1934: 25). Emigration was still seen as the principal way in which the island population could mitigate poverty. While it relieved pressure on the resources of the islands, it had the positive effect of generating a flow of remittances sent by emigrants to families in the islands.

More significant was the fact that Cabo Verdeans had by that time gained a reputation for being well educated and, as the colonial administration in Africa developed and widened its scope, Cabo Verdeans were recruited into the colonial service, being sent to Mozambique, Angola and Guiné (Portuguese Guinea). Although Cabo Verdean labourers contracted to São Tomé continued to work in conditions that nearly equated to slavery, elsewhere in the empire Cabo Verdeans, in posts as administrators and teachers, clearly belonged to the Portuguese colonial elite, not least in Guiné.

Tarrafal

Meanwhile, the Estado Novo had written the final chapter in Cabo Verde's story as a convict colony. Throughout the nineteenth century criminals and political prisoners continued to be sent into exile in Cabo Verde—a total of 2,433 between the years 1802 and 1882, according to António Carreira (2000: 311). However, in this the islands were not alone, as convicts were also sent to Angola to try to boost settlement there. So, perhaps it was only to be expected that in the 1930s the dictatorship would also want to have a convict colony to which to consign its political opponents.

Political prisoners began to be sent to the islands after the mutinies in Madeira, the Azores and Guiné in 1931. At first they went to São Nicolau and then were dispersed throughout the archipelago. The decision to establish a penal colony was only made in 1936, when the term *colónia penal* was used to disguise the reality that it was a concentration camp. The camp was to be sited at Tarrafal in the north of Santiago. This was to be a special prison run by PVDE (later PIDE), the secret police, and was to be specifically for political prisoners, leaders of labour unions, strikers, communists and other opponents of the regime. It was subsequently claimed that the authorities deliberately chose a site that was marshy and where malaria was endemic. Conditions in the camp were deliberately made harsh, and there was no protection against malaria (Oliveira 1974: 17–24, 87). Detention in an isolation cell was commonly used as a punishment. A total of 340 political prisoners were detained there, and 34 died while imprisoned. The camp was closed in 1954 but reopened in 1961 to house African prisoners during the independence wars. In all, 230 Africans were sent there. Tarrafal was not staffed by local Cabo Verdeans, who were kept at a distance from the prison. Unaware of what was involved, Archibald Lyall thought that the building of the prison was a way of stimulating the economy of the country.

The Tarrafal camp still exists, a gaunt, ruined memorial to the cruelties of the dictatorship.

Second World War

During the First World War, both Angola and Mozambique had become battlefields in the struggle between Germany and the Allies, and in 1940 political leaders in Portugal, Britain and South Africa feared that history would repeat itself. Both the Allies and the Axis powers weighed up the advantages and disadvantages of occupying Portuguese territory or of forcing Portugal into the war on their side. German policy was to persuade Franco to enter the war as an Axis ally, a move which would secure Gibraltar and effectively close the Mediterranean to Britain. Portuguese neutrality then would be unsustainable. In the end the Germans settled for Iberian neutrality, satisfied with the willingness of Salazar to provide Germany with wolfram, a vital strategic mineral.

Britain, unlike the Germans, preferred Iberian neutrality but with the proviso that "should Spain enter the war against us [it was proposed] to seize and hold both the Cape Verde Islands and the Azores as soon as possible, irrespective of the attitude of the Portuguese" (Newitt 2015b: 220).

Salazar was in a delicate position. If Franco entered the war on the side of Germany, Portugal would face the likelihood of a German and Spanish invasion, since, as he was well aware, elements in both Spain and Germany considered the unification of the Iberian peninsula a legitimate war aim. However, he knew that if Portugal tried to save itself by entering the war as an Axis ally, Britain would seize the Portuguese colonies. Accordingly, Portuguese efforts were directed at persuading Spain of the benefits of remaining neutral. In July 1940 a protocol was agreed by Spain and Portugal which extended the Treaty of Friendship and Non-aggression and gave "the belligerents the clear message that the Iberian powers had a common preference to remain at peace and to keep the war from the peninsula" (Newitt 2015b: 221).

Salazar saw his regime as threatened both by Bolshevik communism and by the predatory liberal democracy of Britain and America. With this perspective he welcomed Germany's attack on the Soviet Union while at the same time he sought to ward off threats from the Western democracies. In March 1940 the British ambassador reported a remarkable conversation he had had with Francisco Vieira Machado, the Portuguese minister for the colonies, in which the latter expressed great anxiety about "certain ideas which were being ventilated [in Britain] for a European federation on the basis of the pooling of colonial resources as a solution to prevent the repetition of another great war in Europe". The ambassador had had to reassure him that "Portugal had the absolute guarantee of His Majesty's government as regards her colonies" (Newitt 2015b: 221).

The Cabo Verde islands were strategically important for their airfields, bunkering facilities and submarine cable stations, and the British feared a German attempt to seize one or more of the islands. A report by a British naval officer in January 1941 describes these concerns: "On Christmas Day St Vincent was virtually undefended. The Senior Officer present was the Officer of the Port, [he] is a political exile who will accept little responsibility and who lacks decision, and a lieutenant in charge of the garrison, a man miserable in appearance, who commands fifty native troops, recruited locally ... Four to six determined armed men with iron bars and a can of petrol could put the [cable] station out of commission in from five to ten minutes" (Newitt 2015b: 233). Salazar responded to British concerns by sending a warship and dispatching a force of 3,000 men to defend the islands. In spite of these measures the British complained that German U-boats were operating around the islands and were even receiving aid from the islanders. However, it was not to be a British or German occupation that brought disaster to wartime Cabo Verde but the old enemy, drought.

Wartime conditions made the islands particularly vulnerable. In 1939 the rains failed and the islands faced steadily worsening famine conditions over the next three years. The effects of the famine, one of the most severe in the islands' history, were described in the dispatches of the British vice-consul. In August 1941 he recorded,

> from 70 per cent to 80 per cent of the inhabitants of the Cape Verde Islands live within the poverty zone, dependent on the annual rainfall for their next year's supplies of foods and necessities. A bad year means hunger and shortage, two bad years in succession may bring starvation in many islands ... Towards the end of 1940 rumours were constant of serious want in many of the islands, as 1941 advanced food riots due to want were reported from S. Antão and death from hunger from S. Nicolau and Fogo ... Children from this island [S. Nicolau] are being landed in St Vincent just skin and bone and have to be carried to the houses of their friends. (Newitt 2015b: 234)

By December the situation was worse. Patrols had been out turning back people from the countryside who were trying to get to one of the towns to find relief. "The starving seem to accept the situation with an oriental fatalism. They do not press their claims to live, they scarcely beg, may ask you for alms once or twice, and then simply stare at you as if resigned to what is to happen. [The authorities] are very reticent regarding information about the famine ... and it is evident the government do not wish for any outside assistance" (Newitt 2015b: 234). The only measures being taken were to establish relief works, but many people were too weak to work. Eventually some 1,700 starving islanders were sent to São Tomé to work in the cocoa plantations. The Portuguese were aware that drought was a recurring feature of island life and that the customary survival strategies of the islanders involved emigration. Because the normal emigration routes were closed by the war, emigration to São Tomé was the only option. However, in terms of what was needed to stem the deaths from starvation, this measure was too little and too late.

The vice-consul reported that imported foodstuffs were continually running out because the recently reinforced Portuguese garrison had to be fed and visiting Portuguese ships were not running to schedule or were too full to carry goods for Cabo Verde. However, he was emphatic that "the Island Government can deal with the situation if they wish to ... [and] Portugal can also help if required without any inconvenience, it has no war expenditure and is probably at present one of the wealthiest nations in Europe" (Newitt 2015b: 234). António Carreira estimated that during the years 1941–3 there were 24,643 deaths attributable to the famine (1982: 166).

Salazar was very sensitive that offers of assistance would prove to be excuses for political or military intervention, and throughout the war he feared that any miscalculation on his part might lead to the loss of both Cabo Verde and the Azores. In the end he was prepared to compromise his neutrality by allowing the Allies to establish an air base in the Azores in 1943, but only because he judged that the tide of war was turning in their favour.

Post-war Change

It is often asserted that the Estado Novo politicians had no plans for the development of the Cabo Verde islands and left them in a state of unrelieved poverty. According to Paulo Pinto, Cabo Verde, unlike other colonies, still remained "quite untouched in the 1940s" in terms of government-led development (Pinto 2015: 598). Nevertheless the regime did imagine a role for the islands in the future of the empire and, when famine struck the islands in the 1940s, implementing these plans became a matter of urgency. Henrique Galvão, later a high-profile opponent of Salazar, was sent by the government and, in October, reported that "on the islands of Fogo and São Nicolau, 7,100 and 5,000 people had died in a population of about 23,000 and 15,000 respectively. One third of those died from malnutrition." In 1944 the Portuguese government established an Office for Colonial Urbanisation under the Ministry of the Colonies. This was to be a technical section which would gather information and work on the technical aspects of development plans. The same year a mission was sent to produce a plan to "put an end as far as possible to the crises [the islands] experience during periods of major drought" (Pinto 2015: 604–5). In terms of immediate effective government action, however, little was done.

The famine of 1947–8 followed closely after the famine of the war years. For the first time this resulted in major government initiatives. As the report *Soil and Water Conservation Strategies in Cape Verde* put it:

> Following the 1947–1948 famine, the colonial authorities took measures to mitigate the problem. The first was to employ people locally on the so-called *Frentes de Alta Intensidade de Mão-de-Obra*—FAIMO (High Intensity Labor Fronts) to implement measures, such as terraces, dams, afforestation and irrigation infrastructure to reduce erosion risk, conserve soil and retain water, thus stabilizing the agricultural landscape. FAIMO was a national program that ensured jobs for thousands of people in rural areas, particularly in dry years. A second measure was to expatriate people to other colonies to work in plantations. A third initiative was the installation of an agriculture school to guarantee technical know-how, dissemination and extension. These measures, together with large-scale emigration, led to the eradication of famine from the country. (Baptista 2015)

After the war a series of development plans were drawn up covering Portugal and the African provinces. Cabo Verde was allocated funds to improve its infrastructure of ports, roads and airfields, and irrigated agriculture was also identified as an area for planning. The Livestock Development Station, an agricultural research institute, was established in Santiago. In the second six-year plan (1959–64) 308 million *escudos* of development funds was allocated: science 1.3 per cent; use of resources 32.9 per cent; communication and transport 61.58 per cent; education and health 4.21 per cent. The priorities of the regime are reflected in the fact that only 3 million *escudos* was allocated to education.

Although Italians had built the first airfields in the islands in the 1930s, it was only in 1948 that the International Airport of Espargos was opened on Sal. By 1961 there were airfields on all the islands except Santo Antão. Once again the government prepared the Cabo Verde islands to play an important part in the development of global communications, long-haul aircraft now replacing the shipping that no longer used Porto Grande.

During the 1960s development plans were also produced for the two main urban centres of Praia and Mindelo.

All these plans drawn up in Lisbon for improving conditions in the islands moved slowly and seldom amounted to much more than some infrastructure development. Nevertheless, one commentator has concluded that the "development processes triggered by the Estado Novo over two decades ... notably in its infrastructure, its water supply, sanitation, electrification, and its road network ... provided the new authorities [after independence] with a basis for their first efforts to develop and implement infrastructure, a continuity showing a clear detachment between ideology and infrastructure" (Pinto 2015: 617–18).

Emigration

During the twentieth century droughts were recorded in 1896–1904, 1918–21, 1939–43 and 1945–8, and emigration continued to be driven by the recurrence of famine and destitution. As the United States raised serious obstacles to immigration, Cabo Verdeans sought other destinations, notably Argentina and Brazil and, after the Second World War, increasingly western Europe. However, emigration was never an option for the very poor, as there were considerable expenses involved in seeking to emigrate. The very poor were driven to contract for São Tomé, and between 1900 and 1970 over 80,000 Cabo Verdeans are known to have been forced to take this option.

Once emigrant communities were established overseas, they provided a significant "pull factor", as people from the islands were encouraged to come to join established Cabo Verdean communities overseas. Emigration in this way began to detach itself from the exigencies of life in the islands and became a self-sustaining process. It gradually became a normal expectation for many islanders, the way to dream of and plan for a better life.

As well as the United States, Argentina and Brazil, a favoured destination was Senegal and the port city of Dakar. Dakar was quite close and could easily be reached by small boats, useful for people intent on evading the Portuguese regulations. Cabo Verdeans, especially women, found employment in Dakar, and up to the Second World War more Cabo Verdeans moved to Dakar than to the United States. Emigration to Portugal did not develop until the 1930s, but between 1936 and 1952 57 per cent of all officially recorded emigrants from the islands went to Portugal. The movement of people to Portugal fitted fairly comfortably within the ideas of the Salazar dictatorship, which claimed to see the islands as part of a worldwide Portuguese community.

After the Second World War, Cabo Verdean emigration was largely directed towards western Europe, where the rapidly expanding economy sucked in migrant workers. Many reached Europe via Dakar, others via Lisbon, with final destinations in the Netherlands, Luxembourg, Switzerland and Italy. There was also a major revival of emigration to the United States both from Cabo Verde and from the Azores. A major factor in the relaxation of quotas was the earthquake in the Azores in 1956; this created an emergency to which the US government was willing to respond. Emigration continued after independence. According to Marilyn Halter, in the thirty years following Cabo Verde's independence in 1975, 60,000 Cabo Verdeans emigrated to the United States, though this is rather contradicted by the US census figures for 2000, which recorded only 26,000 people as having been born in the Cabo Verde islands (Halter 2008: 37). The uncertainty over numbers is due to the irregular way statistics were gathered, made worse by the interest that some emigrant groups felt in exaggerating their numbers.

The early days, when working in textile mills or picking cranberries provided employment for unskilled Cabo Verdean immigrants, had passed. Now migrants were to be found in a number of different occupations, though 87 per cent of them were still located in New England. In the United States, Cabo Verdeans, determined to maintain their own separate identity, and refused to be classified as Africans, African Americans or Hispanics. Many insisted on being identified as Portuguese, though this naturally declined after independence (Halter 2008: 36).

By the time of independence in 1975 it was estimated that there were as many Cabo Verdeans located in other countries, some say in the United States alone, as there were in the islands themselves. The transformation from the isolation of island life, where the struggle for survival was often a losing battle, to a world where emigration conferred status and in many cases wealth and at the same time consolidated identity, is the most remarkable aspect of the story of the islands in the twentieth century.

During the century the aspiration to emigrate came to dominate the narrative that Cabo Verdeans created for themselves. The poverty and hopelessness of life in the drought-stricken islands had come to be accepted by Cabo Verdeans and, with it, "the idea that the transition from poverty to plenty can only take place outside the homeland" (Carling and Akesson 2009: 134). Emigration offered hope, and the emigrant who succeeded in making a comfortable living through hard work in America or Europe became a kind of ideal to which people aspired—what has been described as a "well-developed migration ideology that constructs mobility as both natural and necessary". Emigration became "associated with self-fulfillment" (Carling and Akesson 2009: 132, 133).

Although many, possibly most, emigrants never returned to the islands, emigration was not always seen as a permanent separation from the motherland. The idea that one day you would return never went away and was frequently realised in short holidays taken back in the islands. It all contributed to the belief that, although you were settled comfortably abroad, you were still part of the island community. Meanwhile, telecommunications and the internet largely did away with the sense of separation and the nostalgia that this created, and enabled emigrants to take a much more immediate part in the life of the islands—"the cellular phone permits direct contact between a rural village on the island of Santiago and Providence [Rhode Island]" (Semedo 2003: 37).

During the Salazar dictatorship, the idea had been promoted that the inhabitants of the empire were part of a single Portuguese community. After independence severed the connection with Portugal, the old idea of a single nation whose members were located in different parts of the world continued to hold sway and led to the creation of the transnational Cabo Verdean nation which was enshrined in the constitution of the Republic.

From the 1990s the story of Cabo Verdean emigration began to change. Both Europe and America began to raise barriers once again to free immigration, and it became progressively harder for unskilled Cabo Verdeans to breach the walls now erected against migrants. The only practical way was to exploit family connections, and increasingly recourse was had to "document marriages"—marriages contracted simply in order to obtain the documents needed to migrate (Carling and Akesson 2009: 142).

At the same time Cabo Verdeans found themselves caught up in the waves of African migration heading towards Europe. The Cabo Verde islands became a favourite transit point for Africans, who made use of the freedom of movement within ECOWAS countries to head for the islands, where people smugglers operated boats to the Canary Islands (Carling and Akesson 2009: 145).

However, as emigration became more difficult and more problematic, it remained an important aspiration, and those who made it successfully to Europe or the United States were still able to send remittances to families in the islands and in this way help sustain the economy of the new republic. In 2022, $312 million was remitted to the islands, forming 13.54 per cent of GDP (although this represents a percentage decline since 1980, when the figure was

28.17 per cent). So important were remittances from the diaspora that this was undoubtedly a major factor behind granting emigrants a political voice in elections for the island government.

São Tomé and Príncipe during the Estado Novo

As a result of the boom in the market for cocoa and coffee at the end of the nineteenth century, a number of creole landowners in São Tomé had grown very rich. Some of these families sent their children to Portugal to receive education, and by the early years of the twentieth century there was not only a number of people among the *forro* population who had received a good education but there was in Lisbon a cultured group of people from the islands. There they were active in early political movements which sought to give a voice to the grievances of the colonies. The focus of these early organisations was on maintaining the status of educated Africans within the colonies. Educated São Tomeans were prominent in forming the Liga Africana and were in touch with the leaders of black political movements across the Atlantic, like W. E. B. Du Bois and Marcus Garvey.

In São Tomé the *forro* population felt themselves under pressure from European Portuguese buying up cocoa-growing land and using their financial resources to expel the *forros* from their property. For the *forros* in São Tomé the principal issue was to maintain their social status vis-à-vis the contract labourers from Angola or Cabo Verde who were brought in to work on the *roças*. Plantation labour was a sign of servile status, which most *forros* refused to accept. In 1910 an organisation with the name Liga dos Interesses Indígenas (League of Indigenous Interests) was formed in São Tomé to improve the cultural and educational situation and to maintain the social standing of the *forros*. A stated objective was "'the protection of its members from abuses by individuals and the authorities' ... At the same time, they tried to stop their economic losses and preserve their social status" (Nascimento 1999: 419). Among its projects was the formation of a Company of Native Labourers, which in spite of its name was an attempt to create conditions for free labour in the islands.

São Tomé and Príncipe had at one time been Portugal's most profitable colonies. Between 1909 and 1919 the islands had exported over 30,000 tons of cocoa beans every year, with 1919 being a peak year when 55,000 tons were produced. Thereafter, production went into steep decline until in 1940 only 6,900 tons and, by the end of the Second World War, only 4,000 tons were recorded. Many companies now began to produce palm oil as well as cocoa and coffee. While world prices remained low, particularly during the 1930s, the Portuguese companies that owned the plantations failed to invest in new fixed capital and saw the cocoa trees ravaged by disease. For their part, the owners of the *roças* believed, almost as an article of faith, that their difficulties were principally caused by a shortage of labour, although the more realistic of them understood that the problem was actually the very low productivity of the labour they did employ. In the eyes of the more intelligent administrators, the problem lay in the appalling conditions on many of the *roças*, where the workers were still treated as virtual slaves (Newitt 2015b: 234).

During the Second World War a shortage of shipping and a depressed market for cocoa meant that the island economies stagnated. Although 1,700 starving Cabo Verdeans had reached the islands in 1942, the next three years saw hardly any newly contracted workers arrive, while the labour force suffered attrition through death, desertion and some repatriation.

The early years of the war were, therefore, a period of crisis for the *roças*, a crisis that went to the very heart of the colonial system. This is vividly brought out in a report on the *roça* Agua Izé, produced in February 1941 for the Companhia da Ilha de Príncipe, which owned the plantation. This confidential report strikingly illuminates Portuguese colonial practice and the slowness in implementing reform (Newitt 2015b: 235–6; Castro Almeida 1941). Having discussed in detail the situation on each of the "dependencies" of the *roças*, the author, Castro Almeida, addressed the delicate matter of relations with the workforce. He pointed out that each labourer cost the *roça* around 700 *escudos*. Before they would be of any use they needed training, but "if brutality and the whip are brought into action unjustly and without any reason the labourers (and particularly the new ones) flee and take refuge in the forest. They remain completely lost to the *roça* which not only loses the 700 *escudos* but also a worker who, with a bit of patience, would become an item of value." It was important that the workforce should be properly fed, for "if we do not feed properly the cattle we need for work, they will not be productive, so why should we adopt other criteria with the labourers?"

"If formerly the workforce on the *roças* was treated as slaves," the report said, "today this cannot be done, not only for reasons of humanity but for legal reasons, seeing that the supervisors (*curadores*) exercise a strict supervision (more or less, according to which *curador* [is involved])." Complaints made to the *curador* "make a disgraceful impression and damage the prestige of the *roça*". Punishment with the *palmatória* [wooden paddle], which leaves the labourer unable to work for days, is stupid. Much better would be "half a dozen blows administered to each hand daily in front of the other [workers]" rather than privately administered punishment that prevents them from working. "I was present at a scene that was not edifying," Almeida wrote. "A young girl of 10 or 12 was given twenty-four blows of the *palmatória* while Mr Amaro stood behind her with a hippopotamus hide whip to force her to hold out her hand." A halt was called to this scene "when they saw me". However, he adds for the benefit of his employers, "corporal punishment for the black man is necessary because it is the only thing he fears."

To achieve a happy workforce, one should allow them to cultivate gardens and hold their *batuques* (dances) but "punish without sparing them when it is necessary and they deserve it." As for the administrators of the *roça*, their "morals are of the very worst kind". The administrator had a girl with whom he sleeps but he also "has a *moleca* [black girl], a *tonga* [child of a contract labourer born in São Tomé] from the *roça*, who has to sleep on a sofa in the administration office, with the result that when I sat down in the office I saw two bedbugs on the sleeve of my coat and the sofa where the girl slept was infested with insects". "All this would be less important if the good name of the *roça* was not involved." Almost all the administrators of the *roças* had relations with young girls, and this did not affect their reputation if it was an occasional matter and they paid generously, "but what is very bad and prejudices discipline is the selection of one girl who comes to be privileged over the others and is the cause of envy, jealousy and disturbance". Evidently not written *para os inglezes ver* (for the English to see), this report, as well as the language in which it is expressed, vividly tells its own story.

In 1944–5 cocoa production began to recover as the world price experienced a modest rise, but the contract labour force continued to decline as labourers who had served their contracts returned home. As late as 1954 a report from the Emigration Society for São Tomé and Príncipe recommended that to improve the recruitment of Cabo Verdeans, food should be served to them on plates and not on banana leaves, and the humiliating practice of shaving the heads of the *serviçais*, observed on some of the *roças*, should be discontinued (Cruz 1975: 56–7).

Governor Gorgulho and the Batepá Massacre

In February 1945 a new governor, Carlos de Sousa Gorgulho, was appointed to try not only to revive the economy of São Tomé but to deal with the social problems which lay at the root of the island's decline. Gorgulho's energy, enterprise and reforming zeal were to transform São Tomé but were also to lead to a revolutionary situation that would present a dramatic challenge to the whole post-war colonial system (Seibert 2024: 75–99). As Alexis de Tocqueville long ago pointed out, the most dangerous moment for any regime is when it begins to reform itself.

Gorgulho planned to reform the whole system of contract labour. His measures "included stricter enforcement of the labour code, imposition of fines and punishments on the planters and their staffs. Higher wages were also decreed for the *serviçais*" (Eyzaguirre 1993: 11). The *roça* workers were now allowed to leave the plantations after work and mix with the *forro* population, resulting in a rapid blurring of the distinctions between the social classes. Gorgulho's plans included modernisation of the capital of São Tomé, the development of a whole new quarter, the construction of an airport and the founding of a secondary school. These were part of a radical development plan which had its counterpart in the Estado Novo's plans for Cabo Verde. Gorgulho, however, found himself in competition with the *roças* for scarce labour and sought a solution in using Portugal's vagrancy laws, widely employed in the mainland colonies, to obtain forced labour, which would be organised into gangs for his construction projects. This policy was fiercely resisted by the *forros*, and rumours spread that this was the forerunner of a policy to employ *forro* labour on the *roças*.

In early February 1953 posters put up by the government were torn down in one of the inland villages. When police were sent, there were a number of confrontations, in one of which a customs officer was killed. There followed a hysterical reaction by the governor. Whites working on the *roças* were organised into vigilante gangs, and contract workers from the *roças* were also armed and let loose on the areas of the island where the *forro* population mostly lived. Large numbers of people were rounded up and imprisoned. There were interrogations and torture, and as a result the governor announced there had been a wide-ranging communist-inspired plot to kill all whites and install a creole government. Meanwhile a priest, Father Pinto da Rocha, smuggled a letter to Lisbon calling for the government to intervene. Early in March, the Lisbon authorities, apparently alarmed at the possibility of a major outbreak of rebellion, sent a delegation of the secret police (PIDE) to investigate. At the same time principal *forro* leaders, horrified at what was turning out to be a racial war aimed at the *forro* population, arranged for a lawyer from Lisbon, Manuel Palma Carlos, to come to São Tomé to investigate.

The PIDE agents quickly discovered that there was no conspiracy, while Palma Carlos began taking evidence from those who had been rounded up and maltreated. In an unprecedented move by the Salazar government, Governor Gorgulho was recalled to Lisbon and forced into retirement, while a number of his henchmen were tried and imprisoned.

Although there were many other incidents in the mainland colonies which were to lead to over-reaction by the police and to the killing of protesters, this incident stands out for the readiness of the Estado Novo to take action against one of its most senior figures (Seibert 2024: 56–75).

The incident, usually known as the "Batepá massacre", after one of the *forro* villages where incidents occurred, had the effect of permanently alienating the leading *forro* families and turning the *forro* population in general against the government. It also helped to drive a wedge between the *forro* population and the contract workers, including the Cabo Verdeans, a wedge which led to deep divisions in the population that would last long after independence. Just as a strong and united island identity was beginning to form in the Cabo Verde islands, the events of 1953 in São Tomé were to divide the island population as never before, and to split it along lines of ethnic origin.

In the 1950s the poor economic performance of the *roças* led to a number of bankruptcies, but the Estado Novo continued to defend the system. P. B. Eyzaguirre maintained that this was to consolidate a social structure on which not only the African empire but the very regime itself had come to depend. He quoted the governor Ricardo Vaz Monteiro, who wrote in one of his reports: "The planters' tenacity and persistence in the fight against adversity caused by their heavy production costs and falling [cocoa] prices is cause for admiration and places them among the greatest of Portuguese colonizers ... If it were not for this spirit, agriculture on the *roças* would have been abandoned by now ... He [the planter] hopes for better days, continuing to work in the hope that his efforts and investment may some day be recompensed" (Eyzaguirre 1993: 304).

The hierarchical society of the *roças* has been compared to the *fazenda*, which was a socio-economic model that some geographers and historians, among them Francisco Tenreiro, a distinguished São Tomean scholar and poet, traced back to the Roman empire and its rural complex of villas. The *fazenda* was a self-sufficient community producing much of what it consumed and supplying its own needs from its own resources, presided over by the *fazendeiro* and his European Portuguese staff (Eyzaguirre 1993: 9).

Another comparison, not too far-fetched, might be made between the survival of the rural *fazenda* and the determination with which the Estado Novo continued to subsidise the White Fleet of small fishing boats that went annually to the Newfoundland and Greenland fishing grounds. This preserved the centuries-old way of

The Eve of Independence: The Legacy of History

During the first three-quarters of the twentieth century, Cabo Verde changed radically. The machinery of a modern government was established and, in spite of the changes brought about by the World Wars and the fluctuations of the world economy, the islands retained some importance in the global communications network. Meanwhile, migration opened the door to worldwide opportunities for the islanders and to the establishment of a thriving literary culture. Nevertheless the islands still remained in many ways prisoners of their history with their fundamental problems unresolved.

Among the issues facing Cabo Verdean society, which had their roots deep in the islands' history, was the question of landownership. Although the old *morgadios* had been abolished in 1864 and a relatively free market in land had been established, the number of landowners was still small. In 1920 there were 8,186 proprietors out of a total population of 159,675 (5 per cent of a population that was still overwhelmingly dependent on agriculture). In 1970 there were 10,000 proprietors in a population of 179,000 (5.6 per cent), but in 1969–70 the island of Santiago was still largely controlled by 52 large landowners. Moreover, agriculture was dominated by the old systems whereby land was rented to small farmers or was farmed by the share-cropping system—a system on which a large part of the population depended for its livelihood. The old practices of hiking rents every year continued, rents which were still payable even during periods of drought. The tenant farmers were trapped in debt and were regularly penalised with fines for alleged damage caused by cattle and goats. Half of the land that was irrigated was devoted to sugar cane, used for the manufacture of *grogue*, a spirit sold internally in the islands. Other historical practices continued, like the forced sale of produce to the proprietor and even corporal punishment, still from time to time administered on recalcitrant tenants. Such historical rural practices, many deriving from the days of slavery, continued unchecked, as the local administration in the *concelhos* was usually dominated by the large landowners (Silva Andrade 1996: 229–33).

The islands remained largely dependent on imported food, and in the last years before independence food imports ranged from 26.8 per cent of total imports in 1967 to 40.2 per cent in 1970. The deficit in the economy of the islands remained crippling. In 1964 exports had covered 18 per cent of imports, but by 1974 they covered only 3 per cent. Remittances from emigrants played a huge part in sustaining the economy, ranging from 33 per cent of the cost of imports in 1968 to an average of 22 per cent between 1970 and 1974 (Silva Andrade 1996: 235, 254). However, perhaps the most serious of the legacies of history was that, until the final years of Portuguese rule, there was a failure to develop any sustained strategy to cope with drought and water shortage. Although the government was prepared to spend considerable sums on communications, very little was allocated to measures to tackle drought. This reflected the role allocated to the islands in Portugal's overall imperial strategy. Cabo Verde was seen as a major transport and communications hub, and drought and famine were to be mitigated by emigration.

The Eve of Independence: Famine and National Identity among the Cabo Verdean Elite

Between 1894 and 1924 there were six serious famines, but it was those of the 1940s (1939–43 and 1947–8) and a subsequent one in 1956–8 that played a major role in changing the outlook of educated Cabo Verdeans.

From the late 1930s Cabo Verdeans had been recruited into the colonial service in all the Portuguese African territories and had filled many of the administrative posts in the Cabo Verde islands themselves. For the most part they had seen themselves as part of the Portuguese administration and, as Alexander Keese puts it, "would fully embrace the rhetoric of the Estado Novo". However, because of their position in the administration, inevitably some began to raise questions about the nature of Portuguese policies towards the islands which were their home. Others had begun to draw attention to the shortcomings of education, which was seen as the major factor holding back development, though this was still widely attributed to the "passiveness and apathy" of the population (Keese 2012: 53, 55).

The onset of drought brought home the failures of the government to anticipate, or make any provision for dealing with, the consequences of famine. In Santiago during the famine of 1947, those driven to beg for food had been rounded up as vagrants and imprisoned on an island off the coast, where many had simply died. António Policarpo de Sousa Santos, the Cabo Verdean appointed as interim administrator of Praia, reacted strongly to this policy.

> When arriving here [at the islet] my hairs stood upright as I saw the state of some hundreds of those creatures who had been thrown on this land for the simple crime that they had begged for things they lacked: that is, for food, which would help them kill the hunger that tormented them. Moreover, your excellency, in no other land of the world, including even Soviet Russia with all its barbarian practices, in savage Germania, or in Asia with all its exotic manners, would the fact that they beg us to stop their hunger be enough of a grave crime to merit such horrible punishment. (Keese 2012: 57)

The reaction of the authorities was the same in São Vicente, where starving refugees trying to enter Mindelo from the neighbouring island of Santo Antão were rounded up and returned to the island they had tried to leave (Keese 2020: 86).

In 1947 an anonymous official wrote to the British consul and referred in his letter to "liberation of the islands from Portuguese mismanagement"—a portent of things to come (Keese 2012: 55). During the 1950s there were more and more incidents of Cabo Verdean administrators speaking out against the absence of serious development policies and reflecting on how the neglect of welfare provision was playing into the hands of those opposed to the whole idea of empire and the Portuguese civilising mission. In 1959 the Cabo Verdean administrator in Fogo, Luís Rendall Silva, called "for improvement of the Cape Verdean land for the benefit of its population, and for a more visible advancement of the civilising mission" (Keese 2012: 49).

Opposition to the policies of metropolitan Portugal was finding other ways to express itself. In 1969 workers seeking employment as casual labour rioted and burnt down the home of the administrator in Santo Antão. Although the Portuguese political police were determined to believe that the rioting was inspired by agitators, Alexander Keese, who has investigated the issue, found that "the anger of local workers who feared being deprived of an opportunity to earn at least a basic wage was an important factor"—possibly the most important factor (Keese 2020: 86).

However, already by this time, events had begun to overtake the slow process of reform within the colonial administration. A group of Cabo Verdeans in Lisbon and Guinea had formed the PAIGC and were calling for total independence from Portugal.

7

INDEPENDENCE

Amílcar Cabral and the PAIGC

Throughout four centuries of history, Cabo Verdeans had always thought of themselves as Portuguese, and this identity had followed them when they emigrated. The only moment when this identification had been in doubt was in the 1820s when Brazil broke away from Portugal and threatened to carry Portugal's African territories with it. Although individual Cabo Verdeans may have been increasingly aggrieved about the neglect of the islands and the failure to deal with the problems of drought and famine, this resentment was aimed at the fascist regime of Salazar rather than the Portuguese connection itself.

So, as the British and French African colonies organised politically and achieved their independence, there was no move in the islands to follow these examples. It was rather among expatriate Cabo Verdeans that a movement for independence gradually came into being, initially among students in Lisbon and then among a small group of Cabo Verdeans in Portuguese Guinea. After the Second World War, the Portuguese regime had begun to provide opportunities for students from Cabo Verde and the other African territories to study in Lisbon. The idea was to encourage the training of technical personnel who would then be employed on development projects in Africa. Among these was Amílcar Cabral, the son of a well-known Cabo Verdean intellectual and writer called Juvenal Cabral. Amílcar went to Lisbon in 1945 and trained as an agronomist. In Lisbon he met students from the other Portuguese African territories, among whom ideas for establishing independence movements in Africa were beginning to be formulated and discussed. These students formed a very small and tightly knit group. They were much influenced by French Marxists, but they had very few links with any popular organisations in Africa itself.

In Portuguese Guinea many Cabo Verdeans were employed by the administration in a variety of capacities, reflecting the close association that had always existed between the islands and the communities of the mainland coastal towns, where a Portuguese creole language, related to Cabo Verde Crioulu, was spoken by local people. Cabral, whose family had close connections with Guinea, believed that an independence movement could be organised in that colony rather than in the fragmented islands of the archipelago. As a trained agronomist, he worked for the Portuguese administration in Angola and Guinea, where he carried out an agricultural census. By the late 1950s he and his associates were beginning to plan a campaign among urban workers in Guinea, but this was rudely interrupted in 1959 when a demonstration by dockworkers in Bissau was broken up by the police with a number of casualties.

Meanwhile the French colonies were moving towards independence. Guinea-Conakry and Senegal, the two countries bordering Portuguese Guinea, became independent in 1958 and 1960 respectively. Both countries harboured political exiles and economic migrants from the Portuguese colony, and a number of independence movements were formed under the patronage of the newly independent states.

It was in this context that the PAIGC (the African Party for the Independence of Guiné and Cabo Verde) was formed in Guinea itself, not in Cabo Verde. The year when it was most likely founded was 1959, though, like the MPLA in Angola, the formation was later backdated to 1956 because of the propaganda value that could be extracted from being the first independence party to be formed.

INDEPENDENCE

Among the various groups that claimed to be organising independence movements, Cabral and his associates soon stood out and Cabral's leadership became an important factor. Cabral's strength lay in his diplomatic skills. He built close links with nationalists in Angola and Mozambique, and was instrumental in the creation of CONCP, the umbrella organisation under which the independence movements in the Portuguese colonies operated on the world stage. Cabral was also tireless in organising support from other newly independent African countries, from European liberal democracies and from Eastern bloc regimes. In Guinea itself, Cabral had to sell the idea of a war of independence to different social groups, all of which had different sets of grievances, different ideals and different visions of the future.

As a spokesman, he was tireless in fashioning ideas and ideologies behind which African and Western intellectuals could unite and which helped in the orchestration of an effective propaganda campaign. One of the most important aspects of this propaganda was Cabral's claim, once the armed struggle began, that the PAIGC had established liberated areas where a new and independent government was delivering health services and schools for the people. Whether there was any real government in the so-called liberated areas is open to doubt, but the reality was not important so long as the section of public opinion which Cabral was aiming to rally to his side believed it to be true. As António Tomás, in a recent biography of Cabral, puts it, "a great deal of what we know about nationalism in Lusophone Africa may have been fabricated" and "the way we recall the revolutionary process today is largely based on the 'facts' which were produced as propaganda" (2021: 4, 5).

Cabral also had a ruthless streak, and in 1964, at the so-called Cassaca Conference, he imposed his political control and that of his Cabo Verdean associates on the fighters, who were largely drawn from the Balanta ethnic group. At least two dissidents were tried and executed. The new "freedom was limited, the ruling party was the purveyor of the people's aspirations and political dissidents, if not killed, were exiled. The party had in a way replaced the church, and those who dared to challenge its mystifications could expect harsh punishment" (Tomás 2021: 13).

However, Cabral, for all his diplomatic skill and leadership qualities, had what proved to be a dangerous obsession. He believed that Cabo Verde and Guinea should move towards independence together as one state and one nation. He defended this on the grounds that, until the 1870s, Guinea and Cabo Verde had been treated as a single administrative unit by the Portuguese, and that a large part of the Cabo Verde island population had its origin in Guinea. However, the idea that they could be a single, united nation was a denial of the distinct identities people had developed over 400 years of history. This was all the more ironic as Cabral never ceased urging Cabo Verdeans and Guineans to rediscover their history and resume its trajectory, which had been interrupted by colonial rule. That there was another way to understand Cabo Verde's history, however, had been articulated by Cabral himself in an early essay published in the *Boletim de Informação e Propaganda de Cabo Verde* "on the cultural similarities between Cape Verdeans, Afro-Brazilians, and Afro-Americans" (Tomás 2021: 48–9). This identified the Cabo Verdean people with the Atlantic creole diaspora rather than with continental Africa.

Cabral's ideas were unrealistic for another reason. The Portuguese administration in Guinea had largely been staffed by Cabo Verdeans. "Cape Verdeans took hold of the entire life of the province. They made up a large part of the military units and occupied the majority of the posts in public administration. This arrangement, which prevented the emergence of a native elite, suited the Portuguese and the Cape Verdeans alike" (Tomás 2021: 18). For many Guineans, Cabral and his Cabo Verdean associates in the PAIGC were simply another manifestation of Cabo Verdean overrule—Cabo Verdeans seeking to take control of their country once the Portuguese left.

Although Cabral realised that Guineans saw that it was their country, not Cabo Verde, that had become the locus for the armed challenge to the Portuguese, he believed it might be possible to start a guerrilla campaign in Cabo Verde itself, possibly in the mountains of Santiago. He invested a lot of effort in trying to train a group of Cabo Verdean fighters to invade the islands. However, this proved wholly impractical and the effort was abandoned in 1968.

Cabral had no illusions that the PAIGC and its military could ever completely conquer Guinea or drive the Portuguese out. Instead the tactic was to tie down colonial forces to their bases and to the coastal towns, while the countryside became increasingly a "no-go" area for the Portuguese administration. This, it was hoped, would bring an end to the colonial regime through a form of attrition. "The schism that existed in these movements [was] between those who made the war and those who publicised it. Cabral was in the second group, and, as Reiland Rabaka has put it, he was a "reluctant soldier": he spent much of the war promoting, but not actually participating in, the fighting. Cabral was not a military man, nor did he have any military training, and even though he was commander of the rebel forces, he was convinced that the independence of Guinea could only be obtained by diplomatic action" (Tomás 2021: 5).

In January 1973, tensions within the PAIGC between Guineans and Cabo Verdeans came to a head, and Cabral himself was murdered by members of his own party outside his house in Guinea-Conakry. However, Cabral's death did not immediately displace the Cabo Verdean elite from control of the PAIGC, and he was succeeded as head of the party by his brother Luís.

In the months that followed the assassination, the party moved towards the most dramatic realisation of its plans and in July 1973 declared Guinea to be an independent state occupied by a foreign power. In November the independence of Guinea was accepted by 93 members of the United Nations.

Cabral, the Idea of Revolution and Modern Cabo Verde

With the possible exception of the singer Cesária Évora, Amílcar Cabral remains the only Cabo Verdean with worldwide recognition. Everyone who has studied the history of the last fifty years and, in particular, the story of the end of the western European colonial empires, will have heard of him. In some quarters he is considered a great intellectual and theorist of both African political thought and social revolution. He is still the subject of a steady flow of books and articles that seek to explain his importance and the cogency of his ideas. However, although most Cabo Verdeans would recognise him as a figure of great national significance, what he achieved and what he stood for has remained controversial.

Although there seems to be widespread agreement that Cabral was an important theorist of the independence struggle, there is less consensus about what his theories actually were. His writings continue to be analysed and re-examined, at least in part because they contain confusing and even contradictory ideas. Cabral was first and foremost a publicist for the cause of independence. To achieve his objectives he tirelessly addressed audiences around the world over a period of more than a decade. Much of what he said and wrote was addressed to particular audiences, and his words were often chosen to suit that audience. This explains the uncertainty and even confusion over what he actually thought and believed.

What his relationship was with the Marxist ideas of his day remains uncertain, as he had to canvass the support of the Soviet bloc, the so-called non-aligned countries and the liberal democracies of the North Atlantic. In a recent essay, Rita Narra explains that by refusing to call himself a Marxist, Cabral was looking for "a means to carve out a sphere of autonomy for Guinean and Cabo Verdean affairs within the Cold War". The Marxist idea of class struggle was not relevant to the struggle against colonialism, which was the struggle of a whole people, though he would also talk about the "negative unity of anticolonialism" (Narra 2024: 63, 69).

What did he really mean by saying that Cabo Verdeans had to rediscover their African roots? How did this match with the ideas adopted by the other revolutionary parties in the Portuguese colonies, which emphasised the non-racial, non-tribal nature of the struggle and denounced many traditional African practices and institutions as reflections of the colonial past? What did Cabral really mean when he said that the *petit bourgeoisie* had to commit suicide while at the same time identifying its members as the necessary leaders of the revolution (Silva Andrade 1996: 280–1; Chabal 1983: 177)? And when Cabral said "to hope that the *petite bourgeoisie* will just carry out a revolution when it comes to power in an underdeveloped country is to hope for a miracle", how was this to be reconciled with his identification of this very class as alone being capable of carrying through the changes he envisaged (Chabal 1983: 176)? In the light of what happened after independence, attempts to unpick Cabral's ideas on class and revolution can read like remote scholasticism removed from the realities of political power structures and ethnic identities, of which Cabral ought to have been aware.

One recent commentator has emphasised that "Cabral had a dynamic conception of societies (and consequently of cultures) as evolving entities, and ... Cabral was a proponent of the development of a 'technical, technological, and scientific culture' and [his] teachings were unhesitatingly directed towards the dismantling of socially retrograde structures" (Nabolsy 2020: 7). But this is not how it always sounded at the time.

Most controversial of all was Cabral's apparently firm belief that the people of Cabo Verde and Guinea should be united as one nation. M. Cardina and Inês Nascimento Rodrigues have described how "the armed struggle emerged as the birth certificate of the postcolonial nation, simultaneously constituting itself as a great symbolic narrative of the return of Cape Verde to 'Africa', which would materialize through a project of binational union with Guinea-Bissau" (2021: 3). This union became the foundational idea of the PAIGC but was widely opposed by most Cabo Verdeans and Guineans. Cabral's continued belief in the desirability and viability of this union has always raised question marks over his real understanding of the forces of change that he was calling into being and attempting to control.

Like Che Guevara and other leaders of revolutions, Cabral became even more influential after his death than he was when alive. For the PAIGC, Cabral was a cross between a martyr and a hero of myth. His image was used in every possible medium to give weight and legitimacy to what the PAIGC (and, after its name change, the PAICV) stood for and whatever policies it pursued. Cabral's name was invoked in every aspect of national life.

> Amílcar Cabral was a constant presence in this period. He appeared in the Cape Verdean song-book and on commemorative stamps and was mentioned as an example to follow in the 5 July celebrations. The newspaper *Voz di Povo* regularly published excerpts from his writings, speeches and interviews, and the preamble of the 1980 Constitution mentions him as the "founder of the nationality" ... The image of Cabral was displayed on one side of all notes, with other African revolutionary figures adorning

the coins. This homage was in line with the re-Africanization supported by the PAIGC and was also present in street names, music, political speeches and sporting competitions in the first years of independence. On the island of Sal, the airport was renamed "Amílcar Cabral International Airport" and throughout the archipelago, public buildings, monuments, streets and squares acquired names associated with the liberation struggle. (Cardina and Rodrigues 2021: 3–4)

The Road to Independence

The future of Cabo Verde was not decided by the 1973 declaration of independence, which concerned Guinea alone, but developments the following year soon directly involved the islands. In April 1974 the Estado Novo regime in Portugal collapsed and two rival factions struggled for supremacy in Lisbon. One group, headed by President Spínola, who had been governor of Guinea, wanted to keep the African territories in some kind of association with Portugal, while the radical, leftist officers of the Armed Forces Movement (MFA) favoured a rapid decolonisation and full independence for the colonies.

The position of Cabo Verde was not straightforward, as independence had never been seriously considered by the population, most of whom still looked on themselves as Portuguese. It is possible to speculate that, had there been more time for decisions to be made, Cabo Verde might have opted for the same relationship with Portugal as that enjoyed by the Azores and Madeira, in which case it would in due course have joined the European Union, with all the special funding arrangements and other benefits that came with membership.

However, in 1974 the only organised political movement in the islands was the PAIGC, which had strong support in Portugal among members of the MFA. The PAIGC, which claimed revolutionary legitimacy in assuming power in Guinea, offered a socialist future for an independent Cabo Verde. It was a future that tied Cabo Verde to Guinea in a close federation—the same political party controlled by the same leaders in charge in both countries. The idea of a union with Guinea was not popular, and during the short six months of his presidency in Portugal, Spínola tried in a rather chaotic manner to resist the claims of the PAIGC that Cabo Verde should be decolonised along with Guinea. He appointed Sérgio Duarte Fonseca, a Cabo Verdean, as governor, and when the independence of Guinea was recognised by Portugal in July 1974, the islands were not included. As Richard Lobban described the situation: "In Cape Verde, the PAIGC had no military strength, only a clandestine political organization … The PAIGC leaders were well aware of their weakness in the islands, but they also knew the precarious state of the Portuguese during these critical months. The situation resulted in a power vacuum which in turn created a classic revolutionary moment" (1995: 102).

During the autumn months of 1974 there were strikes and demonstrations organised by the PAIGC, while in Portugal a very uncertain situation followed the resignation of Spínola from the presidency in September. During the summer months attempts had been made by some Cabo Verdeans to organise opposition to the PAIGC, drawing on widespread hostility to the idea of a union with Guinea and to the avowed socialist programme of the PAIGC, which made no secret of its desire to turn both countries into one-party states. This opposition found a lot of support among Cabo Verdeans in the United States (Lobban 1995: 104–5; MacQueen 1988: 110–15).

In December 1974 it was agreed by the new revolutionary government in Portugal that there would be elections in Cabo Verde prior to independence, but in the meantime the PAIGC was given a place in the interim government, which was tantamount to formal recognition of its claims. The other opposition parties were excluded from the interim government and from contesting the elections for a National Assembly, which were held in June 1975 (Lobban 1995: 107–8). Inevitably the PAIGC won all the seats with 92 per cent of all votes cast.

Cabo Verde became formally independent on 5 July 1975 and moved into a future in which democracy was understood as the expression of the will of the people through the agency of the ruling party. The newly independent state was led by two former guerrilla leaders, Aristides Pereira, who was secretary general of the PAIGC and became president, and Pedro Pires, who became prime minister. Luís Cabral became president of Guinea.

The PAIGC owed a great deal to the support of the radical politicians in Portugal, who recognised it as the only legitimate political party in Cabo Verde. Similarly, in Mozambique only Frelimo was recognised, and in that former colony there was not even the pretence of holding elections. In both countries a relatively smooth transition to independence was achieved, but in the long term the total exclusion of opponents of the one-party socialist state was shown to have been unwise. In Mozambique civil war of a particularly violent kind broke out within five years, while in the same five years the PAIGC's visionary union of Guinea and Cabo Verde collapsed. Cabo Verde then experienced ten years of increasingly authoritarian rule until the PAIGC (since the split with Guinea, now called the PAICV) lost power peacefully at the ballot box in 1991.

Following that election, Cabo Verde experienced a cultural counter-revolution which dismantled much of the ideological framework on which the PAICV had depended.

The Failure of the Union of Guinea and Cabo Verde

The idea that there should be a union between Cabo Verde and Guinea had been central to Amílcar Cabral's whole political vision, and such was his prestige internationally and within the party that the idea of this union was carried over into the era of independence. Although Luís Cabral became president of Guinea, as Amílcar's brother he was perceived by most Guineans as being Cabo Verdean even though he had been born in Guinea. His prime minister was "Nino" Vieira, a Guinean from Bissau of Papel ethnicity. In Cabo Verde, Aristides Pereira had become president, but in both countries the government was controlled by the PAIGC, of which Pereira was the general secretary. It was not difficult to see in this arrangement the continued dominance of Cabo Verdeans over the union.

The union survived for five years, but already in 1977, at the party congress, unity was clearly fractured, and in November 1980 Luís Cabral was ousted by prime minister Vieira (Foy 1988: 36–43). This coup effectively ended the union, in spite of some attempts to save it, though the PAIGC continued to be a dominant force in Guinean politics. Luís Cabral was imprisoned and then granted asylum in Cuba the following year. Eventually he settled in Portugal. Although he subsequently visited Guinea on one occasion, he never returned to Cabo Verde and he died in 2009. In Cabo Verde the party also continued to govern but changed its name in January 1981 to PAICV.

João Madeira and Bruno Reis sum up the reasons for the 1980 coup which ended the union.

> It should be noted that this event was the consequence of a process that had been dragging on since the colonial era, in an intensification of distrust and competitiveness between the two countries. An asymmetrical distribution of power contributed to this situation. Administrative posts were generally occupied by Cape Verdeans, since they had higher levels of education, participation and access to the labour market, and because they spoke Portuguese correctly. Even within PAIGC, there were early incompatibilities between the Guinean wing and the Cape Verdean wing, the first being formed by members of the popular class that obeyed the military party hierarchy, and the second, composed of a bourgeois elite with a more cohesive leadership. (Madeira and Reis 2018: 180)

Cabo Verde and Guinea finally separated peacefully, if not cordially, in 1982 after intervention by Mozambique's Samora Machel. Although Amílcar Cabral's former associates in Cabo Verde deeply regretted the abandonment of what had been the fundamental policy for which Cabral had fought, most people at the time and since have seen the break-up as inevitable and Cabral's belief in the natural unity of the two countries as being deeply flawed. As António Tomás put it: "Cabral had not taken the resentment between Cape Verdeans and Guineans seriously, but at a deeper level, this showed that Cabral was incorrect in his explanation of the social process in Guinea. He was convinced that a process of cultural osmosis would make the Cape Verdeans and Guineans into a community; in reality Guineans took advantage of the anti-colonial war to advance their own agenda of power. But it also shows that Cape Verdeans and Guineans, pushed apart by colonialism, were culturally irreconcilable" (2021: 201).

The One-Party State in Cabo Verde

Cabo Verde's independence was declared on 5 July 1975. From that moment the PAIGC was in effect the state, though no formal constitution was adopted until 1980. The party controlled all the levers of government, from the president and prime minister downwards, and as new administrative bodies were created, so members of the party took control of those as well. And whatever the rhetoric may have been, the party was not a mass party. Membership was difficult to achieve, and large numbers of educated Cabo Verdeans were excluded.

As Elise Silva Andrade has remarked, at the party congress of 1983 the role of the party-state in the immediate post-independence period was made clear through an "ever greater preponderance of the state in the economic life of the country … in all areas: the organisation of the economic apparatus, investment, implementation and management of units of production, and the control of external trade, money and financial activities" (Silva Andrade 1996: 282). Between 1976 and 1980 the government was responsible for 75 per cent of all investment, and proceeded on the basis that it must be the prime mover in the economy. As the 1983 congress report stated, "the state sector alone finds itself in a position to guarantee the economic and social development of the country" (Silva Andrade 1996: 283).

However, even though the party reinvented itself as the PAICV, the break with Guinea had weakened it. It found increasing difficulty in maintaining internal unity, and the fiction that it and it alone spoke for the people of the islands became ever more distant from reality. The PAICV continued to court China and Cuba on the international stage, but this increasingly alienated opinion among the Cabo Verdean diaspora, particularly in the United States. The resignation of the senior judge Carlos Veiga from the party in 1982 was a portent that change was on the way.

Political Change

The comparative success of the Cabo Verde economy was put down by most observers to sound policy combined with good governance and the participation of the population in the programmes for change. It is clear from this that the role of the political leaders and the new institutions that had been created was of paramount importance. However, this did not mean that the political process was entirely one of consensus.

When Portugal decided to withdraw, there had been opposition in the islands to the political project of PAIGC, in particular to the union with Guinea. Embryo political parties were formed, particularly among emigrants in the United States, who were alarmed at the prospect of a party taking power that seemed to conform to the idea of a Marxist one-party state. In the event these groups were excluded from the elections that preceded independence, but they did not go away. Gradually they came to offer the Cabo Verde islanders an alternative political vision, one which was more securely rooted in Cabo Verde's historical experience than Cabral's urgings that islanders should turn to Africa and rediscover their African roots.

By the late 1980s various winds of change were blowing. International aid givers were now demanding greater liberalisation not only of the economy but also of political institutions—and Cabo Verde was one of the biggest recipients of foreign aid (per capita). There was also growing unease among sections of the Cabo Verde population concerning the direction of land reform and the long-term intentions of the government towards the considerable numbers of those who owned property in the islands, among whom were many emigrants working in Europe or America. From the start, land reform was a minefield and there was no easy way of negotiating the tangle of customary rights and practices, which in Santo Antão included rights to water and access to irrigation *levadas* (Keese 2020: 93). The early years of independence brought a fresh onset of drought, and in Santo Antão, although the government responded with organised work schemes, there were inevitable problems over implementation. Attempts to resettle the rural population of the worst-affected areas were particularly strongly opposed. According to Alexander Keese, the causes of resentment "include early frustrations of local expectations, anger about a combination of more police control paired with the absence of certain juridical and administrative services, resistance to the creation of structures of the ruling party in certain places, resettlement initiatives and the effects of unwanted agrarian reform" (2024: 3).

To meet the increasing demands for a more liberal politics, the PAICV allowed independents to stand in elections in 1985. In March 1990 a new party was formed, the MpD (Movimento para a Democracia), led by Carlos Veiga. In January 1991 other parties were allowed to contest the election for the National Assembly and the presidency. The result was the shock defeat of the PAICV, which had assumed that it would be rewarded by the electorate for the successful transformation of the islands' fortunes that had taken place under its guidance. Aristides Pereira, who had been a close associate of Cabral since the founding of the PAIGC, was replaced as president by António Mascarenhas Monteiro, a judge in the Cabo Verde Supreme Court, who had been educated at Coimbra University in Portugal and Louvain in Belgium. The MpD won decisively in all the islands except Boa Vista and Fogo.

The MpD was barely six months old, but the motivations which had led to its landslide victory soon became apparent, not only in the economic liberalisation and privatisation policies it implemented but also in what amounted to a cultural revolution. The MpD was perceived as the party of youth and of change. Its leaders were determined to alter the Africanist direction that had been pursued by the PAICV and to rediscover the history of Cabo Verde as an Atlantic nation with deep roots in Portuguese history and culture and a more recent but nevertheless strong influence from the United States. As Jørgen Carling and Luís Batalha put it, "ties with the diaspora were a critical lifeline for the newly independent country, and instrumental in the transition to multi-party democracy" (2008: 13).

The change of government was accompanied by a change in the national flag. "One of the most symbolically important changes introduced under the MpD government was the new flag, designed in red, white and blue with a circle of ten yellow stars representing the islands of the archipelago. The more European and American layout of the new flag matched a redirection of the country's foreign policy and development strategies" (Carling and Batalha 2008: 15). As well as a new flag, a new national anthem was adopted. Cabral's image now disappeared from stamps and banknotes, and there was a marked change in other national symbols.

> In S. Filipe, on the Island of Fogo, the bust of Serpa Pinto (a soldier who had played a role in putting down revolts against the Portuguese colonial presence in Africa, and a former governor of Cape Verde) also reappeared in 1991. On August 1992, the busts of Luís Vaz de Camões and the Marquis Sá da Bandeira returned to the centre of Mindelo, on the Island of S. Vicente, reoccupying their places in a square that had previously been named after Amílcar Cabral. In the same decade, the statue of another Portuguese discoverer, Diogo Afonso, returned to a prominent place in Mindelo … The return to a symbolism that so unambiguously recalled the colonial period was a phenomenon virtually unparalleled. (Cardina and Rodrigues 2021: 5)

Policies were developed that encouraged trade links with Portugal, while the islands joined the group of Atlantic islands collectively known as Macaronesia. Cabo Verde withdrew from the ECOWAS protocol allowing free movement of people in western Africa. Changes were also made to the constitution in 1999 to entrench the rights enjoyed by emigrants as citizens of a transnational Cabo Verde.

Whereas the PAICV had claimed legitimacy from its armed struggle against the Portuguese in Guinea, the MpD, for its part, claimed they were "double combatants: liberation combatants, on the grounds that they had taken part in the struggle for national independence, and—more importantly in this context—as combatants for democracy. Indeed, they claimed that the 'true' liberation of the archipelago was not achieved until 1991, through their incentive and pressure" (Cardina and Rodrigues 2021: 8).

Although much of this cultural programme amounted to a truly revolutionary turn, when the MpD lost the elections in 2001 there was no attempt by the PAICV to put the clock back. The new direction was followed most notably in the encouragement of private investment in tourism. The peaceful transition between rival parties in 1991 and 2001 and then back again to MpD in 2016 gained Cabo Verde the reputation for being the most democratic country in Africa.

The most striking footnote to the cultural turn that the MpD had brought about and to the economic success of Cabo Verde governments since independence was written in 2005 when Mario Soares joined with Adriano Moreira, who had been a minister in the Salazar government, to suggest publicly that Cabo Verde should enter into negotiations to join the European Union, of which the other three Macaronesian territories were members.

Agriculture and the Environment

After independence, the development priorities of the PAICV had been in the sector of agriculture and the environment, with an emphasis on land reform, water management and labour-intensive initiatives that would create employment. Among the projects immediately set in motion were terracing to prevent soil erosion and the planting of trees, a measure that had been called for by observers ever since the early nineteenth century. Those travelling from Mindelo across the narrow strait to Santo Antão were soon to see the arid lowland landscape of that island completely covered with small, promising thorn trees. By 2012 three million trees and 92,000 hectares of forest had been planted (Baptista 2015).

Land reform had been seen by the new government as necessary to deal with the problems faced by the 6,000 tenant farmers and the 26,000 sharecroppers. The land reform that was passed into law in 1982 proposed the acquisition by the state of land not worked by its owners, and new contracts of tenancy for sharecroppers. However, this measure ran into strong opposition from emigrants who owned land in the islands and even from the sharecroppers, who resisted the change in the arrangements by which they farmed their plots. Land reform was particularly contentious in Santo Antão and was a major cause of opposition to the PAICV government (Keese 2024: 14). "Under the conditions of change between 1974 and early 1976, [this] included intense and sometimes very violent conflicts between larger and smaller landholders, of which the former shared in the privileges of the older, 'feudal' landlords (including rights to water), while the latter had been sharecroppers or de facto tenants and were thus dependent, even in the final decades of colonial rule, on the former's water distribution practices" (Keese 2020: 93). In the end, little land was actually transferred, and most of the provisions of the reform were never implemented (Silva Andrade 2002: 278–81).

A programme of building terraces and small dams to capture rainfall was also begun with the objective of increasing the availability of water for irrigated crops. The search for water resources soon ran into the problem that, once water was extracted from deep underground wells, there was an invasion of seawater and the wells threatened to become brackish. The management of water resources proved as difficult as land reform. In the end a hybrid management system grew up. While water was declared to be a national resource, private control of springs and traditional management of *levadas* and local irrigation systems continued alongside government control of the drilling of deep wells (*furos*). Moreover, water from these wells was managed by municipal water and sanitation services (Bosa 2015). The centralising water policies of the PAICV government ran into local resistance, especially on Santo Antão, which was the only island where there was a relatively plentiful water supply.

The government also embarked on a much larger project to counter desertification. The idea was to reclaim a whole sector of the island of Santiago. The work was partly funded through the sale of food gifted by aid organisations during the famine years of the late 1970s (Baptista 2015). The initial project was a top-down approach, providing the population with paid work, but this was succeeded between 1985 and 1995 by attempts to involve the local communities in decision-making. "From the late 1990s onwards … local communities were involved in drawing up a national action program to combat desertification. Since then, a full partnership with the population has been established, with community-based organizations playing a major role not only in implementing and maintaining SWC (Soil and Water Conservation) works, but also in contributing local knowledge and choosing the best local measures" (Baptista 2015). As the report on the project observed, "There is general consensus that success in combating land degradation and natural resource management can best be achieved with active involvement of affected populations in developing solutions, leveraging their knowledge and experiences and combining them with the knowledge of researchers and managers in all planning steps" (Baptista 2015).

As part of its environmental policies,

> the government constructed large dams to collect and store runoff from the watersheds, with a total of five dams already built in the two largest islands. Ribeira Seca encloses one of the largest rainwater collecting dams built in the country, with a capacity of 1.2 million m^3. The construction of this large piece of infrastructure completely changed the surrounding landscape, allowing 188 ha of irrigated land. Drip irrigation was introduced in the 1990s as a more efficient and water-saving irrigation system, and has been promoted since. In rain-fed areas in the downstream section of the watershed, large concrete water reservoirs were built to collect and stock rain water for supplementary irrigation, human and animal consumption. (Baptista 2015)

In spite of the relative success of these policies, it was soon clear that the future prosperity of Cabo Verde would not lie with agriculture, which could neither feed a rapidly growing population nor provide a significant export sector. In 2007 agriculture accounted for only 5 per cent of GDP, although it still accounted for 45 per cent of employment (Bosa 2015: 2646).

Remittances

For most of the twentieth century, remittances from emigrants had provided relief for Cabo Verdean families and helped to cover the islands' deficit in foreign trade. Remittances sent directly to families and bank deposits held by emigrants continued to rise in the post-independence era, but as the GDP of the islands grew, the proportion deriving from remittances declined from 23 per cent of GDP in 1995 to less than 10 per cent a decade later. Although remittances from families working abroad were part of the expectations involved in the culture of migration, the long-term significance of this form of income had become uncertain, not to say controversial.

The African Development Bank report of 2012 had this to say about the role of remittances in the development of the Cabo Verde economy since independence.

> These remittances, combined with the high levels of ODA [Official Development Assistance] per capita, permitted the government to cover the expanding fiscal and external deficits. Much of the expanding deficits of this period were the result of the major infrastructure investments carried out, such as Sal international airport and the upgrade of Mindelo port, both of which became major revenue earners. These also enabled Cape Verde to sustain significantly higher fiscal and external deficits and provide for some alleviation of the persistently high unemployment—which, however, remains a problem even now. In the first phase of Cape Verde's development, it would appear that the steady flow of remittances was driven by family connections and a commitment to the "home country" among the Diaspora … Cape Verde was thus far ahead in its practice in relation to remittances as compared to other developing countries in the early 1990s. These resources are then channeled by the banking system for investment, particularly in the construction sector. (African Development Bank 2012: 8)

Large inflows of remittances can have an inflationary effect if they are used to increase consumption rather than to invest. One report published in 2015 concluded that "despite increases in remittance inflows, their relationship with GDP is negative. This is because in Cabo Verde recipients do not use the money they receive from remittances for productive purposes but rather they use it as a way of supplementing their incomes for consumption purposes" (Adarkwa 2015). In general, it is now believed that for many countries remittances can create a state of dependency which does not contribute to the development of the economy.

Tourism

During the early part of the twentieth century, few people who knew the Cabo Verde islands would ever have considered taking a holiday there. British residents in Mindelo, working for the coaling companies or the telegraph, seem to have hated the place, describing it as a "cinder heap", while there were few attractions for passengers on the ships that called to fill their bunkers, beyond a few bars and brothels.

Archibald Lyall, a linguist and author of guidebooks, who stayed in the islands for some weeks in 1936, was an exception. He liked the Cabo Verde islands and took a real interest in their poetry and literature, but his portrayal of the rather sad community of expatriates and exiles in Praia and the poor coal heavers of Mindelo would hardly have attracted tourists to the islands (Lyall 1938). At independence it was alleged that there was only one hotel in the capital, and this had only twelve beds.

It took some years for the tourist potential of the islands to be discovered, and it was only around 2000, when the islands had opened up to foreign investment, that tourism really took off. Between 2000 and 2008, the average annual growth rate in the number of tourists entering the country was 11.4 per cent. Over 300,000 tourists arrived in Cabo Verde in 2008, totalling nearly 2 million bed nights. Despite the global economic crisis, over 475,000 tourists arrived in 2011. The government's strategic plan called for half a million annual arrivals by 2013 (African Development Bank 2012: 11). By 2016 there were 644,000 arrivals, and tourists outnumbered the country's population of half a million (Resende-Santos 2019: 148).

Tourism transformed Cabo Verde and rapidly overtook remittances and ODA (Official Development Assistance) in its contribution to the Cabo Verde economy. In 2015 it was estimated that 6,353 people were employed in tourism. So successful was this development that, according to João Resende-Santos,

> Cape Verde has been among the top five performers in sub-Saharan Africa across nearly all social, economic, and political indicators. It has consistently ranked among the regional leaders in terms of the Human Development Index (HDI), low poverty rates, and growth performance. Cape Verde's 6% average annual growth rate during 1991–2010 far outpaced the regional average of 3.5%, and even surpassed the 4.5% average

of Mauritius ... Indeed, Cape Verde's development success has been so robust and multifaceted that in 2007 the United Nations General Assembly graduated the country from the list of Least Developed Countries (LDCs). (Resende-Santos 2019: 152)

Almost all the tourism was concentrated on Sal and Boa Vista—the two islands which for centuries had appeared to be irredeemably locked into poverty and desertification. Sal was where the international airport was located, and from there it was a short ride to the vast sandy beaches that tourists craved. Sal also turned the famous *salinas* of Pedra Lume into an attraction where tourists could float in the saline lakes, while the conservation of turtles provided a niche attraction for some tourists. Boa Vista had fewer advantages but, as well as fine sandy beaches, there was the grandeur of the Sahara-like desert interior of the island.

The other attraction that established Cabo Verde in the consciousness of the world tourist industry was the volcano on the island of Fogo. Tourists could be driven into the Chão crater and marvel at the vineyards planted in the volcanic lava. In 2014, following a major eruption, the sight of the old town in the Chão, submerged up to its rooftops in lava, provided another attraction. Along the roads travelled by tourists in Fogo, mothers with blond children (alleged by the guidebooks to be the descendants of a French aristocrat, the Comte de Montrond) stood by the roadside tempting the passers-by to photograph their children and give alms.

Meanwhile, a canny local authority refurbished the decaying colonial grandeur of São Filipe, where the old *sobrados* of the Fogo landowners were saved from destruction and restored to give the town a historic and architecturally interesting appearance.

Many tourists are also attracted by Cabo Verdean music and its performers, the singer Cesária Évora having established a worldwide reputation. However, playing for tourists introduces a different set of cultural incentives and trends from those created by a purely indigenous culture.

Santo Antão boasts an old sugar mill still operated by oxen, where the cane juice is converted into *grogue* and sold to the unwary visitor. There has been an attempt to market a more healthy form of tourism for those wishing to hike in the mountains and visit the lush valleys where Cabo Verde's only perennial streams run down from the cloud-covered heights. In Santiago it is also possible to visit the Tarrrafal concentration camp or take a taxi ride out of Praia to the site of Ribeira Grande—now known as Cidade Velha—a sad expedition where you are invited to visit the well-preserved fortress built during the reign of Philip II and the little medieval church with its few *azulejos* (decorative tiles) and monuments to long-dead Portuguese *fidalgos*—the only truly medieval church in sub-Saharan Africa.

Tourism has its downside. The benefits are not widely distributed between the islands; the import bill rises sharply to meet the requirements of the visiting foreigners; and the jobs created are at best only semi-skilled. Tourism increases dependency on imports, and although the political stability of the islands and the year-round fine weather are huge assets, the industry would be very vulnerable to changes in the world economy. Moreover, the scatter of nine islands makes it difficult for the benefits of tourism to have a concentrated multiplier effect.

Tourism has tied the economy of the islands closely to Europe, which reinforces the political turn away from Africa that began with the change of government in 1991. Roughly 90 per cent of foreign direct investment now comes from Europe, and the European Union accounts for over 85 per cent of the country's imports and exports and 90 per cent of its tourists.

Privatisation

The economic transformation of the Cabo Verde islands since independence is one of the relatively rare success stories in Africa's struggle against underdevelopment. The process began under the government of the PAICV. "In less than two decades Cape Verde transformed itself from one of the poorest countries in the world, declared 'unviable' after independence in 1975 by the then US Secretary of State, and thereafter by some international financial institutions, to one of the fastest growing economies in Africa" (African Development Bank 2012: 1).

In this transformation the election of a new party to govern in 1991 was a significant moment. In the late 1980s, the ruling PAICV had initiated changes to the rigid one-party politics and state-led economy that had marked the first decade of independence, but the newly formed MpD, which started to govern after the elections of 1991, began a programme of change that was radical and swift. When the PAICV returned to power after the 2001 elections, the new programme was continued. The African Development Bank report in 2015 describes the changes to the economy that were undertaken.

> There were four distinct phases of the privatization process in Cape Verde: the early 1990s, the follow-on phase of 1997–2000, the so-called "second generation reforms" of 2001–2008, and the period after 2008. The first phase involved the initial and sudden process of the state's divestiture from a number of industries and sectors. The state divestiture process was formally initiated with the 1992 Privatization Law. Privatization during this first phase focused on the two critical areas of infrastructure, principally telecommunications and energy, and financial services. The first divestiture took place in 1993, followed in rapid succession by much larger numbers of privatizations in 2004, 2005, and 2006. At the beginning of the privatization process, Cape Verde had 50 SOEs (State Owned Enterprises), estimated to employ over 6,000 people and accounted for 25 per cent of GDP. From 1992 to 2004, the number of SOEs in Cape Verde fully controlled by the state was sharply reduced from 50 to 6, primarily during the first two phases of privatization. The subsequent phases since 2001 have focused primarily on enhancing economic regulation, liberalizing sectors to spur competition, and improving the business and investment climate. (African Development Bank 2012: 21)

In particular, the tourist industry has been built up with the help of foreign capital: Italy has been one of the most important investors. In the space of just over a decade Cabo Verde's per capita income rose from $175 at independence to $1,000, and in 2008 the UN reclassified Cabo Verde as a Middle Income Nation. "Cape Verde became the first country in the world whose upgrade is an outcome of efficient economic and social policies and strategies" (African Development Bank 2012: 5).

Education

The first government of Cabo Verde after independence invested heavily in the development of human capital, especially in education at the primary and secondary levels, to boost labour productivity. By 1990 some 87 per cent of the population had completed primary and 22.8 per cent secondary education. But education remained a challenge, as the population of Cabo Verde was so dispersed. There was a lack of library and information resources (MacGregor 2022), and it was not until 2006 that there were moves to create a university. Initially this involved merging three, and eventually four, institutes that had been created to train teachers, engineers, agriculturalists and administrators. The construction of a university campus with a capacity for 5,000 students was completed in 2020. The university had six faculties covering science and technology, humanities, engineering and maritime science, agriculture, business, education and sports.

In addition, since 2000, nine private university institutions have been established, all located in either Praia or Mindelo and offering qualifications at advanced level.

Transnationalism

The idea that people should be citizens of the country where they reside was essential to the so-called Westphalian structures of international politics, but the existence of European overseas empires had made this idea obsolete even before it was born. Not only did the Spanish and Portuguese crowns have vast subject territories which they controlled beyond their borders, but through their patronage over the Church, they claimed jurisdiction over populations that had no direct links with their kingdoms at all. The transnational nation took many shapes, but in one form or another it was built into European imperial systems. As part of the Portuguese empire, Cabo Verdeans were used, until independence, to think of themselves as being Portuguese. And still today there are French *départements* inhabited by French citizens in the Caribbean, the Indian Ocean and the Pacific.

It is not, therefore, surprising that the notion of a transnational Cabo Verde should have taken hold. In 1975 emigration was part of the life expectancy of the islanders, and emigrants, even when in fact they settled permanently away from the islands, never entirely lost the idea that one day they would return. The Portuguese had encouraged Cabo Verdeans to emigrate as part of a policy to reduce population pressures in the islands and provide some form of relief from poverty and famine. After independence there was a shift of emphasis, but emigration continued to be seen as an essential tool to be used by the government to secure the islands' future. The flow of remittances, which at one time had amounted to more than 25 per cent of GDP, was essential not only for the support of poor families but also for the economy of the islands. Would remittances continue if the islands cut ties with their citizens who emigrated? Nobody knew the answer to that, but it seemed sensible to try to maintain the ties between the homeland and the emigrant community.

From the start PAIGC had sought the support of emigrants in the struggle for independence, and there was emigrant participation in all the multi-party elections, beginning in 1991. These ties were strengthened in the revision of the constitution in 1999. Now Cabo Verdean emigrants up to the third generation could claim Cabo Verdean citizenship. Various criteria applied, but having two Cabo Verdean grandparents was usually enough. When it came to election time Cabo Verde emigrants were grouped into three regions—the Americas, Africa and Europe plus the rest of the world—and were encouraged to register as voters.

As the number of emigrants and their descendants grew, the potential extra-territorial vote threatened to be larger than the number of voters in the islands. So, there had to be provisions to prevent the votes of those not resident in the islands from, in effect, providing the island government. It was decided that the emigrant vote could not contribute more than 20 per cent of the total votes cast. However, this proved to be enough to influence the overall results in a significant way on two occasions. In the presidential elections of 2001 and 2006 the extra-territorial vote swung the result against Carlos Veiga and allowed the PAICV candidate, Pedro Pires, to win. On both occasions Veiga won the vote in the islands. In 2001 the margin by which Pires eventually won was 0.1 per cent (Borges 2022).

The Cabo Verde islands are one of only thirteen countries in the world which make provision for extra-territorial constituencies, but with migration becoming an ever more global phenomenon, this number is likely to rise as countries seek to retain the loyalty and support of emigrants.

São Tomé and Príncipe as an Independent Nation

In 1975 the creole islands of São Tomé and Príncipe were also given their independence by Portugal, which handed the government over to a political party formed in exile and known as the MLSTP. Like Cabo Verde, São Tomé began its life as an independent nation, as a one-party state organised on principles of socialist self-sufficiency. Like Cabo Verde it inherited a weak economy which had been supported by budgetary grants from Portugal. The economy was entirely dependent on the export of cocoa, which was still produced on large plantations with a contract labour force recruited from outside the islands. With a population of around 90,000 (1977) and a land area of 372 square miles, São Tomé and Príncipe ranked as one of the smallest independent countries in the world. Contrary to the experience of Cabo Verdeans, the São Tomean *forros* had not been recruited into the administration of the islands nor had they entered the Portuguese colonial civil service in the other African territories. Moreover, the islands did not enjoy the important assets that Cabo Verde possessed in Porto Grande, the Sal International Airport, and the large emigrant population in America and Europe, which provided a flow of remittances and contacts with the wider Atlantic world. São Tomé was an isolated country that few people in the world had heard of. The only real asset that it possessed was a potentially rich agricultural export sector, which Cabo Verde could not match. In 1975 the islands were still sometimes able to produce around 10,000 tons of cocoa beans in a good year (Seibert 2024: 134).

Cabo Verde, even during its one-party phase, had drawn on the administrative experience that islanders had acquired both in the islands themselves and in other Portuguese territories. They also benefited from their European heritage and the experience of emigrants and returnees, who brought the islands into line with the economic, administrative and cultural practices of the developed world. São Tomé, on the other hand, turned increasingly to its African heritage. From the start its ruling party, the MLSTP, formed close ties with the MPLA in Angola. Angola provided the islands with oil at low cost, and Angolan military personnel underpinned the rule of the MLSTP with a permanent presence in the islands. São Tomeans had little experience of running the government, and the political scene was dominated by the few wealthy *forro* families. Not surprisingly, the rule of the MLSTP, under its president and party leader Manuel Pinto da Costa, came to reflect the patrimonial politics of Angola and other newly independent African states. Politics was seen as a matter of rent-seeking and reward for the patronage networks of the leading politicians. As Gerhard Seibert, the leading commentator on São Tomé affairs, puts it: "Local political culture has been characterised by personalistic politics, neo-patrimonial relations, clientelistic networks, corruption, and rent seeking to the detriment of economic rationality and administrative efficiency" (2024: 121).

There was one more important difference between the two creole island states. In Cabo Verde, although its population was distributed across nine different islands, each with its own individual character, the people enjoyed a strong sense of a common identity and from the start had a government focused on their welfare. In São Tomé, however, more or less 40 per cent of the population did not enjoy citizenship or political rights and was excluded from the economic and cultural life of the *forro* majority. The contracted labourers brought from Angola, Mozambique and especially Cabo Verde to work on the cocoa plantations were left in limbo when the islands became independent.

At independence most of the Portuguese administrators and plantation managers left, and among the first acts of the MLSTP in September 1975 was the nationalisation of the cocoa plantations.

Significantly, the largest of them was renamed Agostinho Neto, after the president of Angola. The dilemma facing the country was spelt out in an interview that the president gave to the British economic journalist Tony Hodges, which was printed in *Africa Report* in January 1976.

> In the health sector we had only three São Tomean doctors, and one Portuguese doctor who stayed. In the administration you could count the people with a university level education on the fingers of one hand ... It was the same story in education. The Portuguese all left. Although we had very few São Tomean teachers, we declared that schooling would be free for everyone. We had a huge number of students and almost no teachers ... So ours was a country with no financial means, with no specialised people, totally disorganised. This was our starting point, which has to be recalled when judging what was achieved. We started from practically nothing. (Newitt and Hodges 1988: 131)

The MLSTP proved unable to manage the plantations, let alone provide the investment they needed. Although world cocoa prices remained high until 1979, thereafter there was a rapid fall which coincided with an equally rapid decline in the workforce, many of whom abandoned the plantations, as they were unfed and unpaid. Cocoa production went into freefall. The fifteen state-owned plantations, far from contributing to the economy, had to be subsidised by the government to stay operational. Between 1980 and 1984 GDP declined by 25 per cent; by 1988 cocoa production had fallen to 4,560 tons and by 2000 was only 2,883 tons. The decline was not arrested when, with the encouragement of the World Bank and other donors, foreign management contracts were made with European companies, beginning in 1986. The nationalised enterprises were also beset with problems in recruiting agricultural labour. Of the approximately 15,000 labourers needed to run the plantations, two-thirds were Cabo Verdeans, while the rest were recruited from the Tonga population (descendants of contract labourers) and *forro* women, as the *forro* men still refused to accept any work except in administrative roles (Eyzaguirre 1993: 15). Between 2005 and 2013 exports never rose above 2,728 tons (Seibert 2024: 136).

With the collapse of the production of cocoa, other aspects of the economy went into steep decline. Imports could not be paid for, and the consumer side of the economy also failed. Visiting the island ten years after independence was a revelation. The shops were all empty (I remember shop windows where the only item on display were dressmakers' snap fasteners) and the markets offered little more than bunches of bananas.

From the mid-1980s São Tomé suffered from almost continual financial crises. While inflation remained high, the economy steadily weakened and standards of living and of public services inexorably declined. Nevertheless, unlike many African countries during this period, society remained peaceful and political life was not only non-violent but was carried on in relatively free and democratic conditions. The often bitter war of words waged between the leaders of the political factions was to a large extent a front behind which there was a broad political consensus on matters of policy (Newitt 1996–8: B290).

In 1991, with the country effectively bankrupt, a multi-party constitution was adopted, as it was in rather different circumstances in Cabo Verde. Since then, numerous political parties have been formed while others have changed their names, but politics have been dominated by four major political figures. Manuel Pinto da Costa of the MLSTP was president from 1975 until 1991 and again from 2011 to 2016. In 1991 he was replaced by Miguel Trovoada, a veteran politician of the MLSTP, who formed a party, the PCD, to defeat Pinto da Costa but then fell out with his own supporters and founded another party, ADI, to reflect his interest. Trovoada was president from 1991 to 2001, after which ADI became the political vehicle of his son Patrice Trovoada, who held the office of prime minister four times between 2008 and 2022 under various presidents.

The fourth major political figure during the early twenty-first century was Fradique de Menezes, who was president from 2001 to 2011. Menezes, who was half Portuguese and had been educated in Belgium, was a businessman like Patrice Trovoada. In 2003 he was briefly ousted by an attempted military coup before being restored to power.

Elections for president have been held at regular intervals, and elections for the National Assembly rather more often. "Far from being reluctant to go to the ballot box, the main parties see elections rather than day-to-day compromise as the way to resolve political differences. Preparing for the next set of elections is one of the factors that paralyses effective government and prevents the making of hard decisions" (Newitt 1996–8: B290).

Although the frequency of elections and changes of government may give the impression of a healthy democratic culture, comparable to that of Cabo Verde, there are aspects of political life in São Tomé that are markedly different. One is the "particularly São Tomean form of electoral practice in which the wealthy parties bought up the electoral registration cards of known supporters of the opposition. *The Economist* described how 'voters crowded into the various campaign headquarters demanding cash in exchange for their votes'" (Newitt 1996–8: B291).

Another difference is the recurrence of coup attempts by disgruntled politicians and military men. Gerhard Seibert lists "two bloodless military coups, two police revolts, a coup attempt, and an assault on the barracks", and he comments that "the six incidents revealed both the fragility of local institutions and the weakness of the government" (2024: 130). However, none of these violent incidents received any significant support from the population at large.

The patrimonial politics of São Tomé have, since 1997, been dominated by the anticipation of oil wealth. It was thought that São Tomé shared in the geological formations that provided Nigeria and Gabon with their oil reserves. In 1997 the first oil exploration contracts were signed. Since then major oil companies like Exxon-Mobil and Total have been involved, as well as smaller entrepreneurs. Agreements have been reached with Nigeria to share the revenues from disputed international waters. Exploration drillings have been carried out and signature bonuses have often been gratifyingly large. However, by 2024 no exploitable oil had yet been found.

All attempts at economic development seem to have stalled. Land reform has not yielded significant results. Tourism, in spite of the enervating climate, has considerable potential. The islands have beautiful beaches, rich tropical vegetation, spectacular scenery, and the extraordinary architecture of the old Portuguese *roças*, now decaying and crumbling away. However, tourism numbers peaked in 2019 with 35,000 visitors, less than a twentieth of the numbers visiting Cabo Verde (Seibert 2024: 133).

Meanwhile, for a quarter of a century, the elites of São Tomé have fed their patrimonial networks in the hopes of a rich oil bonanza. It seems clear that this has stood in the way of any sort of realistic approach to economic development in the islands and even to simple good governance.

8

SOME ASPECTS OF THE CULTURAL LIFE IN THE CABO VERDE ISLANDS

The hundreds of thousands of tourists who now visit the Cabo Verde islands see an increasingly prosperous and well-ordered community which offers a secure and peaceful environment, where the visitor can enjoy a pleasant climate and all the amenities of a middle-range holiday resort. What the islands have to offer is well covered in tourist guidebooks, and there is very little that tourists will experience that refers back to the islands' history, to the centuries of slavery and the slave trade, the violence of pirate raids, the famines and the relentless poverty that left so many of the islanders on the verge of starvation. Perhaps only a visit to the ruins of the Tarrafal concentration camp provides a window onto a disturbing and less happy past. Nevertheless the uniqueness of the Cabo Verde islands' culture can only be understood by looking into the past and retelling the historical narrative that gives their identity some context.

The islands were, from their very first settlement in the fifteenth century, at a crossroads between Europe, Africa and the New World, and the creole culture that developed drew on elements from all three continents. However, the islands were not just recipients of the cultures of others but developed their own unique creole culture, which in turn was exported and which influenced all the countries of the lusophone South Atlantic world. No culture is static; all are in a permanent process of change as they absorb new ideas, new influences and new materials that come to them from beyond their immediate cultural home. Languages also evolve in a similar way through a process of constant creolisation. Italian and Portuguese are creolised forms of Latin, and English is a creole language, Germanic in form and heavily loaded with a Latinate vocabulary. Studying Cabo Verde's history is a reminder that history cannot be understood in terms of the binary confrontations of black and white, slave and free, coloniser and colonised, African and European. In between these harsh opposites there has grown up a rich creole culture that has profoundly influenced the whole South Atlantic world.

After fifty years of independence Cabo Verde is now a forward-looking country, well administered and enjoying unprecedented prosperity. Education and the close contacts the islanders have with Europe and the United States have made Cabo Verdeans recognisably citizens of the modern world. For them the past has receded into the memories of the older generation and, beyond that, into images evoked by poetry, song and fictional writing—and history.

Africa and Europe

However often a book, like the present one, asserts that Cabo Verdean identity is neither African nor European nor Brazilian—nor even Macaronesian—the question of whether Cabo Verdeans are really Africans keeps turning up in discussion. In the last quarter of the twentieth century this discussion acquired a deep political significance, as Amílcar Cabral and his followers were intent on urging Cabo Verdeans to rediscover their African roots. After independence, the PAICV tried to assert Cabo Verde's African identity both in the ill-fated union with Guinea-Bissau and as a member of ECOWAS. In contrast, the founding of the MpD and the aftermath of its victory in the polls in 1991 seemed to be in many ways the assertion of a European heritage, even European identity, for Cabo Verde.

Two examples from the writings of recent historians show how this discussion is often formulated. For the historical geographer

Orlando Ribeiro, the two strands of Cabo Verdean culture are symbolically represented by the way that grain is turned into flour.

> At dawn whoever turns his attention to the noises in the house, while still half asleep, will hear, before the chatter of the children, the hollow and monotonous beat of the pestle. This cadence, so typically African, will have to be prolonged through the first hours of the morning while the corn is prepared for the day's *cachupa* but the attentive listener will be able to discern, in the intervals of the steady beat, another sound, soft and continuous. It is another woman who, crouched at the foot of the hand mill, is making the flour for the porridge and cakes. These two instruments brought together in the interior of all the *"funcos"* [outside kitchen huts] and humble dwellings are symbols of the civilisations which, meeting each other in these islands, have shaped their vigorous human originality. (Ribeiro 1997: 146)

Writing in 1996, Elisa Silva Andrade, after discussing the African roots of Cabo Verdean music, makes a list of contrasting African and European cultural traits. From Africa came

> the "uril" game played on a wooden board with twelve holes ... the use of the pestle and mortar and the calabash; the custom of carrying infants on the back; cereal based food, above all maize and beans, and no utilisation of bread. Africans also brought with them from the continent the craft of weaving, the manner of preparing dyes for cloth and pottery. From the Portuguese, Cape Verdeans received their way of dressing ... their principal type of house ... the way of laying out villages and towns and the disposition of houses and streets and public places ... the patriarchal family structure as it was defined in the Portuguese civil law, monogamy de jure but polygamy in practice; many traditional festivals like Christmas and Epiphany and many folk tales. (Silva Andrade 1996: 157)

However, although these cultural traits were thus placed into neat pigeonholes, she found so many exceptions and modifications as to render the exercise of dubious value.

What many commentators have noted is a contrast between the *barlavento* and *sotavento* islands. The latter include Santiago and Fogo, which were the first to be populated by importing large numbers of slaves. There the African influence has continued to be strongest and the influence of slavery has lingered. In contrast, the *barlavento* islands, including São Nicolau, São Vicente and Santo Antão, were settled later, and the European, or rather Atlantic, influences are strongest and most obvious in the physiognomy of the people. Already in the eighteenth century this distinction was being made: George Roberts commented that on São Nicolau, "the best Portuguese is spoken here in all the Cap de Verde islands" (Green 1745–7: 664).

Elsie Clews Parsons records that among Cabo Verdean immigrants in the United States individual identity was very strong. "In the Leeward [*sotavento*] islands," she writes, "folk-lore in a more primitive form appears to flourish. Cab'Verde [Santiago] in particular is described by other islanders as *brut* ('savage' i.e. primitive)." But, she adds, "In my own partial observations this differentiation is not apparent." However, she goes on, "Inter-island marriage is disapproved of. I have been told that the houses of kinfolk are apt to be grouped together. In this country there is a marked tendency for immigrants from the same island to keep together. A group of Fogo men will board in a Fogo family, S. Antão men in a S. Antão family etc. In collecting tales we would go to what we called a Cab'Verde house, a S. Antão house etc. when we wanted a variant" (Parsons 1921: 89, 94).

It was in Santiago and Fogo that slavery made the deepest impression on society, but slavery declined in importance from the seventeenth century and slaves came to constitute an ever smaller percentage of the population. However, it has been claimed that it was the experience of slavery that helped to determine the structure of the typical Cabo Verdean family (see below). In contrast, the population of São Vicente was entirely formed in the nineteenth century around the supply of coal to international shipping, while that of Brava had close contacts with the American whaling industry and looked outward towards the United States. Neither of these islands was burdened with the inheritance of slavery or the hierarchies of plantation society. In contrast, in the Guinea islands, slaves continued to form 70 per cent or more of the population well into the nineteenth century.

Slaves who escaped from the plantations formed communities in the inaccessible areas of the interior of Santiago, but it was only in the Guinea islands that a permanent maroon community grew up. These called themselves Angolares, based on a tradition that Angolan slaves, escaping from a shipwreck in the seventeenth century, formed the core of the community. The Angolares developed their own creole speech and developed a separate community around the bay of Angolares on the west of the island. Like the *forros*, the Angolares refused to work on the plantations and made a living from fishing as well as agriculture.

In the Cabo Verde islands, there does not appear to have been any permanent maroon community, and the slaves who freed themselves merged with the free black rural population. However, in the nineteenth century, as a result of relentless drought and famine, many of the people of Santiago became vagrants—*vadios*. Francisco Travassos Valdez commented, metaphorically holding his nose as did so: "There are a number of persons called 'vadios', or vagrants, who live collecting the orchilla and purgueira, which they bring to the various ports for sale. These vadios have a great partiality for intoxicating drinks, their immoderate love of which, and their mania for the well-known *batuque*, or stamping dance, have been the cause of much licentiousness, and consequent disease" (Travassos Valdez 1861: I, 105). Many of the forms of Cabo Verdean music are supposed to be linked to the former slave communities. However, the *vadios* were not necessarily of slave origin nor were the so-called *rabelados* (rebels)—religious dissidents who kept alive the ancient Cabo Verdean way of life in opposition to the modernising influences that were transforming society in the twentieth century (see below).

In Travassos Valdez's eyes, the slaves, still an element in the population when he visited the islands in the 1850s, were part of the mix in the creole world of Santiago, which he loved to depict in exotic colours but which defied classification as either African or European.

> A bull-fight was appointed to take place that day at Tarrafal, to which I was invited, as were all the passengers and officers. We

were informed that the officers of the American cruisers were also to be there, with their band ... I had thus an opportunity of seeing many varieties of the rational and irrational animals of Africa. Among the former were beauties of various shades, all in their holiday attire; some of the fair sex were adorned with their manilhas, or arm-bracelets, of gold, silver and coral. Their heads were dressed with curious feathers, fastened in the hair. Some wore a kind of cotton shirt, with sleeves reaching to the wrists; petticoats of printed calicoes, and large handkerchiefs of red or yellow cotton, disposed in a very coquettish manner ... sashes of native cloth being thrown across the shoulders covered the bosom, and gave the fair wearers quite a military appearance. The nhanhás, or white and mulatto ladies, were dressed in European style, though not quite à la mode de Paris. The slaves wore no shoes. (Travassos Valdez 1861: I, 117)

The Cabo Verdean Family

An enduring feature of the history of the Cabo Verde islands has been the demographic resilience of the population. Within a short time of the heavy mortality that accompanied the droughts and famines, the population recovered and began to grow again. Although there may be a Malthusian explanation for this in the improving living conditions in the nineteenth and twentieth centuries, the same resilience appears in earlier centuries when the islands were even more isolated and neglected. As there was never significant in-migration, apart from the dwindling import of slaves, the explanation for the population increase has usually been attributed to the family structure. It was common for young women to have their first pregnancies in their teens and to have large families; the families were traditionally matriarchal and matrilocal, headed by the mothers and grandmothers. In São Tomé the figure of the godmother (*madrinha*) was also at one time important among the *forros*, and "the wealth of the wealthy women (*sinhas da terra*) was measured by the number of girls who followed them around" (Galvão 1950–3: I, 282).

Although similar family structures can be found in West Africa, where matrilineal lineages are common, the comparative weakness and even absence of the typical Portuguese patriarchal family structure in the islands has been variously interpreted. Basil Davidson, the inspirational champion of the independence movements in the Portuguese African colonies, discussed this issue in his book *The Fortunate Isles*. He records meeting a male emigrant who had returned for a holiday. "It transpires that our host has twenty-one living children 'or maybe it's more', he adds with great cheerfulness, 'you can't always keep count'. His father was thought to have had as many as sixty-three children. 'But again, it could have been more.' I recall that Amílcar Cabral's father Juvenal had scored about as many as that, and I remain puzzled" (Davidson 1989: 171). He then asks why so many women put up with this "informal polygyny", which allows men to behave in this way and to take no responsibility for the children they father.

Before the twentieth century the only accounts of life in the Cabo Verde and Guinea islands were written by outsiders, either Portuguese who came to the islands as officials or priests, or foreign visitors who arrived to trade, legally or illegally, in the islands. As a result there is more than the usual distortion involved, as outsiders reported what they saw through the lens of their own values and understanding.

Most observers commented on the informality of marriage and the perceived sexual promiscuity of the women. Nowhere is the difficulty of understanding these observations more acute than when foreigners reported on the origins of the mixed-race creole population. Already in the sixteenth century, royal decrees against "prostitution" show the level of official concern at the absence of formal marriages in the islands. One curious *alvará* of D.Sebastião, dated 1559, while decreeing that "public women" (*mulheres públicas*) should not be allowed to live in the towns in São Tomé, also tries to forbid the immodest dress of the island women—"the skirts and cloths open in front from the waist downwards ... in the manner of heathen women" (Caldeira 1999: 206–7).

The fact that the Cabo Verdeans share both an African and a European heritage, both a cultural and genetic DNA, is one of the determining factors in their identity. Nowhere is this more apparent than in descriptions of relations between the sexes. An early attempt to address this topic is contained in the report, written by Francesco Carletti for the Grand Duke of Tuscany, of a trading voyage which began in 1591 and in the end continued round the world. Carletti describes in detail the society of Ribeira Grande as he saw it.

> It is a certain thing that they place more value upon a Moorish woman of that region than on a white woman from Portugal ... It seems ... that heaven disposes and wishes that they should appreciate more those who are native to the place than those who are foreign to it, as one sees by sure experience that those who do not have native women as wives quickly arrange to have them as concubines. And in the end, overcome by affection, they marry them and live with them much more contentedly than they would with women of their own nation. (Carletti 1964: 9)

He goes on to speculate on the phenomenon of skin colour. "Some of them seemed to me very beautiful, and that black covering did not annoy me at all ... [because] like others, who see nothing else from day to day and with such frequency, it does not appear so strange" (Carletti 1964: 9).

A rather different understanding of the sexual mores of the islands can be found in the anonymous *Notícia corográfica e chronológica* of 1784. "Apart from idleness, the vice to which people who live in the '*zona torrida*' are most inclined is sensuality. The women of this island [Santiago] have no shame in practising this '*vicio horrendo*' [and in being] dishonest and dealing with men who are not their legitimate husbands, because they consider that only those who live for gain are to be admired" (Carreira 1985). And, the author continues, among the ordinary people fathers did not concern themselves with the marriage of their daughters, nor are they ashamed or feel injured when the "fruit of their belly" appears, but instead help them to bring up these children. He then adds, rather surprisingly, that if these women are admonished and corrected, they mend their ways (Carreira 1985: 28).

Archibald Lyall, writing in the 1930s, also reflects on this topic:

> Among the lower classes marriage is looked on as an entirely unnecessary bother and expense. The latest statistics show that at

least two-thirds of the children born in the Islands are technically illegitimate, and a priest ... in 1912 put the proportion here as high as 98 per cent. This does not matter to them, for the Cape Verdeans are very fond of children, and no stigma attaches to bastardy ... Among the upper classes, too, the old slave morals persist. Marriage is the rule rather than the exception, though a cynic told me, "There is no need to get married in Cape Verde," but the average man has children by his mistress as well as his wife. That is the recognised thing. I knew a man in Praia who had several children by his Creole mistress. Eventually he married a *branca*, a white lady from Portugal; she had brought up his brown bastards with her own children. (Lyall 1938: 54–5)

These foreign observers were seeing a social reality which they only partially understood. It was a reality that had its roots in the culture of slavery and that persisted long after slavery ceased to be the defining characteristic of Cabo Verdean society. In the slave-owning society that grew up in the sixteenth century, it was common for slave owners to have sexual relations with slave women; this fundamental social relationship persisted through to the nineteenth century. António Correia e Silva mentions Baltazar Correia, "the proprietor of the estate of Boca Larga and the founder of the *capela do Pico Vermelho*, who in the middle of the sixteenth century lived intimately with his slave Catarina, and the judge (*ouvidor*) José da Costa Ribeiro, who was in Cabo Verde at the end of the twenties and thirties of the eighteenth century and who was described in an anonymous source as 'very self-indulgent, principally with women, participating recklessly in their vices to such an extent that he was vulgarly known as the King of Guiné'. He had six girl slaves whom he taught to play musical instruments" (Correia e Silva 2014: 91–2).

Equally notorious was the governor João Zuzarte de Santa Maria, who held the office from 1741 to 1751. According to Senna Barcellos, the prolific chronicler of Cabo Verdean history, "he always lived in good comradeship with his pretty slaves, by whom he had many children, and, as a good and pious father, he took them to Mass on Sundays, giving them the place of honour next to himself". When he died early in 1752, the chronicler commented, "we do not know if today there exist descendants of that glorious phalanx of beautiful slaves" (Senna Barcellos 2003: II, part 3, 8). Francisco Travassos Valdez, writing in 1861, records being invited to a marriage party where "the principal amusement ... during the early part of the day was playing at cards ... often making large stakes, and not infrequently risking or staking their slaves, who are in some instances their own children" (1861: I, 119).

Correia e Silva explains that the institution of slavery prevented a male slave from supporting a wife in the way expected of a conventional nuclear family. And this remained largely true during the long years of poverty among the peasantry who were nominally free. "If the seigneurial family was patriarchal and patrilineal, it had its opposite in the matrifocal and matrilineal nature of the slave family" (Correia e Silva 2014: 101).

If an informal polygamy was common in both Cabo Verde and the Guinea islands, polyandry was not unknown. Among the Angolares in São Tomé, the shortage of women led to raids on the *roças* to abduct women; and in some areas of Brazil, where the gender imbalance was most marked, there were examples of semi-formalised polyandry (Caldeira 1999: 78–9, 85–94). In São Tomé in 1901, it was recorded that a native of the island "who wants to be considered a big man will be polygamous, although he will appear to be married in the eyes of the Church", while a woman will be considered an important person if she can have four or five children by different men (Castro e Moraes 1901: 8–10). In his study of sexuality in São Tomé, Arlindo Caldeira stresses that in the slave society of the Guinea islands marriage, as Europeans understood the institution, only existed among people of European origin and then only as a marker of social status (1999: 128–40).

In his book *Recreating Africa*, James Sweet also reflects on the prevalence of pregnancy and childbirth outside marriage among slaves in colonial Brazil, but he sees this less as a result of the oppressive consequences of slavery and more as a result of the continuation of traditional African practices and family values. "African societies celebrated a sexual freedom that was rare in the West. The offspring of these relationships were by no means marginalised. Indeed they were readily accommodated into existing family and kinship arrangements" (Sweet 2003: 37).

The sexual lives of island women and the complexities surrounding this topic are clearly brought out in the story of the French nobleman Comte Armand de Montrond. Montrond came to Cabo Verde in 1872 and settled on the island of Fogo. There he used his wealth and skills to promote the cultivation of vines, to build houses and roads, and to improve the water supply. One writer has described him as "a true man of the people, a figure beloved by the people of the island of Fogo". Another writer refers to his surprising decision to choose to live in an inhospitable place, far from all that was considered "civilisation at that time" (*Euronews* 2020; RFI 2021; Fogo 2018).

However, there is a backstory to this tale of romance and philanthropy. This was the free rein he allowed himself in his exploitation of the women of the islands. According to one account, he had twelve children with six different women during the twenty-eight years he lived on the island. That these women were rewarded by having houses built for them merely underlines the complexity of these relations in a community where formal marriage was at best optional. A hundred and fifty years later, exaggerated claims were being made for the sexual prowess of the count. Up to a third of the population of Fogo claimed descent from him, and the incidence of blond hair and blue eye-colouring among islanders is often attributed to the count, although the only extant photograph of him shows that he had dark, perhaps black hair. The entry for Montrond in the *Dictionnaire encyclopédique et bilingue. Cabo Verde / Cap-Vert* begins, "Almost nothing is known for certain about this Frenchman," and concludes acidly, "How was he able to have blond descendants? Perhaps the laws of Mendel [on the inheritance of physical characteristics] do not apply in Cabo Verde" (Massa and Massa 2001: 190).

The count was not, of course, alone. In São Tomé, when the first Baron Agua Izé, one of the pioneers of cocoa production, died in 1869, he left no legitimate children but had eleven illegitimate children by various black women, thereby establishing a dynasty of São Tomean nobility. His eldest son became the viscount of Malanza, who, following the traditions of Portuguese royalty, married his niece (César 1969: 66–7).

The incidence of blond-haired mulattos in Santo Antão was noted by Travassos Valdez in 1861 before the arrival of Montrond: "One now meets with a number of mulattos, with fair hair and blue eyes, the offspring of such white men as have occasionally called there, and of the low, immoral beings with whom they have associated" (1861: I, 50–1).

One factor in the resilience of the population, although unproven, must have been the early pregnancies that became common in Cabo Verdean society. Adolescent pregnancy, referred to in the *Notícia corográfica e chronológica* of 1784, precluded the traditional delays until formal marriages could be arranged. The birth of children was a more urgent requirement for the society than any concerns about legitimacy.

Statistics for the twenty-first century show how this pattern of reproduction has persisted even into the radically changed circumstances of the post-independence era. Between 1933 and 1950, 66 per cent of births recorded were illegitimate, with a peak of 70.4 per cent in 1946 (Medina 2009: 42). Figures for 2005 show that 39 per cent of women were mothers by the age of 19, and 20 per cent before the age of 17 (Challinor 2017: 11).

The study of marriage, sexual relations and "informal polygyny" is a complex issue. For both men and women this can be understood as a form of freedom: for men, a freedom to "scatter their maker's image through the land", as Dryden famously phrased it, and not to take any responsibility for their actions; and for women, the freedom to have children without the oppression so often involved in patriarchal married relationships. Davidson quotes a Cabo Verdean woman who explained to him that "tradition has taken it as axiomatic that a woman's self-respect goes with her having children, however fathered. The outcome has been a hallowed acceptance of a more or less complete sexual liberty" (1989: 172). This custom may have grown up during the era of slavery when family relationships in the slave population were difficult, if not impossible; and during the centuries of recurrent drought and famine, the birth of large numbers of children was seen as essential for the community's survival. The custom continued once emigration began and men went abroad in large numbers to seek work. Although the newly independent Cabo Verdean government passed laws to strengthen marriage, lone women left caring for children (with the help usually of grandmothers) continued to be the norm. As Irineo Gomes, the minister for health, put it, "A man goes for a time, say for six months, and takes care to leave his wife pregnant so that, when he comes back, he'll know the child's his own" (quoted in Davidson 1989: 173). The absentee father is still a very recognisable figure. As Andrea Lobo (2012) put it, "the meanings of masculinity include the relative distance from the domestic universe, especially concerning child rearing."

Since independence, the government has passed a number of laws to strengthen the rights of women and to make men take responsibility for the children they father. "These laws advance and protect women's rights in marriage, divorce, inheritance, and in the condition of being an unmarried mother" (Davidson 1989: 173). In law there has to be a father registered for every child, and the father has to accept responsibility for its upbringing. Formal marriage is now encouraged and has been given a boost by the requirements of some countries that formal marriage to a man already resident is a prerequisite if a woman wishes to emigrate.

However, the traditions surrounding early pregnancy and the mother as the principal focus of family life are very deeply rooted, though the wider family is also important. As more and more women emigrate in search of work, the grandmother assumes many of the roles of the mother, and the wider network of family members is brought in to manage the care of children. Andrea Lobo (2012) describes the persistent characteristics of the Cape Verdean family as "mobility of men, women and especially children among many domestic units as part of family dynamics; [and] constant sharing among houses".

Being "White"

During the first hundred years of settlement there were clear racial distinctions in Cabo Verdean society. There were white-skinned Europeans, including Jews and New Christians, and there were

African slaves, who were black. However, as the population became more mixed, the perception of race and skin colour became more complex. Because white-skinned Europeans had, for a hundred years or more, made up the social elite, so the idea of whiteness became attached to wealth and social status. If you had wealth or enjoyed a position of importance, this made you white.

Among the Afro-Portuguese traders of the West African coast, the term "white" was used not only to indicate wealth and social status but as descriptive of traders in general. According to Olfert Dapper, writing in the seventeenth century (as reported by John Green), islanders always claimed that they were Portuguese, not Africans: "they scorned to be accounted any other than Portuguese; for if any man call them Negros, they will be very angry, saying they are white Portuguese" (Green 1745–7: 634).

Writing about São Tomé before the nineteenth century, Arlindo Caldeira, in a chapter headed *casamento/branqueamento* (marriage/bleaching), conflated formal marriage with the claims of the wealthy for the high social status of being "white" (1999: 128).

In his book on the island of Fogo, the geographer Orlando Ribeiro described the complexity of the situation as it was before independence.

> In the island of Fogo, because of the existence of some old families various classes could be distinguished, the *whites* who formed the traditional aristocracy; the *mulatos* (*mestiços*), children of a white father and a slave mother; *mulatos* properly called, children of slave mother and father; and the *povo* [ordinary people] ... This division was not one of ethnicity: "white people" indicated people who lived better, in good *sobrados* [double-storey houses], went about well dressed and shod, who during crises do not die of hunger; black people are the children in rags and without shoes who play in the street, the men and women who live in the poor *funcos* [round thatched huts], possess nothing and live in a state of misery which punishes them severely; among the first are to be found dark-skinned mulattos; among the second are to be found people who might pass for whites if one was not

forced to see in them faint traces of *mestiçagem* [miscegenation]. (Ribeiro 1997: 155)

Miguel Cardina and Inês Nascimento Rodrigues (2002), commenting on the dilemmas of Cabo Verdean ethnicity, maintain that the concepts of "white" and "black", "which generations of intellectuals have shaped particularly since the nineteenth century ... tended to be based on the combination of two archetypes: Europe (or Portugal), symbolising reason, fatherhood and science; and Africa, seen as a place of emotion, motherhood and tradition".

Such obsessions with race and the cultural distinctions between "white" and "black" might be thought to have disappeared from Cabo Verdean discourse in the fifty years since independence. However, they rose to the surface again during the cultural debates that took place after the MpD victory in the 1991 elections, when the PAICV's policies of moving closer to an African identity for the islands— the inheritance of Cabral—were challenged and in part reversed. Writing in 2003 about the controversy over the use of Crioulu as the primary medium for teaching literacy in schools, Donaldo Macedo could say, "Colonial schools were successful to the extent that they created a *petit-bourgeois* class of functionaries who had internalised the belief that they had become 'white' or 'black with white souls' and were therefore superior to Africans who still practised what was viewed as barbaric culture" (2003: 398). In his view, the use of the Portuguese language was holding back real emancipation and cultural growth in Cabo Verde, and this could still be expressed in terms of the historical racial binaries of "white" and "black".

Religion

Most Cabo Verdeans are still nominally Catholic Christians, though the Evangelical Nazarene Church made an appearance as early as 1908 on Brava and now has branches in all the islands. At one time the Catholic Church was the only permanent visible presence of the state in the lives of many of the islanders. In the twenty-first century, many of the Church's functions in welfare and education have been taken over by the state, but popular saints' festivals are still celebrated and religion is woven inextricably into the music and songs of the islands.

To get an idea of the deeper history of Cabo Verdean religion, one has to look back into the historical record. In the sixteenth century, there had been a large number of Jews and New Christians among the early settlers from Europe. The Crown had tried to impose restrictions on their numbers, and after the founding of the bishopric in 1533 there had been increasing confrontations between Old and New Christians as well as cases of intervention by the Inquisition (although no branch of the Holy Office was ever established in the islands). New Christians had been particularly active in the slave trade in Guinea, where many of them had settled and where Judaism had been openly practised along with syncretic forms of religion, combining elements of Christianity mixed with the traditional beliefs of mainland Africa. Along with the Crioulu speech, these syncretic religious practices became an intrinsic part of the Afro-Portuguese society that was formed in Guinea.

Back in the islands, adherence to religious orthodoxy and identification as Old Christians became increasingly important as the social structures of island society evolved. As more and more of the population had a mixed racial origin, Old Christian orthodoxy increasingly replaced a European ethnic origin as a way of maintaining social status (Green 2009).

However, as most of the population had an African ethnic origin in at least part of their make-up, many African beliefs and practices continued to influence the practice of Christianity, particularly in the remoter islands and rural areas where the presence of the Church was minimal. Even on the plantations in Santiago, where there were large concentrations of slaves, the proprietors resisted efforts to Christianise newly arrived slaves, regarding this as an expensive waste of time and money (see chapter 3).

In the islands settled in the eighteenth century, the Church gradually established a presence. George Roberts, describing Brava in the early part of the century, records that a priest made regular visits to the island and got paid for his trouble until the roof of the cave where services were held collapsed; this gave the islanders "an Opportunity of mingling the Pagan and Romish superstitions so intimately together that to this Day they remain inseparable". He goes on to describe the role of the priest: "He baptises, marries and buries; but the Natives have intermixed, with Popish rites, some of their own, such as washing before Baptism, decking the Bride with Flowers and a Garland; on the Marriage Day giving her bodily Worship; stripping her of all at Night and putting Earth on his [the bridegroom's] Head in token of subjection" (Green 1745–7: 665–6; Defoe 1726: 425).

By the early nineteenth century foreign observers were sceptical that Christianity existed at all in the islands. The author of the *Notícia corográfica e chronológica*, having described at some length the ruinous state of the Misericórdia and churches of Ribeira Grande, wrote:

> the whole mountain population is extremely rustic and savage and totally ignorant of Christian doctrine because as they live in the mountains ... right there they bring up their children as brutes without communion or doctrine. And this savageness is principally the result of the priests, because of whose negligence and lack of education the vineyard of our Lord in these parts is barren. However, although these people are brought up like animals and almost according to the laws of nature, they are nevertheless very obedient and treat with the greatest respect everything that is sacred. (Carreira 1985: 28)

Another outsider, Francisco Adolfo Varnhagen, a distinguished historian of Brazil, commented: "The islanders are totally ignorant of religion; and their ideas relating to this are limited to making the sign of the cross and using the words God, Jesus and Our Lady—along with other superstitious rites from Guinea which they practise by tradition and by continuous dealings with the newly arrived slaves" (Santos 2017: 159). As for religious marriage vows, as Marius Valkhoff (1975) expressed it, Cabo Verdeans "have very successfully succeeded in reconciling their Christianity with customs which are rather more relaxed in the domain of love".

In the 1940s, during the final phase of Portuguese rule in the islands, the Catholic Church received strong government backing as the official religion of the Estado Novo. This was part of a drive to bring life in the islands more into line with the values and practices of continental Portugal—a counterpart of the greater emphasis on education and the involvement of Cabo Verdeans in their own administration and in the administration of the wider Portuguese empire.

With the arrival of mission priests from Portugal, orthodox liturgical reforms and Catholic orthodoxy were increasingly imposed. This led to a group of dissidents breaking away from the Church and establishing communities in the remoter mountain regions of Santiago, where they also expressed their separatism by refusing to pay taxes, to be conscripted into the armed forces, or to submit to public health measures. The dissidents became known as *rabelados* (rebels), and in 2001 became the subject of a very detailed and sympathetic film entitled *Rabelados*, made by German filmmakers Ana Rocha Fernandes and Torsten Truscheit, who lived for some time among them. The *rabelados* were the first organised group in the history of the islands who actively rebelled against the government, but, by practising a withdrawal from "modern" life, they were not really a political movement and contributed only very indirectly to the eventual independence of the islands (Lobban 1995: 61–2).

The Nazarene Church was introduced into Brava early in the twentieth century by João José Dias, an emigrant returning from the United States. In the following 120 years branches were established in all the islands, though as late as 1998 it had only 2,783 active members. However, the Cabo Verdean Nazarenes also established branches elsewhere in Africa and undertook missionary work. Other Protestant-leaning churches appeared, mostly with origins in the United States. These include Adventists (who were first established in Brava in 1941), Mormons (since 1989), Pentecostals (since 1990) and the Assembly of God (since 1989). And there are others. These sects have proliferated since independence, when the official support which the Catholic Church enjoyed before 1975 was removed (Almeida 1998: 154–60).

Feitiçaria

As Cabo Verde became fully acclimatised to the modern world and as education was extended to the whole population, beliefs and values that were once common have become so modified as to have virtually disappeared. This is certainly true of *feitiçaria* or the belief in witchcraft and the evil eye.

The words *feitiço* and *feitiçaria* describe happenings that cannot be explained by normal rational causation—"an event that cannot be reduced to its natural causes" (Sansi-Roca 2007: 23). When something untoward occurred, explanations were to be sought in the work of the Devil or of individuals who, it was believed, wielded his satanic power. *Feitiço* could also be used proactively to achieve some desired outcome. "*Feiticeiros* are not priests but private practitioners of the arts of magic—people who make charms of love, wealth and death. The objective of *feitiçaria* is not worship but the solution of practical problems of life" (Sansi-Roca 2007: 31). There was also another dimension to *feitiço*. It could be used to safeguard oneself against the sorcery of others or even against the natural hazards of living—physical danger, misfortune, illness and death. In this case ordinary people would seek the protection of *feitiço* by wearing an amulet or charm, which might take the form of a Christian rosary, crucifix or image of a saint or a so-called *bolsa de mandingo*, which was an amulet given power by the *feiticeiro* who supplied it.

In 1722 George Roberts recalled a meeting with some Brava islanders to whom he showed an hourglass.

> They said, They believ'd all White Men were Fittaseers (i.e. Conjurors). I told them, We utterly detested having any Correspondence with the Devil, and in our Country when anyone was found guilty of Sorcery, he or she was by Law of the Land immediately burn'd. They said, It was a very good Law, and they wish'd they would do so there also. But, said they, we do not mean, when we say all White Men are Fittaseers, that they are such evil Persons, or commit such Mischievousness as our Fittaseers do, or that you are beholden to the Devil for your Skill ... and therefore we do believe, that it is not in the power of our Fittaseers ... to hurt a White Man especially if he be Scholastico (i.e. an Artist or Man of Learning).

They then hoped that if Roberts went into the town, he would do something to scare the "Fittaseers", "to make them forbear hurting them and their Cattle, and especially their Children, against whom they had such a Spite, especially if their Parents had anyways offended them, that in some Families they would not suffer a Child to live, but would so bewitch it, that in a little Time it would pine away, and die" (Defoe 1726: 158. Green 1745–7: I, 617). This account, albeit possibly from the colourful pen of Daniel Defoe, is a remarkably vivid account of the beliefs in the power of *feitiço* and *feiticeiros*.

Elsie Clews Parsons, collecting Cabo Verdean folklore among immigrants in the United States in the second decade of the twentieth century, found belief in *feitiçaria* and the powers of *feiticeiros* to be all-pervasive in the minds of her informants. "Black magic is believed in all the Islands to be practised by *f'itice'ra*, who may be old or young but who are always women (just as the *saib* practitioners of white magic are always men)." She recorded numerous stories of people who had been affected by *feitiçaria* and the measures they took to protect themselves. The behaviour of *feiticeiros* was bizarre, to say the least. Apparently they were believed to remove their own entrails to make themselves light enough to fly. So if dirt was put into them, the *feiticeiro* would die. Scissors stuck in a door would prevent the *feiticeiro* from leaving a house, and so on. The *feiticeiro* can enter the body of a black cat. Human beings who are thought to be possessed are whipped with a length of grapevine. Pigs and cows can also be possessed and are whipped to exorcise the spirit (Parsons 1921).

One may well wonder to what extent these strange tales were anything but rumours that circulated at second or third hand, but they clearly grew out of a fertile soil of belief in the ever-present evil eye and the ill will of jealous neighbours. They were stories told by the final generation of Cabo Verdeans who were relatively untouched by modernity.

Tomé Varela Silva, writing in 1998, described how the ideas of magic and *feitiçaria* travelled into the twentieth century, though he emphasises that "today they are totally discredited" (Silva 1998: 146). Two sorts of magic were practised. The *Korda* was magic designed to manipulate the future for some individual—to avoid the penalties of the law, to obtain the favour of some man or woman, or to obtain "certain powers or assets". It was practised in secret and the *korderus* were "almost always considered to be liars and charlatans" (Silva 1998: 146). The other sort of magic was the *feitiçaria*, whose effects were invariably maleficent. It was apparently believed that *feiticeiros* were born with these powers and inclinations, but they carried certain signs on their bodies and their identities could be discovered. In this case the *feiticeiro* might be hunted out of the community or forced to undo the sorcery that had been inflicted.

And beliefs in *feitiço* are ever-present in folk tales and in the fiction of those writing about the islands.

Folk Tales and the Preliterate World of the Imagination

After fifty years of independence Cabo Verde has largely left behind its past, scarred by famine, poverty and illiteracy. It is now a thriving modern state with a basic education system, strong contacts with Europe and the Americas, in touch electronically with its own diaspora, and increasingly in tune with the ideas and trends of the modern world. The realities of an earlier world, recorded in folklore traditions and values, are now a distant memory, but looking back at them enables one to obtain a broader understanding of what, over a period of four centuries, helped to make the creole culture of the Atlantic. Germano Almeida, one of Cabo Verde's best-known writers, who came from Boa Vista, reflected in one of his stories that for a child "the whole world was summed up on the island of Boa Vista". The island was nothing less than "the centre of the world where everything ended and came to die", a sentiment that Russell Hamilton described as "one of the paradoxes of the Cape Verdean ethos ... that the archipelago is both the center of the world and a group of obscure little islands scattered on the ocean at a continent's periphery" (Hamilton 2003: 318–19).

African oral traditions are often focused on stories of origin and reflect the desire to secure a group's identity. These oral stories are as much about the present and its concerns as they are about the past. A story recorded in the early eighteenth century about the origins of the volcano on Fogo, although ostensibly about the past, reflects contemporary attitudes towards the Church. "It is by them believ'd as undoubted Fact, that the first Dwellers upon this Island were two Fryers ... Whether these two Fryers were Mineralists, Metalists, or Alchymists, or any, or all of them, I can't tell, but the Story goes they were Conjurers ... but whatever the Fryers were they found a Gold mine, and there took up their Hermetical abode." After they had obtained enough gold "they concluded to put an end to hermetick Life", but they quarrelled over the division of the gold, "whereupon the Contest grew so high, that they fell to conjuring to do each other Mischief, and conjur'd so long, that they set almost all the Island in a Flame, in which they both perish'd, after which the Fire went out, except where the Peek now stands" (Defoe 1726: 416).

In the second decade of the twentieth century, the American folklorist Elsie Clews Parsons interviewed a number of Cabo Verdeans working in the United States. She got them to tell her traditional stories, and they provided her with a wide range of information about life in the islands as they remembered it. Her informants came from five of the islands, Brava, Santo Antão, São Nicolau, Fogo and Santiago, which she unaccountably called Cap' Verde. What she was recording was the memories of the islands' past rather than the living realities, and they were clearly coloured by the attitudes of her informants, who were busy adjusting to life in the United States and absorbing a whole new set of cultural values. The way her stories were gathered, and the inevitable uncertainties resulting from the material being presented in English, raise problems that have led some writers to avoid using them altogether. Nevertheless, although modern criticism tends to throw doubt over the "authenticity" of any and every text, and questions whether any writer or compiler can escape the biases and distortions of authorship, there seems to be a perfectly good case for making use of her collection simply as a portrait of how the culture of Cabo Verde was understood and remembered by emigrants in the United States in the early twentieth century.

What emerges from the traditions that Elsie Parsons recorded was, not surprisingly, a hybrid culture borrowing extensively from Portuguese and European traditions of oral storytelling but with added elements from Africa, the Caribbean and Brazil. As such, it provides a rich tapestry of the culture of the creole Atlantic world.

The prevailing theme in a large number of the stories is the subversion, or attempted subversion, of the existing social order by cunning and unscrupulous individuals. These resemble "trickster" tales from the oral literature of other former slave societies in the Caribbean and the Indian Ocean. The cunning is not necessarily condemned and is represented as one of the strategies for survival of the poor. An example would be tale 19, "The Interrupted Dinner under the Hat", in which a man is tricked out of his wealth by an old soldier who turns his old drill manual into an instrument for fortune-telling (Parsons 1923: 54–6).

Tânia Macedo has taken the series of stories that feature Uncle Wolf (*Tîlobe*) and his Nephew, and has shown how there is a recurrent theme of hunger which drives Uncle Wolf in his escapades. Uncle Wolf is usually unsuccessful and is punished by his cunning being turned against him (Parsons 1923: 324–6; T. Macedo 2003: 103–8). Though the parallels with the story of Red Riding Hood spring immediately to mind, it is clear that hunger was the experience to which Cabo Verdeans would most directly relate. There are other dimensions to these stories. Cannibalism occurs again and again, and is not treated as anything abnormal, while casual cruelty is described without any sense of horror or revulsion, as in tale 58, "The Girl without Hands, Breasts or Eyes" (Parsons 1923: 180–1). African notions of matrilineal social relations colour many of the stories. Representing the protagonists of the stories as "uncle" and "nephew" makes most sense in a matrilineal world where these, rather than biological fathers, are the two most important male figures in any family.

Otherwise the tales feature plot lines familiar from European folk tales in which the poor escape from their poverty and low social status through displays of abnormal strength or intelligence. The route to social advancement is marriage to the king's daughter, a largely symbolic way of describing how the trajectories of life can be transformed. What most characterises these stories is the prevalence of magic and the supernatural, which is present in the lives of ordinary people and which the fortunate are able to use to their advantage. And there are sexual themes in many of the stories which may or may not speak of a Cabo Verdean reality—most notably in tale 54, "The Girl Who Did Not Like Men" (Parsons 1923: 163). In the tale "The Lady Visitor", Uncle Wolf is deceived and duly punished because, as the Nephew puts it, "he desires women excessively" (Parsons 1923: 19).

Apart from her collection of stories, Elsie Parsons assembled notes on Cabo Verdean life provided by her informants. These are a potpourri of the memories her informants had of everyday life, and the beliefs and practices which guided the social relations of the islanders. Prominent among them was the importance attached to the figure of the *saib* or *curador*, an amalgam of folk doctor, white witch and simple adviser to the community, and the *f'itice'ra* (*feiticeira*), who practises black magic (Parsons 1921: 97).

It is not surprising to find that *feitiçaria* and the world of the supernatural form a theme that recurs not only in these folk tales but also in some modern fiction. Orlanda Amirilis (1924–2014) is one of the best-known women writers from Cabo Verde. Her life included a period of six years living in Goa, where she qualified as a teacher, an example of the global reach of the Portuguese empire in the twentieth century.

Her short story "Cais do Sodré" evokes the way folk tales and ancient beliefs in the supernatural lurk in the memories of people from the islands. Andresa, herself from Cabo Verde, meets a woman from São Vicente on the Cais do Sodré station platform in Lisbon. The meeting brings back childhood memories of the woman's father and sister. The father was believed to be a freemason and, as such, in league with the Devil, while the sister had a fiancé in Guinea who had taken a black lover—"any single man abroad would get himself a girl, and often one or two children". The sister falls mysteriously ill and dies. Witchcraft is suspected—"a Guinean will curse someone for next to nothing," she is told by the house servant, who is the purveyor of endless folk tales. These are memories of a world haunted by magic, nightmares and stories of the supernatural from which there is no escape for islanders even in Lisbon, where she is told that the woman's brother, a qualified doctor, has married a *mondronga*—a witch (Hopkinson 2019: 141–55).

Language and Music

There are at least eight creole languages based on Portuguese that have taken root in the Atlantic world. In São Tomé there are Forro and Angolar (and a dialect spoken by the Tongas, the descendants of contract labourers). In Ano Bom a language known as Fa d'Ambu is spoken, and in Príncipe there is a creole called after the name of the island. In Cabo Verde there is the language spoken throughout the archipelago known as Crioulu. In Guinea-Bissau and in the Casamance region of Senegal there is the creole language, usually called Kriolu, spoken by the urban Kriston community, which is rapidly becoming the lingua franca of the coastal areas of the whole country. And in the Caribbean there is Papiamento, recognised as an official language in the islands of Aruba, Bonaire and Curaçao, which is now thought to be a creolised Portuguese language probably brought by slaves traded across the Atlantic from Cabo Verde.

It is now largely accepted that Crioulu was in existence and widely spoken as early as the sixteenth century, when it was the lingua franca of the islands and the trading communities of the mainland. It was through speaking Crioulu that slaves became integrated into the population of the islands, and it was through this language that the landowning and mercantile class could converse with the lower strata of society. Although there are rival theories that hold that the language originated in Europe, where slaves were taken in the fifteenth century, or in Africa, the most likely story is that the language grew up over two or three generations in the social context of the islands, "the result of a dialectic in a plurilingual context ... in part the result of the ethnic diversity [of the slaves]. But above all from the necessity of communication from a social, economic and cultural perspective. In this context linguistic tolerance between the parties (dominant and dominated) was demanded by very survival itself." Communication was needed not only between master and slave but between "the white man and black woman in the intimacy of the bed, shared not by love, certainly, but above all by the force of circumstances" (Veiga 1998: 102). The emergence of the language, according to this evolutionary concept, began with a simple pidgin and gradually acquired the grammatical and lexical stability of a fully grown language during the seventeenth and eighteenth centuries.

However, little detail is known about the history of Crioulu. The first attempts to study it go back to the first half of the nineteenth century when José Feliciano de Castilho began work on a dictionary of Crioulu with the help of a religious from the convent in Ribeira

Grande, presumably the cleric who in 1841 was reported to have compiled a vocabulary and grammar (Santos 2017: 181).

Crioulu may have been the language which people used in their everyday lives and in their homes, but until the twentieth century it was seldom written down. In the mid-twentieth century it was given literary status by the writers who founded *Claridade*. Baltasar Lopes, one of the most famous of these, began his novel *Chiquinho* with the couplet in Crioulu "Corpo, qu' é nêgo, sa ta bai: Coraçom, qu' é fôrro, sa ta fica" (The body which is a slave can go, the heart which is free remains). However, there remained problems in the use of the language, as there was no agreed or authorised spelling, and significant dialect differences existed between the language varieties spoken in the various islands.

This problem has contributed to making language policy more complex. As Manuel Veiga has pointed out, although in general terms Crioulu is used in everyday speech and Portuguese is reserved for formal and intellectual contexts, the two languages endlessly merge without hard and fast boundaries. It is a case of the "invasion of one language by the other" (Veiga 1998: 110). There has been considerable debate about whether Crioulu is primarily an African language with Portuguese vocabulary or vice versa. This discussion resonates with wider debates about Cabo Verdean culture, which were given a political dimension by Amílcar Cabral. To what extent were Cabo Verdeans Africans, and their culture, language and music essentially African?

The status of Crioulu became more complex when the language situation of the diaspora was considered. In the islands Crioulu predominated, and many people found problems in using Portuguese. However, knowledge of Portuguese was essential for a modern, outward-looking country firmly set on the path of development. Speaking Crioulu, however, was considered the very essence of Cabo Verdean identity. Among the diaspora it was this that raised questions, as second- and third-generation Cabo Verdeans experienced the weakening or even disappearance of the use of Crioulu, its place being taken by the languages of the host nations, English, French or Italian. Can anyone still claim to be Cabo Verdean if they cannot speak Crioulu? This is a key cultural question.

SOME ASPECTS OF THE CULTURAL LIFE

There has been discussion not only of the recognition of Crioulu as the official language of Cabo Verde but also of the extent to which it should replace Portuguese entirely. It is a debate familiar in Africa, where local languages, spoken by the whole population, are not widely known outside the continent and do not give access to the wider world, where knowledge of a European language, especially English, is increasingly seen as essential. In the United States, English and not Portuguese is the language of business, technology and education; and in Dakar, where there is a large Cabo Verdean community, it is French. Cabo Verdeans seem trapped in a trilingual, even a quadrilingual, dilemma, one familiar in much of the modern world.

Today Cabo Verdean identity is most clearly expressed by the Crioulu language, by the music of the islands, and in the social relations of Cabo Verdean families and their international networks. Crioulu is not only the language of everyday use but is also the language of song and, as such, has become part of the rich island musical tradition. Music and language are inseparable, as most of the music is an accompaniment for song, and songs were for a long time the principal means of expression for the Crioulu language. In the language and music of the islands, the influences of Europe, Africa and the wider creole world of the South Atlantic come together to form unique cultural patterns.

Although Crioulu has always been the language of songs, there is very little historical record of what Cabo Verdean music was like before the twentieth century. An exception is Charles Darwin's account of his visit to Santiago in 1832. He described a group of young women performing a dance in the village of São Domingos in Santiago.

> It happened to be a grand feast-day, and the village was full of people. On our return we overtook a party of about twenty young black girls dressed in most excellent taste; their black skins and snow-white linen being set off by their coloured turbans and large shawls. As soon as we approached near, they suddenly all turned round, and covering the path with their shawls, sung with great energy a wild song, beating time with their hands upon their legs. We threw them some vintems, which were received

with screams of laughter, and we left them redoubling the noise of their song. (Darwin 1989: 44)

What Darwin witnessed was clearly an example of the *batuko* music and dance performed by groups of women.

Francisco Travassos Valdez gave another description of *batuko* in his account of a wedding, which makes it clear that this was music performed by slaves to a wider creole audience.

> After tea, the young female slaves, mulattos and blacks belonging to the house, were introduced into the drawing room, for the purpose of exhibiting their favourite dance, the batuque. The dance was conducted by a smart, clean, genteel-looking female slave, who, in an inaudible voice, ordered the formation of the various figures; the dancers formed a circle at each end of the room, the leader standing in the centre. After the first set the whole party united, and formed into a *grand ronde*, singing and dancing round the leader. Their music was composed of guitars, flutes, and the batuque, or tom-tom, which gives its name to the dance. The instrument is formed of part of a tree hollowed out, one end of which is covered with skin; the music (pardon the expression) is produced by striking this end, so as to keep time with the other instruments—all equally unmelodious ... When the slaves had finished their dance, the bride was conducted in great state to the nuptial chamber. (Travassos Valdez 1861: I, 119)

In the nineteenth century the *morna* became a popular form of music and song. *Morna* performers used Crioulu, making this form of poetry one of the principal modes of expression in that language. The *morna* belongs distinctly to a typically Portuguese tradition to which the *fado* and various forms of Brazilian music also belong. Tolerated by the Estado Novo regime, it became one of the most important vehicles for Cabo Verdean literature and tradition in the decades before independence.

Otherwise popular music was not encouraged by the Portuguese authorities, as it too easily became an expression of discontent and opposition, even if not outright rebelliousness. The Church also objected to the overly erotic nature of some of the dancing, especially the rhythmic *batuko* music performed by women and the *finason*, which involved improvised song. In 1866 the government placed a ban on the public performance of the *batukos* in Praia, describing them as "an entertainment opposed to the civilisation of our age … offensive to morality, public peace and order … It is in the interest of society that they should be suppressed for ever because they are performed, for the most part, by slaves, freed slaves and other similar people and because such an entertainment performed by the least civilised is not suitable for people who are honest and of good manners who might witness them and sink into drunkenness and immorality" (Lima 1998: 119).

It was only after independence that Cabo Verdean music in its various forms was able to find full expression and was encouraged by the PAICV as part of its campaign to rediscover the African roots of Cabo Verdean culture.

Simone Caputo Gomes has given a succinct description of the genres of modern Cabo Verdean music:

> the *tabanca* on the island of Santiago (ritualistic, repetitive, with seashells blown in counterpoint, drums and bass bugles), the party rhythms of the beat of the *pilão* [pestle or crusher] on the island of Fogo (the pestle that is used to pound the corn is also used as a musical instrument), the drums of San Jon, the mazurka and quadrille (both of European origin) developed on the island of Santo Antão, the *coladeira* (exuberant, sensual, with hints of the *cumbia* and Afro-Cuban music), the *batuque* on the island of Santiago (the African cry, the women playing percussion on their thighs with cloths and plastic pouches), the *finason* (the lament of the slaves), the *funaná* (a hypnotic trance), the Christian chant—*divina*—of the island of São Nicolau (four women's voices), and the nostalgic *morna* from the island of Boa Vista with its harmonies that are the result of musical syncretism (which originated with the Brazilian *modinha* and subsequently crossed with the *lundum*, the fado, the samba, the foxtrot and the mambo). (Gomes 2003: 267)

Some musical genres have flourished, principally because they are linked to the type of group which performs them. These include the *coladeira* and the *tabanca*, which are performed at religious festivals.

Cabo Verdean music had always had a following in Portugal, but it was the extraordinary career of the singer Cesária Évora that gave it a worldwide audience. Cesária's troubled life was so typical of the lives of many Cabo Verdean women that it added a deep authenticity to her music. She was born in 1941 in Mindelo, one of seven children. When her father died, her mother struggled to bring up her large family and Cesária spent some time in an orphanage. She began her singing career at the age of 16, singing *mornas* in bars and clubs in Mindelo. During this time she had three children by three different men, again an experience which linked her with the lives of so many island women, and was forced to give up singing to look after her children. She returned to an active music career in the 1980s and spent twenty years performing in many countries to increasing acclaim until she became one of the best-known and most popular performers on the international circuit. Évora received a total of six Grammy Award nominations, and she won the award for her album *Voz dámor*. Évora was made an ambassador of the World Food Programme in 2004, and was declared a cultural ambassador by the Cabo Verde government. She received the Portuguese Grand Cross of the Order of Prince Henry in 1999, and became a member of the French Legion of Honour in 2009. She died in 2011. Often singing without wearing shoes, she seemed to represent in her life the story of the ordinary women of the islands, and this, in many people's eyes, added meaning to her singing.

The essential nature of Cabo Verdean music has been described by Carlos Felipe Gonçalves. "Rhythms and melodies of ancestral African rites are mixed with profane and religious European songs resulting from repression and the imposition of Western cultural models. From this sad interaction between the force of the white man and the cultural repression dictated by the 'civilising' mission, and the resistance of the black man, has been born throughout the centuries the different creole cultural elements. Today this is a specific universe which touches all forms of art … where Africa and Europe are intimately linked" (Gonçalves 1998: 164).

Cabo Verdean music has remained a very popular genre, but this has brought some disadvantages with it. As more and more tourists visit the islands and cruise ships have begun to put in an appearance, musicians perform increasingly for a foreign audience, separating the roots of the music from the lives of the people. Carlos Gonçalves suggests that the *batuko* in particular is losing "most of its primitive elements", which were closely associated with marriage and sexual rituals (Gonçalves 1998: 109). And the recurrent themes of homesickness, nostalgia and longing are now becoming more muted as a result of electronic communication, which enables exiles and emigrants to keep in touch with families. As José Maria Semedo puts it, "the relative distance that separates any part of the world has become the time needed to dial a number on the telephone" (Semedo 2003: 37).

This, of course, is the fate of all musical genres which become widely popular, but it remains an issue of which performers and composers need to be conscious.

Folk Theatre and Dance of São Tomé under Threat

Those knowledgeable about creole music and culture have long been fascinated by the folk theatre and dance of São Tomé. At regular intervals drama groups located in the *forro* community have staged public performances of what is known locally as *tchiloli*. This is a rendering of a drama written originally in the sixteenth century by Baltasar Dias, a blind writer from Madeira, who developed a play called "The Tragedy of the Emperor Charlemagne and the Marquis of Mantua". The play has evolved in the hands of the *forro* communities to incorporate many musical and dramatic influences from Africa, but the players are still very distinctive in their black European-style costumes and white face masks, while many modern artefacts like telephones are used in the drama.

The fact that the original of *tchiloli* was a play written in Madeira in the sixteenth century led many commentators to imagine a centuries-long history, a unique survival of a sixteenth-century Renaissance drama. The Calouste Gulbenkian website (2020), for example, describes it in this way: "Tchiloli has been part of São Tomé and Príncipe's tradition for more than 500 years. Based on a medieval text … that probably reached the islands in the sixteenth century."

This idea has been supported by a large number of writers since the 1960s and has been elaborated: according to some, the play was introduced by travelling players from Madeira, who were brought to São Tomé by Madeiran sugar growers early in the sixteenth century. However, just as the enthusiasm of the folklorists reached its height, it was pointed out that there is no mention of this drama in any document or by any writer before the very end of the nineteenth century, and the earliest known text dates only from 1907 (Seibert 2009).

It is more probable that this play, which reappeared in a collection entitled *Romanceiro* by Almeida Garrett in 1843, was adopted by *forro* communities in the late nineteenth century and became instantly popular. The reasons for this, and the circumstances which led to its adoption, remain entirely unknown. The belief that this play has had a continuous existence in São Tomé since the sixteenth century is really only evidence of the passionate desire of folklorists to believe in the possibility of such a continuous history.

How *tchiloli* is interpreted also depends very much on whether it is believed to be centuries old or whether it was introduced more recently during the height of the colonial period. The anthropologist Françoise Gründ, who was a firm believer in the sixteenth-century origin of the play, saw it as

> a magic ceremony functioning at various levels of codification. In her opinion, Charlemagne symbolises the King of Portugal, far off but tolerated and almost always considered by the local people as a just father for the half-caste children of the land. His son, D. Carloto, is the Portuguese governor of the island, a kind of cynical dictator, a cruel, grasping man, hated by the local people who suffer daily from his behaviour. The Marquis of Mântua is, in fact, the leader of the "children of the land" (the new inhabitants born of the union of white men and slave girls). He brings the first breath of independence, demanding and getting justice. Along with his followers, he represents the half-caste families, of high origin, raised to the position of rulers on the plantations and defenders of local interests. (Buala 2010)

Readers would be forgiven if they saw in this an example of over-interpretation.

However, in spite of the worldwide interest in the *tchiloli* and the support of the Gulbenkian Foundation, it appears that the number of societies still staging performances has dwindled. The fact that, in its traditional form, performances could continue for six or seven hours may be one reason for the decline in its popularity.

A similar question mark hangs over other traditional dances and dramas. "In Ilha do Príncipe, there is the *Auto de Floripes*, first mentioned in 1858 and known locally as 'São Lourenço'" (Buala 2010), as well as the dances associated with the figure of Captain Congo, known as the *danço-congo*. Again, this rich dramatic rendering, clearly deriving from African culture, attracted a lot of folklorists during the twentieth century, who found in it the perfect expression of creole culture, blending themes from Europe and Africa into something unique. Once again it is under threat from the click-button availability of world music in electronic form.

9

THE CHANGING CREOLE WORLD OF THE SOUTH ATLANTIC

Over five centuries the Cabo Verde islands developed as part of a South Atlantic world of commercial and cultural exchange. This chapter looks at the nature of creole cultures and the eventual fragmentation and disintegration of this world as both sides of the Atlantic and the island communities adjusted in their own ways to the pressures of modernity in the nineteenth and twentieth centuries. Although European imperialism in Africa and European emigration to Brazil largely displaced the creolised populations, the end of the Portuguese empire in the 1970s gave a fresh opportunity for the old creole families to regain something of their former importance.

Population Movement in the Creole Atlantic World

The most important innovation that the Portuguese creole traders brought to Africa was the commercial links with the New World, which opened up vast new markets for exported African produce and labour, and led to the introduction of American food crops into Africa. The creole communities in the islands were of fundamental importance in determining how the initial contacts with the New World developed. Seamen from the Azores pioneered the exploration of the western Atlantic, and later the Cabo Verde islands became regular stopping places for ships plying between Europe and the Americas. The earliest settlements on the coast of Brazil followed a pattern already familiar in mainland Guinea. Traders, many of them New Christians, made camps on the coast to collect dyewood and formed relations with Indian women; these led to the emergence of a mixed creole population in which the culture and way of life of the native Brazilians was the predominant feature. The system of captaincies, which had been used in the settlement of the islands, was replicated in Brazil in the 1530s and gave the settlements there the same degree of autonomy enjoyed at that time by the creole islands. Towards the end of the century sugar growers from São Tomé moved to Brazil and promoted the development of the sugar industry in the northern coastal districts. The sixteenth century saw, therefore, an extension of the semi-autonomous creole commercial world across the Atlantic, linking Africa to the emerging societies in America not just commercially but culturally and institutionally.

The forced migration of African slaves to Europe, the Atlantic islands and the New World was only one aspect of the extensive population movements that characterised the early modern world. The slave trade has to be seen alongside the emigration of Portuguese and Castilians from the Iberian peninsula and the diaspora of the Sephardic Jews, with which it became inextricably involved. As migrants left Portugal to settle the islands, to travel East to the Estado da India and to settle in Brazil, African slaves arrived in Portugal to fill gaps in the labour force, and joined Portuguese and New Christians in the peopling of the islands and the New World.

The very approximate guesswork that has to take the place of real statistics suggests that between 1400 and 1640 perhaps between 600,000 and 700,000 people may have left Portugal while rather fewer left Spain. As a result of the 1492 decrees, 70,000 Jews and people of Jewish origin left the Iberian peninsula, with a steady stream of departures thereafter. Meanwhile, as the Slave Trade Database suggests, 280,000 slaves were exported during the sixteenth century, with three times that figure in the following fifty years. Although by the seventeenth century the number of African slaves came to exceed the "free" emigration of Portuguese and Spanish, it is important to see the slave trade in the context of a diverse and hitherto unprecedented movement of populations within the Atlantic basin which provided the ingredients for the creolisation that took place (Newitt 2015a; Newitt 2017).

Cabo Verdeans

Writers often give the impression that the Cabo Verde islands were isolated, adrift in the Atlantic at the mercy of droughts and famines, and enduring centuries of poverty and neglect. Although this is an image of their history that has a certain romantic appeal, it is far from being the whole of their story, for the islands were at the heart of an ever-widening and expanding world of creole economic and cultural influence.

Although the slave trade was at the heart of this creole Atlantic world, the flow of people and cultural influences was not all one way. As Kristin Mann and Edna Bay say, "earlier generations of scholars had posited a unidirectional movement of enslaved persons stripped of identity and culture", but as a result of new research "we are beginning to understand movements of peoples and cultures in the south Atlantic instead as a series of interactions and influences back and forth across seas and cultures from the earliest period of the slave-trade up to the present" (Mann and Bay 2001: 1).

From the time of their first settlement, the Cabo Verde islanders had close links with the mainland societies and established permanent trading posts and settlements along the rivers of upper Guinea. The traders who settled there married into local lineages, and by the sixteenth century there was a large, if thinly scattered, population of mixed ethnic origin, speaking Portuguese creole dialects as well as local African languages. These trading families attracted to themselves elements of the local African populations who formed the labour force of the creole settlements and who acted as servants, carriers and boatmen. These were known as *grumetes*, and of necessity they shared in some aspects of creole culture. The creoles settled on the mainland developed a syncretic religion which was an amalgam of Christian, Muslim and local African religious beliefs and practices. Although for the most part they retained their Portuguese names, continued to dress in the Portuguese fashion, and built rectangular houses in the European style, in most other respects they adopted the cultural practices of the communities among which they settled. In particular there was no introduction of European technology, so that transport, weaving, pot-making, ironworking and agriculture continued to be carried on according to local practice.

Meanwhile, the settlements in São Tomé became another point from which creoles established themselves on the mainland, while the official royal missions to Kongo led to the widespread adoption of elements of Christian culture by the elites of the Kongo kingdom. Although the Kongo kingdom was the most important African monarchy that experienced a degree of creolisation, it was not the only one. The small Warri kingdom of the Niger delta region also saw the adoption of Christianity by the ruling elite and formed a close alliance with the Portuguese in the Gulf of Guinea region (Ayida 2022).

The seventeenth century was, in many respects, the golden age of creole influence in West Africa, and the Cabo Verde islands were the centre from which creole culture spread. Not only did traders constantly move between the islands and the mainland, but there was a wider movement of population as the creole population of Cabo Verdean origin spread out along the coast. Until the end of the sixteenth century, the maritime trade of the upper Guinea regions was dominated by the Portuguese. The Cabo Verde islands provided warehousing and bases for trading ships as well as much of the personnel who operated the ships. Creole-speaking Afro-Portuguese became the leading class of brokers in maritime trade, and the Portuguese-based languages were the trading languages of the coast. Other Europeans wanting to trade in this part of West Africa found it was best to operate through Afro-Portuguese intermediaries, who became not only brokers in the trade but also, to some extent, power brokers in local politics.

However, by the end of the sixteenth century, English, French and Dutch traders were increasingly present, and in the seventeenth century, although the Afro-Portuguese continued to be active along the whole West African coast, the centres of direct Portuguese participation were increasingly confined to the area south of the

Casamance river. Here significant changes gradually reduced the importance of the islands in this commerce. First, there was the inexorable growth of contraband trade, especially by slave traders who avoided the Cabo Verde islands, where they would have to pay duties on their cargoes, and who traded directly from Africa to the New World. During the union of the Spanish and Portuguese crowns between 1580 and 1640, the Spanish for the first time had direct access to Portuguese-controlled ports, and by the seventeenth century Spanish slavers had come to dominate the trade.

The second factor was the determination of the African rulers of the Guinea coast to retain an active role in the trade in order to maintain the flow of imports. Although the Portuguese had tried to formalise their presence in the Guinea rivers by establishing fortified towns and appointing officials, these settlements remained entirely dependent on the goodwill of the local African rulers, who frequently threatened to burn the towns if the Portuguese became too independent.

Aware that customs duties paid on the slave trade were in sharp decline, the Portuguese Crown eventually decided to move its customs house from Santiago to Cacheu on the Guinea coast, a move which effectively cut the Cabo Verde islands off from any significant role in the Guinea trade.

There is a marked contrast between the Portuguese trading operations in Guinea and those in Angola. In Angola the Portuguese established their own towns and occupied and ruled over significant areas of the mainland together with their populations. In Guinea there was never an independent Portuguese settlement the equivalent of Luanda or Benguela and no territory was permanently conquered and occupied by Portugal, even though half-hearted attempts to build forts and send soldiers to protect the trading towns were sometimes tried.

Although the trade of metropolitan Portugal was in inexorable decline, the Afro-Portuguese trading families prospered, "capitalizing on the advantages of their African kinship networks, their superior knowledge of African languages, cultures and markets, their greater resistance to tropical diseases and, always of paramount importance, their monopoly or near monopoly in kola trade and *panos* manufactured in Cape Verde" (Brooks 2003: 124). These Afro-Portuguese traders and brokers considered themselves to be "white", meaning that they belonged to the same commercial networks as the traders who came from Europe. In this community an important role was played by women (known in creole by the courtesy title of *nharas*), who would contract marriages with European traders in order to secure luxury European goods and find outlets for their trade (Havik 2007b). Through these marriages and the wealthy households that these women maintained, creole influence continued to spread in the areas otherwise dominated by French and English traders, and the creole language in its various dialects became widely used along the coast. As Philip Havik has pointed out, whereas creole languages developed in the islands in the context of plantation slavery, the creole language of the Guinea mainland "emerged in and around riverine trade settlements on the continent" in free commercial communities (2007a: 46).

Although Afro-Portuguese traders operated along all the coast, from the region of Dakar in the north to Sierra Leone and even beyond, and although many of them grew rich, their position as a special privileged class was always precarious. In particular, the local custom was for the property of anyone who died to revert to the ruler of the land, a factor which limited the emergence of wealthy and independent commercial dynasties. The Afro-Portuguese "white" traders could also have their freedom of movement restricted and be liable to fines for crimes or breaches of custom committed by themselves or their slaves (Brooks 2003: 134–8). It was for this reason that the Portuguese tried to regulate affairs within their settlements by appointing officials, and to fortify their settlements to make them more independent.

Through the next 200 years the creole trading communities along the Guinea coast, distinct in their creole speech and their syncretic Catholic worship, struggled to maintain peaceful relations with the local Africans and to keep a foothold in the trade of the region, but increasingly they were under pressure, as the outside influences were no longer coming from Portugal or the islands but from the French to the north and from the English in the Gambia river region and Sierra Leone. In the nineteenth century, Portuguese who had settled in Africa and adopted African customs, those of mixed race, and indigenous people who had adopted Portuguese names, Portuguese customs or spoke a Portuguese creole language, were all recognised as members of Portugal's global community, their Portuguese-ness ultimately depending on their adherence to the Catholic faith and, in some cases, an expressed loyalty to the Crown. In many such "Portuguese" diasporic communities which survived in Africa and Asia, the specifically Portuguese element in their culture was so diluted that it often amounted to little more than the use of Portuguese names, a nominal Catholicism, and the wearing of hats or shoes, and yet these people often claimed affiliation with Portugal when it suited their needs (Newitt 2017).

The Creole World of Brazil

After 1575, when Luanda was founded, the Portuguese creole trading network in Angola and the Kongo region grew to supply the great expansion in demand for labour from the sugar economy and, later, gold mining in the interior of Brazil. The settlement of the coastal regions of Brazil took place from the middle of the sixteenth century, and although a few important port cities were established, in the north at Olinda and Bahia and in the south at Rio, the major area of settlement was in the sugar-producing regions of the north where the plantations and the *engenhos* formed the framework for society.

Over one million slaves were sent to Brazil between 1575 and 1700, and a further million in the first half of the eighteenth century. The slaves joined a society that was already substantially creolised through mixture with the native Indian population, and they themselves underwent a process of creolisation. In spite of a marked rise in racial consciousness among European Portuguese during the sixteenth century, the black slave population of Brazil never became a distinct social caste, separate from the creole population or even from the whites of direct European descent.

A creolisation of great complexity took place in the societies of the New World and in Spanish America. This complexity is reflected in the series of so-called Casta paintings, which were produced in the eighteenth century and which illustrated every type of racial and ethnic mix in the population. A rare and seldom seen set of Casta paintings can be found in Braemore House in Hampshire in the UK. Although slavery and the slave trade have usually been seen as a process which dehumanised the captives, turning them into chattels and denying them human rights, slaves nevertheless found ways of resisting that dehumanisation, often through adroit forms of cultural appropriation and synthesis that resulted in remarkable examples of creolisation. Many slaves came from communities already partly creolised and knew that, to survive, they had to adopt the patois of the new society and adjust to its religious beliefs and material culture.

The slaves who were sent to Brazil did not all come from the same region in Africa. During the sixteenth century most came from upper Guinea, but from about 1580 onwards the trade shifted to central Africa and the ports of Luanda and Benguela. At the end of the seventeenth century, the numbers of slaves coming from central Africa declined and the trade refocused on the Mina and Lagos regions of West Africa. In the nineteenth century, increasing numbers of Yoruba were enslaved and sent to Brazil, and slaves were also brought from eastern Africa in large numbers for the first time. This shifting focus of the slave trade meant that Africans entering Brazil came from widely separated regions and from different African cultural zones (Sweet 2003: 17–18).

During the first two or three centuries of Portuguese settlement in Brazil, the population remained very diverse. Although there were cultural pressures to conform to the norms of European Portugal, notably from the Church and from the royal government in the cities, the culture of Brazil was heavily influenced by the beliefs and practices of the black population, many of whom had arrived via the Cabo Verde islands. Racial mixing and manumission resulted in the growth of free black populations, more integrated into the prevailing creole culture than the newly arriving slaves, who often strove to retain elements of the languages, religions and cultural practices of Africa. In Brazil the partial absorption of the Amerindian populations added further ingredients to the mix. There were also marked distinctions between people of African origin born in Brazil and those born in

Africa, while the different African regions from which slaves came created further distinctions of language and culture. As there was no common creole language in Brazil, differences arose between those born in Brazil who knew Portuguese and the newly arrived slaves who did not. And above everything else, there was the fundamental legal distinction between slave and free, a distinction that survived until the end of the slave trade in 1851 and slavery itself in 1888 (Russell-Wood 2007: 185–6).

It was among free Afro-Brazilians and people of mixed race that the process of creolisation was most prevalent. This section of the population had many ways of enhancing their status that were denied to slaves. They could join religious brotherhoods or militia regiments and become certified members of craft guilds, while literacy also opened fresh opportunities for them (Russell-Wood 2007: 193). Afro-Brazilians also used the Portuguese language, which not only facilitated their interactions with Portuguese-Brazilians and people of mixed ethnicity, but set them apart from the newly arrived African slaves, who often took time to adjust to the new linguistic environment.

In spite of the continued creolisation of the population, the constant arrival of slaves from Africa meant that the African element in Brazilian creole culture remained strong, and the distinctions between Afro-Brazilians and newly arrived slaves continued. These distinctions were not so much in the occupations followed by each group but in things like dress, hairstyle and, of course, religious practice.

In spite of the subordinate position of newly arrived slaves, African values and practices continued to influence the way in which Brazilian society evolved. Many African slaves cultivated reputations as healers, and healers and diviners were in great demand and often commanded a large following. African practices in the realms of health and diet, and the wearing of amulets and protective charms, were prevalent throughout the society. African notions of kinship and community were also important in providing support for people who might otherwise have become completely deracinated. Although the different religious brotherhoods provided a way in which Catholicism could open itself to African beliefs and value systems, the religious beliefs of African slaves continued to draw "on religious and linguistic commonalities from the Old World to construct a cosmology unknown and unknowable to their masters [though] in the process they changed the meaning of West Central African religious practices" (Mann 2001: 9). "Religion was inalienable from African cosmology, rituals, cultures, kinship and lineages, and permeated into value systems and behaviours" (Russell-Wood 2007: 176, 197). In time these might be modified in the context of the life they lived in Brazil, but for most they would remain with them throughout their lives.

African influences in Brazilian visual culture and music were also important, and visitors to Brazil were made aware that beneath the high society of wealthy white families was a world still dominated by ideas, customs and values derived from Africa. After the Portuguese royal family moved to Brazil in 1807, "the theatricality of the Braganza court was enriched by themes derived from the tropics and the New World, and lost nothing from an environment that included the celebrations of the black slave population and even the forest cults of the Indians. D. João VI also revived the conservatory at Santa Cruz where slaves were taught to be musicians and singers. The highly accomplished slave orchestra performed at church services and public celebrations" (Newitt 2019b: 186).

Yet, even though very large numbers of slaves continued to arrive in Brazil until the slave trade ended in 1851, and although it seems that slave marriages were very frequently made between men and women of a similar cultural background, while religious and ritual activities were often specific to one African ethnic group, it was never possible for slaves wholly to recreate an extension of Africa in the New World. Even the *quilombos*, the communities that escaped slaves established in the *sertão*, were too small and remote for this to be possible. Slaves came from too many different regions of Africa—they were anyway separated by the locations where they were sent to work—ever to establish a homogeneous African society.

The Portuguese embrace of creolisation contributed to a demographic dynamism lacking in the British colonies. In the seventeenth and eighteenth centuries Britain struggled to establish communities in the New World: immigration rates were low and racial segregation prevented the emergence of a dynamic creole population. This was in marked contrast to the lusophone areas of the Atlantic where strong Portuguese creole communities were established. As Nancy Naro has written, "the breadth of Portugal's multicultural empire attested to centuries of cultural pluralism, integration and unity under a sovereign head of state" (2007: 131). By 1800 the population of Brazil was approximately twice that of the thirteen colonies which formed the United States. One highly visible consequence of this was the rapid territorial expansion of Brazil beyond the Tordesillas line of 1494. This was recognised in the 1777 Treaty of San Ildefonso, and allows contrast to be made with the British North American colonies, which at that time were still largely confined to the eastern seaboard.

Brazil and Africa

If it was creole merchants from the islands who introduced sugar growing to Brazil and organised the mass (forced) migration of Africans to the New World, the tide of creolisation soon flowed back to Africa through many different circuits. New World food crops and plants, first introduced into the Atlantic islands, were from there taken to Africa and Europe. Maize, manioc and peanuts spread in Africa and became a staple of the African diet. The pineapple, first mentioned by Columbus, was taken by the Portuguese to Africa and India early in the sixteenth century. Sweet potatoes were being cultivated in the Azores as early as 1538. The ordinary potato made its appearance in Europe towards the end of the sixteenth century; other American plants included cashews, guavas and chillies. Tobacco was being widely used in Europe for medicinal purposes by the 1530s and by the end of the century had become widely diffused in Europe, Africa and Asia. Tomatoes, first encountered by the Spanish in Mexico, were to become an essential ingredient in European cuisine, while sunflowers were brought from the New World to Portugal, initially as a decorative flower.

In the seventeenth century, Brazilians were appointed as governors of Angola; Brazilian soldiers, including Amerindians, fought in African wars; Brazilian merchants traded tobacco for slaves and even settled in the West African ports; and Brazilians brought the cacao tree to São Tomé and set in motion the great boom in West African cocoa production. Atlantic influences were passed along trade routes from one part of Africa to another. Creolisation was, therefore, not a uniform or one-way process limited to a few island communities, but a natural and organic cultural exchange, affecting whole continents, that was inseparable from the growth of a global economy.

When Portuguese influence faded with the decline of Portugal as a major trading nation in the seventeenth century, the influence of Brazil gradually rose. By the nineteenth century Brazil was the main market for slaves in the South Atlantic and the main supplier of tobacco, which was one of the chief items of commerce on the coast.

In West Africa, Brazilian influence became focused on the port of Whydah (Ajuda or Ouidah), which was founded in 1721 by a Brazilian and which became the centre of the Brazilian slave trade on the West African coast. Robin Law has estimated that a total of a million slaves may have left the port of Whydah throughout its history, while "directors of the fort were appointed by and reported to the Viceroy (later Governor) of Bahia" (Law 2001: 22–3). Brazilian tobacco was the major commodity in demand in the West African market, and Brazilians made use of São Tomé island to support their shipping. São Tomé became more closely linked to Whydah and to Brazil than to Portugal, and it was from Brazil that coffee and cacao were introduced into the island.

In the early nineteenth century the Brazilian presence in Whydah grew in a significant way as the British and French slave trade largely ceased and Brazilians were left as the only major operators. Slavers settled in the town and a leading slaver, Francisco Felix de Souza, established close ties with the king of Dahomey, acquiring the title of "Chacha", which made him in effect the king's representative in the city, a position inherited after his death by his heirs. The Brazilians continued to dominate the port of Whydah throughout the nineteenth century, their families growing through the marriages contracted with African women and the creole community expanding, as the creole communities in the upper Guinea rivers had done, through the large numbers of slaves and *grumetes* in the service of their families. The Brazilian community was also boosted numerically by numbers of slaves sent there from Brazil after the slave rebellion of 1835 (Law 2001). This Brazilian creole community in Whydah became the subject of Bruce Chatwin's fictionalised story *The Viceroy of Ouidah*.

Although Dahomey became a French protectorate in 1892, the fort established at Whydah (known to the Portuguese as Ajuda) remained technically a Portuguese enclave until 1961, while the inhabitants of the town continued to maintain the traditions of their Brazilian origin.

Creole Angola and its Links with Brazil

Angola had been established as a Portuguese kingdom, founded initially with soldiers and settlers from Portugal in the late sixteenth century. However, after the Dutch occupation in 1640 and the reconquest by a Brazilian army in 1649, the Portuguese presence in Angola weakened and commercial activity in Angola was dominated by Brazilians. "These links included the deployment of soldiers from Brazil to fight wars in the Luanda hinterland, the continued arrival in Angola of Brazil-based merchants, bureaucrats and political and criminal exiles, and the ownership of ships used in the Angolan trade" (Ferreira 2007: 101).

During the eighteenth and early nineteenth centuries Angola became increasingly a creolised society. The coastal cities were dominated by local creole families who filled administrative posts and controlled the town councils and prestigious institutions like the Misericórdias. Attached to these families was an underclass of slaves and free Africans, who provided the workforce of the cities, the crews for ships, and porters for the inland trading expeditions. The leading families, all of mixed ethnicity, clung to their "Portuguese" identity and to the family networks on which their local wealth and status depended. However, no creole language established itself in Angola, and Kimbundu became the locally used language of the creole community as well as of the African societies who lived under Portuguese control.

As Brazilian influence grew in Angola, Brazilian merchants and shipowners, operating out of Luanda and Benguela, constituted the overwhelming majority of those involved in the slave trade (Ferreira 2007: 100–1). Also significant was the role of people of mixed ethnicity in the trade, so that the Angolan slave trade became increasingly an affair not of Europeans but of the creole Atlantic community. The networks of the creole families in Luanda and Benguela provided Brazilian traders with local access to African markets and "allowed them to conduct business in cultural and social environments radically different from the ones they might have known in Brazil and Portugal" (Ferreira 2007: 114).

By the nineteenth century the influence of Portuguese creole culture had extended deep into the interior of west-central Africa. The establishment of settlements (often referred to as *presidios*, which emphasised their quasi-military character) as bases for trading activities led to the growth of creolised communities far in the interior. From there the leading traders organised caravans which travelled as far as the upper Zambezi, bringing back ivory and slaves to the coast.

Of particular importance was the settlement at Ambaca, 300 kilometres inland from Luanda, which had originally been established in the seventeenth century. The creole community there, known as Ambakistas, was "made up largely of black Africans (a large proportion of whom were freed slaves) and 'mestizos', but also of a few whites ... As a symbol of their elevated status these Luso-Africans wore shoes (this being a particular privilege) and European clothes. They regarded themselves as Christians and spoke Portuguese. Many of them could read and write" (Heintze 2007: 128).

By the early nineteenth century Ambakistas were active across a swathe of the interior, inland from the ports of Luanda and Benguela. "The influence they exerted on 'traditional' African societies was significant both in political and economic terms, since they often served as secretaries, interpreters and advisors to the chiefs and married into the latter's families. They also occupied unpaid leadership positions in the colonial auxiliaries ... They were joined by numerous specialised African craftsmen, such as tailors, cobblers and carpenters" (Heintze 2007: 128).

The Luso-Africans of Angola (and of Mozambique) accompanied many of the European exploratory expeditions during the century, playing a major part in the opening up of the African interior, as guides and interpreters. In this way they performed a function similar to that of the *lançados* and Afro-Portuguese brokers who had facilitated the European trade in West Africa from the fifteenth to the eighteenth centuries.

The trading caravans that criss-crossed the west-central African interior in the nineteenth century were mostly organised and led by men from local creole families, though some were of Portuguese or Brazilian origin, like the famous António Francisco Ferreira da Silva Porto. Silva Porto had adopted the suffix Porto when in Brazil, where he grew up, to distinguish himself from others with the name Silva. Silva Porto married an African wife, a practice common among many of the creole traders from the coast who contracted marriages with women from important local families and in this way built their commercial networks, as the *lançados* of earlier centuries had done in the Guinea region. The mixed-race children of these unions swelled the numbers of the creole population in the interior, all identifying as Portuguese and adopting the usual markers of Portuguese identity—names, European-style clothing and a nominal Catholicism. However, in the nineteenth century, the most important of the creole traders and caravan leaders wielded far more political power through their armed followers than the *lançados* had ever done.

In the 1840s a survey of the creole community in Viye in the Angolan interior was conducted by Joaquim Rodrigues Graça.

> The people listed by Graça composed a heterogeneous group with four things in common: they were all men, with Lusophone names, considered *moradores* of foreign origins (even if these origins were located in the past, as in the case of the Portuguese immigrants' descendants) and involved in trading activities. Graça considered three trade-related occupations: *negociantes*, i.e., traders who made up the majority of the group, also known as *sertanejos*; *agencias*, a term that probably referred to men responsible for recruiting porters, also known as *pombeiros*; and finally, fewer in number, there were *caixeiros*, or clerks or bookkeepers. (Amaral 2022: 47)

Almost all of these 100 people were considered by Graça to be black or of mixed race, with only six of recent white European extraction.

Decline and Resurrection of the Angolan and São Tomean Creole Families

During the nineteenth century, in the areas of formal Portuguese settlement in the Cabo Verde and Guinea islands as well as in Guinea itself, creoles made up most of the administrative class and the personnel of the armed forces. They owned the land and the trading ships, formed the merchant and broker classes, and became town councillors, officers in the militia and brothers in the Misericórdias. They also constituted a large part of the priesthood of the Catholic Church (Candido 2013: 114–15, 124–5).

This diverse creole world was not in any sense a world of equality, as it was universally slave-owning, but it was marked by a rich and creative mixture of cultures, which found expression in social customs, including carnival, food, art, music, dance and religious observance, and in social relations, in which the role of women, not only as mothers but as property owners and commercial brokers, often prevailed over the patriarchal presumptions of Portuguese law and custom.

In nineteenth-century Brazil the imperial government of Dom Pedro II struggled to maintain the European credentials of urban Brazilian society, but in the rural areas a mixed creole society predominated. In 1933 Gilberto Freyre memorably described this creole world of the plantations before its values had been critically undermined by the all-pervading racist ideologies of the late nineteenth and early twentieth centuries. However, in the last quarter of the nineteenth century the culture of Brazil was to experience radical change. Slavery was abolished in 1888, while at the same time a flood of immigration from Europe, mostly from Portugal and Italy, soon displaced the old creolised population in the towns and even on the plantations, where contracted European labourers filled the roles once occupied by slaves. The transformation of Brazil from a predominantly creole society into one dominated by immigrants of European origin and culture had begun.

At the same time Britain's campaign against the slave trade merged with the European "scramble for Africa". In order to counter Portugal's claims to central Africa, the British systematically branded Portuguese creoles as slave traders, whose degenerate slaving propensities resulted from miscegenation. This narrative contributed, in turn, to the idea that the Portuguese were not really white Europeans at all and therefore not the standard-bearers of progress, a prejudice that reverberated round the world. Portuguese immigrants in the British Caribbean, for example, were not accepted as Europeans but in census returns received a separate classification of their own (Newitt 2015a: 170–1; Newitt 2017).

The scramble for African territory by European countries began to gather pace in the 1870s, and Portugal determined to play an active part. This involved, among other things, military expeditions to secure control of areas the Portuguese considered to belong to them and an attempt to promote European settlement. As a result European personnel arrived in Africa as soldiers and administrators, and there was also an influx convicts, who were seen as the most readily available settlers. At the same time Portugal adopted many of the current European attitudes towards race. The old traditions which had allowed black people and people of mixed race to be accepted as Portuguese, to call themselves "white", and to play a full part in the life of the colonies were now increasingly replaced by strictly racial attitudes which privileged the claims of people of white European origin. Creoles found themselves replaced in Angola and São Tomé by newly arrived European settlers and administrators, while in São Tomé the old creole population, the *forros*, were displaced from 90 per cent of the land.

To counter any threat to their imperial status, Portuguese politicians were quick to mimic the racial policies of the British and Americans (Williams 2007). Portugal had to be seen to be in the forefront of those bringing "civilisation" and "progress" to Africa. In pursuit of this policy, creoles became an embarrassment and, in places such as Angola and Mozambique, were largely replaced in public offices by metropolitan Portuguese without the taint of African ancestry (Dias 1984). A strong strain of racism emerged in Portugal, giving full expression to all the Manichaean tendencies of twentieth-century thought—setting black against white, civilised against uncivilised, *indígena* against *assimilado*. In many respects the period of Salazar's dominance witnessed racial policies almost as extreme as those in the British colonies (Henriques 2012): almost, but not quite. Salazar, drawing on a long-standing Iberian imperial tradition stretching back to Las Casas and the Dominican theologians, liked to extol the multiracial nature of the Portuguese colonies and recognised *mestiços* and a small minority of educated Africans as Portuguese citizens—a civilised status also granted to the creole populations of the islands, with Cabo Verdeans even being recruited into the colonial service.

As the old creole classes in society lost their status and found their fortunes in sharp decline, they reacted by forming the first movements of political dissent. Political organisations, supported largely by the educated creoles, appeared in Angola, Mozambique and São Tomé. Newspapers were founded and representatives attended the Pan-African Congresses. Loss of status helped to radicalise the creole populations and gradually to create a climate sympathetic to the ideas of nationalism and independence. Of course, not all the educated creole population turned against the colonial regime, as some were successfully recruited into the structures of the empire. This was particularly the case in Cabo Verde, where the educated found employment opportunities in the Portuguese colonial administration, and in São Tomé there was also the example of Francisco Tenreiro, a poet and academic of distinction, who became a deputy in the Portuguese parliament.

Nevertheless, the deep contradictions between Salazarist multiracial ideology and colonial practice were never reconciled, and it is no surprise that it was African creoles, marginalised by the racist policies of late Portuguese imperialism, who became leaders of the nationalist opposition, elaborating their own ideology, which rejected the importance of colour and tribe and espoused a form of modernity that denied the binaries of race and civilisation embedded in the Salazarist project. As nationalist and independence parties were formed, leaders were found in the creolised sections of the communities, in São Tomé from the *forro* population and in Angola from the educated Luanda-based elite families, who formed the core of the MPLA. In Guinea, the PAIGC was also founded by creoles, but they were for the most part Cabo Verdeans, who dominated the independence movement and the country after independence until the coup of 1980.

When the Portuguese wound up their colonial empire following the revolution of April 1974, the successor regimes were the parties with a creole leadership. The former colonies were now again ruled by the creole families which had once been dominant and which now replaced the European Portuguese administrators. The triumph of African nationalism in the 1975 independence agreements was the triumph not only of an elite of creole politicians but of a specifically creole ideology, silencing, or attempting to silence, a more "Africanist" strain of nationalism, which found some expression in alternative independence movements like FNLA and Unita in Angola and Renamo in Mozambique.

GLOSSARY

almoxarife	customs officer
asientistas	holders of contracts to supply slaves to the Spanish Indies
azulejos	decorative ceramic tiles
barlavento	windward
batuko	drum music; also spelt *batuque*
bolsa de mandingo	protective amulet
branca	white woman
buzios	currency shells
cachupa	stew of beans, vegetables and meat; Cabo Verde national dish
caldeira	boiler; crater of a volcano
capelas	entailed estates with obligation to support the Church
capitão-mor	captain-major
cori beads	beads made of stone
corregidor(es)	royal official(s)
curador	supervisor; inspector of labour in São Tomé
degredado/-a	convict
donatário	donatary captain

GLOSSARY

engenhos	sugar mills and plantations
fazenda	farm or plantation
feitiçaria	magic
feiticeiro	magician
feitiço	magic
fidalgos	gentlemen
finaçon	type of music associated with slaves of former times
forros	free people; the free populations of Cabo Verde and São Tomé
fruta de espinho	pitaya or dragon's fruit
funcos	round huts in the African style; also, outside kitchen huts
furos	deep wells
grogue	rum
grumetes	servants of Portuguese creoles in western Africa
indígenas	natives
ladinização	latinisation; process by which slaves acquired elements of Portuguese language and culture
lançados	Portuguese settled in mainland Guinea
levadas	irrigation channels
linguas	interpreters
manilhas	bracelets or anklets of brass or silver
mestiços	people of mixed racial origin
Misericórdia	charitable brotherhood
mocambo	community of escaped slaves in São Tomé
*morador*es	settlers or residents
morgadios	entailed estates
morgados	holders of entails
morna	Cabo Verde poetry set to music

GLOSSARY

nhanhás / nharas	white African and mulatto upper-class ladies
nzimbu	currency shells
ouvidor	judge
padroado real	rights and patronage of the Portuguese Crown in the Church
palmatória	a paddle used for beating the hand
panos	cloths manufactured in the Cabo Verde islands
pilão	pestle
pombeiros	African traders in Portuguese service in Angola
pontas	farms cultivated by Cabo Verdeans in Guinea
presídios	towns in the Angolan interior
quilombos	communities of escaped slaves
rabelados	religious dissidents in the island of Santiago
rendeiros	people who rented the right to collect Crown revenues
roça(s)	cocoa plantations in São Tomé
salinas	salt pans
senado da câmara	city council
sertão	the interior or backlands
sesmarias	grants of wasteland for cultivation
sobas	Angolan chiefs, tributary to the Portuguese
sobrados	two-storey houses in São Filipe, Fogo
sotavento	leeward
tabanca	Cabo Verde music genre
Tongas	descendants of contract labourers in São Tomé
vadios	vagrants
vinculação	process of establishing an entail over land
vizinhos	citizens and property owners

REFERENCES

Adarkwa, Muriel Animwaa. 2015. 'Impact of Remittances on Economic Growth: Evidence from Selected West African Countries (Cameroon, Cape Verde, Nigeria and Senegal)'. *African Human Mobility Review* (online version). http://www.scielo.org.za/scielo.php?pid=S2410-79722015000200003&script=sci_arttext.

African Development Bank. 2012. *Cape Verde: A Success Story*. African Development Bank and African Development Fund. https://www.afdb.org/sites/default/files/documents/projects-and-operations/cape_verde_-_a_success_story.pdf.

Agência-Geral do Ultramar. 1960. *Cabo Verde. Pequena monografia*. Lisbon: Agência-Geral do Ultramar.

Albuquerque, Luís de and Maria Emília Madeira Santos. 1991. *História geral de Cabo Verde* [*HGCV*], 2 vols. Lisbon: Centro de Estudos de História e Cartografia Antiga.

Almeida, João de. 1925. *O Porto Grande de S. Vicente de Cabo Verde*. Lisbon: Imprensa Limitada.

Almeida, José Maria. 1998. *Descoberta das ilhas de Cabo Verde / Découverte des îles du Cap-Vert*. Praia: Arquivo Histórico Nacional.

Amaral, Ana Rita. 2020. 'Um Portuense em África: Notes for a Biography of a Luso-African Archive'. *E-Journal of Portuguese History* 20 (December): 47–67.

Amaral, Ilídio do. 1964. *Santiago de Cabo Verde. A terra e os homens*. Lisbon: Junta de Investigações do Ultramar.

Ambrosio, António, ed. 1970. 'Manuel Rosario Pinto, "Relação do descobrimento da ilha de San Thomé …"'. *Studia* 30, 1: 205–29.

Anon. 1960. *Viagem de Lisboa à ilha de S. Tomé*. Lisbon: Portugalia.

Ayida, Allegra. 2022. 'Pre-colonial Lusophone Kingship and Elite

Migrations: A Case Study of the Warri Kingdom'. *E-Journal of Portuguese History* 20.

Baião, António, ed. 1940. *O manuscrito 'Valentim Fernandes'*. Lisbon: Academia Portuguesa da História.

Baldacchino, Godfrey and Anders Wivel, eds. 2020. *Handbook on the Politics of Small States*. Cheltenham: Edward Elgar Publishing.

Baptista, Isaurinda et al. 2015. 'Soil and Water Conservation Strategies in Cape Verde (Cabo Verde in Portuguese) and Their Impacts on Livelihoods: An Overview from the Ribeira Seca Watershed'. MDPI Report. https://www.mdpi.com/2073-445X/4/1/22.

Barrow, John. 1806. *A Voyage to Cochinchina in the Years 1792 and 1793*. London: Cadell and Davies.

Bialuschewski, Arne. 2004. 'Daniel Defoe, Nathaniel Mist, and the "General History of the Pyrates"'. *Papers of the Bibliographical Society of America* 98 (March), 21–38.

Borges, Aleida Mendes. 2022. 'Emigration and Citizenship: Diaspora Political Engagement in Cabo Verde'. *E-Journal of Portuguese History* 20: 86–112.

Bosa, Miguel Suarez. 2015. 'Water Institutions and Management in Cape Verde'. *Water* 7: 2641–55.

Bosse, Malcolm. 1972. *The Four Years Voyages of Captain George Roberts*, reprint. New York: Garland Publishers.

Boulègue, Jean. 1989. *Les Luso-africains de Sénégambie, XVIè -XIXè siècles*. Lisbon: Instituto de Investigação Científica Tropical.

Boxer, C. R. 1978. *The Church Militant and Iberian Expansion, 1440–1770*. Baltimore: Johns Hopkins University Press.

BPP (British Parliamentary Papers). 1914. 'Report of the Year 1914 on the Trade of San Thomé and Príncipe'. British Sessional Papers 1914–16, 74, no. 5496.

British Foreign Office. 1912. *Portugal Report for the Year 1911 on the Trade of the Cape Verde Islands*. Diplomatic and Consular Reports. London: HMSO.

British Foreign Office. 1920. *Cape Verde Islands*. Handbooks of the Historical Section of the Foreign Office, no. 117. London: HMSO.

Brooks, George E. 2003. *Eurafricans in Western Africa*. Oxford: James Currey.

Bruto da Costa, B. F., J. F. Sant'Anna, A. C. dos Santos and M. G. de Araújo Álvares. 1916. *Sleeping Sickness: A Record of Four Years' War against It in the Island of Príncipe*. Translated by J. A. Wyllie. London: Tindall and Cox.

Buala. 2010. 'Tchiloli of S. Tomé or Charlemagne in Africa'. https://www.buala.org/en/stages/tchiloli-of-stome-or-charlemagne-in-africa.

Bullen, Frank. 1953. *The Cruise of the Cachalot*. London: Collins.

REFERENCES

Caldeira, Arlindo Manuel. 1999. *Mulheres, sexualidade e casamento em São Tomé e Príncipe (séculos XV–XVIII)*. Lisbon: Cosmos.
Candido, Marianna. 2013. *An African Slaving Port and the Atlantic World. Benguela and Its Hinterland.* Cambridge: Cambridge University Press.
Cardina, M and I. Nascimento Rodrigues. 2021. 'The Mnemonic Transition: The Rise of an Anti-anticolonial Memoryscape in Cape Verde'. *Memory Studies* 14: 1–15.
Cardina, M. and I. Nascimento Rodrigues. 2022. *Remembering the Liberation Struggles in Cape Verde: A Mnemohistory*. Taylor Francis, Open Access. https://library.oapen.org/handle/20.500.12657/58591.
Carletti, Francesco. 1964. *My Voyage around the World*, reprint. Edited by H. Weinstock. London: Methuen.
Carling, Jørgen and Lisa Akesson. 2009. 'Mobility at the Heart of the Nation: Pattern and Meanings of Cape Verdean Migration'. *International Migration* 47: 123–55.
Carling, Jørgen and Luís Batalha. 2008. 'Cape Verdean Migration and Diaspora'. In Jørgen Carling and Luís Batalha, eds., *Transnational Archipelago. Perspectives on Cape Verdean Migration and Diaspora*, 13–31. Amsterdam: Amsterdam University Press.
Carreira, António. 1982. *The People of the Cape Verde Islands*. London: Hurst.
Carreira, António, ed. 1985. *Notícia corográfica e chronológica do bispado de Cabo Verde*. Lisbon: Instituto Caboverdiano do Livro.
Carreira, António. 2000. *Cabo Verde. Formação e extinção de uma sociedade escravocrata (1460–1878)*, 3rd edn. Praia: Instituto de Promoção Cultural.
Castro Almeida, P. L. M. 1941. *Relatório sobre as condições em que se encontra actualmente a Roça Agua Izé da Companhia da Ilha do Príncipe*. Typed report in the possession of M. Newitt.
Castro e Moraes, António Maria. 1901. *Um breve esboço dos costumes de S. Thomé e Príncipe*. Lisbon: Typ. Adolpho de Mendonça.
César, Amândio. 1969. *O 1º Barão d'Água Izé, 1819–69. João Maria de Sousa e Almeida*. Lisbon: Agência-Geral do Ultramar.
Chabal, Patrick. 1983. *Amílcar Cabral*. Cambridge: Cambridge University Press.
Challinor, Elizabeth. 2017. 'Caught between Changing Tides: Gender and Kinship in Cape Verde'. *Ethnos: Journal of Anthropology* 82: 1–50.
Chelmicki, João Conrado Carlos de and Francisco Adolfo de Varnhagen. 1841. *Corografia cabo-verdiana ou descrição geografico-historica da provincia das ilhas de Cabo Verde*, vol. 2. Lisbon.
Cornell, Vincent. 1990. 'Socioeconomic Dimensions of Reconquista and

REFERENCES

Jihad in Morocco: Portuguese Dukkala and the Sa'did Sus'. *International Journal of Middle Eastern Studies* 22: 379–418.

Correia e Silva, António. 1998. *Espaços urbanos de Cabo Verde*. Lisbon: Comissão Nacional para as Comemorações dos Descrobrimentos Portugueses.

Correia e Silva, António Lobo. 2004. *Combates pela história*. Praia: Grafica de Mindelo.

Correia e Silva, António Lobo. 2014. *Dilemas de poder na historia de Cabo Verde*. Lisbon: Rosa de Porcelana.

Crone, G. R., ed. 1937. *The Voyages of Cadamosto*. London: Hakluyt Society.

Cruz, Carlos Benigno da. 1975. *S. Tomé e Príncipe. Do colonialismo à independência*. Lisbon: Moraes Editores.

Cunha Matos, Raimundo José da. 1916 [1842]. *Corografia historica das ilhas de S. Tome e Príncipe, Ano Bom e Fernando Pó*, 4th edn. São Tomé: Imprensa Nacional.

Dampier, William. 1937. *A New Voyage round the World*, reprint. London: A. & C. Black.

Darwin, Charles. 1989. *Voyages of the Beagle*, reprint. London: Penguin.

Davidson, Basil. 1989. *The Fortunate Isles*. London: Hutchinson.

Defoe, Daniel. 1719. *The Life and Strange Surprizing Adventures of Robinson Crusoe, of York, Mariner*. London: William Taylor.

Defoe, Daniel. 1720. *The Life, Adventures and Piracies of the Famous Captain Singleton*. London.

Defoe, Daniel. 1726. *The Four Years Voyages of Capt. George Roberts; Being a Series of Uncommon Events, which Befell Him in a Voyage to the Islands of the Canaries, Cape de Verde and Barbadoes, from Whence He Was Bound to the Coast of Guiney*. London.

Defoe, Daniel [Charles Johnson]. 1972. *A General History of the Pyrates*, reprint. Edited by Manuel Schonhorn. London: Dent.

Dias, Jill. 1984. 'Uma questão de identidade: Respostas intelectuais as transformações económicas no seio da elite crioula da Angola Portuguesa entre 1870 e 1930'. *Revista Internacional de Estudos Africanos* 1: 81–94.

Donelha, André. 1977. *An Account of Sierra Leone and the Rivers of Guinea of Cape Verde (1625)*. Edited by Avelino Teizira da Mota and P. E. H. Hair. Lisbon: Junta de Investigações Científicas do Ultramar.

Drury, Robert. 1729. *Madagascar, or Robert Drury's Journal*. London.

Duffy, James. 1967. *A Question of Slavery*. Oxford: Clarendon Press.

Duncan, T. Bentley. 1972. *Atlantic Islands: Madeira, the Azores, and the Cape Verdes in Seventeenth-Century Commerce and Navigation*. Chicago: University of Chicago Press.

REFERENCES

Ellis, A.B. 1885. *West African Islands*. London: Chapman and Hall.
Espirito Santo, Carlos. 1979. *Contribuição para a história de S.Tomé e Príncipe*. Lisbon: Rosa de Porcelana.
Euronews. 2020. 'Armand Montrond, la French Touch du Cap Vert'. https://fr.euronews.com/2020/01/14/armand-montrond-la-french-touch-du-cap-vert.
Exposição Colonial Portuguesa. 1934. *Informação económica sobre o império e alguns elementos de informação geral*, vol. 1: *Cabo Verde*. Porto: I^a Exposição Colonial Portuguesa.
Eyzaguirre, P. B. 1993. 'Plantations, State Farms and Smallholders: Cocoa Production in São Tomé'. Paper presented to Cocoa and Development Conference.
Farr, James. 1983. 'A Slow Boat to Nowhere: The Multi-racial Crews of the American Whaling Industry'. *Journal of Negro History* 68: 59–70.
Ferrão, José Mendes. 1993. *A aventura das plantas e os descobrimentos portugueses*, 2nd edn. Lisbon: Instituto de Investigação Científica Tropical.
Ferreira, José Manuel Silva Pires. 1999. *Geração dourada. Ensaio da história do Paul de Santo Antão*. São Vicente: Edições Calabedotche.
Ferreira, Roquinaldo. 2007. 'Atlantic Microhistories: Mobility, Personal Ties, and Slaving in the Black Atlantic World (Angola and Brazil)'. In Nancy Naro, Roger Sansi-Roca and David Treece, eds., *Cultures of the Lusophone Black Atlantic*, 99–128. Basingstoke: Palgrave Macmillan.
Filho, João Lopes. 1996. *Ilha de S. Nicolau Cabo Verde. Formação da sociedade e mudança cultural*, vol 1. Praia: Secretaria-Geral, Ministério de Educação.
Fogo. 2018. 'François Louis Armand Fourcheut de Montrond'. http://www.fogo.cv/index.php/personalidades/237-francois-louis-armand-fourcheut-de-montrond.
Fonseca, João Gomes da. 1934. *O Pôrto Grande de S. Vicente*. Porto: I^a Exposição Colonial Portuguesa.
Foy, Colm. 1988. *Cape Verde. Politics, Economics and Society*. London: Pinter Publishers.
Freyre, Gilberto. 1946. *The Masters and the Slaves*. New York: Alfred Knopf. Originally published as *Casa-Grande e Senzala* (1933).
Frutuoso, Gaspar. 1939. *Saudades da terra*, vol. 1. Edited by Manuel Monteiro Arruda. Ponta Delgada: Oficina de Artes Gráficas.
Galvão, Henrique and Carlos Selvagem. 1950–3. *Império ultramarino português*, 4 vols. Lisbon: Empresa Nacional de Publicidade.
Garfield, Robert. 1971. 'A History of São Tomé Island, 1470–1655'. PhD thesis, University of Illinois (subsequently published by Mellen Press, 1992).

REFERENCES

Gemery, H. A. and J. S. Hogendorn. 1978. 'Technological Change, Slavery, and the Slave Trade'. In Clive Dewey and A. G. Hopkins, eds., *The Imperial Impact: Studies in the Economic History of Africa and India*, 243–58. London: Athlone Press.

Gomes, Simone Caputo. 2003. 'Echoes of Cape Verdean Identity: Literature and Music in the Archipelago'. In *Cape Verde: Language, Literature and Music*, 265–85. Dartmouth: Centre for Portuguese Studies and Culture, University of Massachusetts.

Gonçalves, Carlos Filipe. 1998. 'Kap Verd Band'. In José Maria Almeida, ed., *Descoberta das ilhas de Cabo Verde / Découverte des îles du Cap-Vert*, 163–91. Praia: Arquivo Histórico Nacional.

Green, John. 1745–7. *A New General Collection of Voyages and Travels*, 4 vols. London: Thomas Astley.

Green, Toby. 2009. 'Building Creole Identity in the African Atlantic: Boundaries of Race and Religion in Seventeenth-Century Cabo Verde'. *History in Africa* 36: 103–25.

Green, Toby. 2012. *The Rise of the Trans-Atlantic Slave Trade in Western Africa, 1300–1589*. Cambridge: Cambridge University Press.

Green, Toby. 2019. *A Fistful of Shells*. London: Penguin.

Green, Toby and Patrick Chabal. 2016. *Guinea-Bissau*. London: Hurst.

Gulbenkian Foundation. 2020. 'Tchiloli: The European Tragedy Which Is Part of São Tomé's Cultural Heritage'. https://gulbenkian.pt/en/news/tchiloli-the-european-tragedy-which-is-part-of-sao-tomes-cultural-heritage/.

Hakluyt, Richard. 1913. *The Principal Navigations, Voyages & Traffiques & Discoveries of the English Nation*, reprint, 8 vols. London: Dent.

Hall, Trevor. 2019. *Before the Middle Passage: Translated Portuguese Manuscripts of Atlantic Slave Trading from West Africa to Iberian Territories, 1513–1526*. London: Routledge.

Halter, Marilyn. 2008. 'Cape Verdeans in the United States'. In Luís Batalha and Jørgen Carling, eds., *Transnational Archipelago: Perspectives on Cape Verdean Migration and Diaspora*, 35–46. Amsterdam: Amsterdam University Press.

Hamilton, Russell. 2003. '"Chronicling" from the Center of the Periphery: *Estórias contadas (Tales Told)* of German Almeida'. In *Cape Verde: Language, Literature and Music*, 315–26. Dartmouth: Centre for Portuguese Studies and Culture, University of Massachusetts.

Havik, Philip. 2007a. 'Kriol without Creoles: Rethinking Guinea's Afro-Atlantic Connections (Sixteenth to Twentieth Centuries)'. In Nancy Priscilla Naro, Roger Sansi-Roca and David Treece, eds., *Cultures of the Lusophone Black Atlantic*, 412–73. Basingstoke: Palgrave Macmillan.

REFERENCES

Havik, Philip. 2007b. '*Mary and Misogyny* Revisited: Gendering the Afro-Atlantic Connection'. In Philip Havik and Malyn Newitt, eds., *Creole Societies in the Portuguese Colonial Empire*, 41-63. Bristol: Lusophone Studies no. 6, Department of Hispanic, Portuguese and Latin American Studies, University of Bristol.

Havik, Philip and Malyn Newitt, eds. 2007. *Creole Societies in the Portuguese Colonial Empire*. Bristol: Lusophone Studies no. 6, Department of Hispanic, Portuguese and Latin American Studies, University of Bristol.

Heintze, Beatrix. 2007. 'Between Two Worlds: The Bezerras, a Luso-African Family in Nineteenth-Century Western Central Africa'. In Philip Havik and Malyn Newitt, eds., *Creole Societies in the Portuguese Colonial Empire*, 127–53. Bristol: Lusophone Studies no. 6, Department of Hispanic, Portuguese and Latin American Studies, University of Bristol.

Henriques, Isabel Castro. 2012. 'Africans in Portuguese Society: Classification, Ambiguities and Colonial Realities'. In Eric Morier-Genoud and Michel Cahen, eds., *Imperial Migrations: Colonial Communities and Diaspora in the Portuguese World*, 72–103. Basingstoke: Palgrave Macmillan.

Heywood, Linda and John Thornton. 2007. *Central Africans, Atlantic Creoles, and the Foundation of the Americas, 1585–1660*. New York: Cambridge University Press.

Higgs, Catherine. 2012. *Chocolate Islands*. Athens: Ohio University Press.

Hopkinson, Amanda, trans. 2019. *Lisbon Tales*. Oxford: Oxford University Press.

Irwin, Aisling and Colum Wilson. 2001. *Cape Verde Islands*, 2nd edn. Bradt Travel Guides. Chalfont St Peter: Bradt.

ISCSPU (Instituto Superior de Ciências Sociais e Política Ultramarina). 1966. *Cabo Verde, Guiné, São Tomé e Príncipe. Curso de extensão universitária*. Lisbon: Instituto Superior de Ciências Sociais e Política Ultramarina.

Keese, Alexander. 2012. 'Managing the Prospect of Famine: Cape Verdian Officials, Subsistence Emergencies and the Change of Elite Attitudes during Portugal's Late Colonial Phase, 1939–1961'. *Itinerário* 36: 49–70.

Keese, Alexander. 2020. 'Imagining a Better Future: Anti-colonial Protest and Social Debates in Santo Antão, Cabo Verde, 1945–1975'. *Itinerário* 44: 80–104.

Keese, Alexander. 2024. 'Between Land Reform and Postcolonial Frustration: Understanding the Social Roots of Local Opposition to the PAIGC/PAICV in Santo Antão, Cabo Verde, 1975–91'. *Journal of African History* 65, no. 1: 1–17.

REFERENCES

Law, Robin. 1980. 'Wheeled Transport in Pre-colonial West Africa'. *Africa* 50: 249–62.

Law, Robin. 2001. 'The Evolution of the Brazilian Community in Ouidah'. In Kristin Mann and Edna Bay, eds., *Rethinking the African Diaspora*, 22–41. London: Frank Cass.

Lima, Humberto. 1998. 'La tradition orale comme patrimoine'. In José Maria Almeida, ed., *Descoberta das ilhas de Cabo Verde / Découverte des îles du Cap-Vert*, 117–40. Praia: Arquivo Histórico Nacional.

Lindskog, Per A. and Benoit Delaite. 1996. 'Degrading Land: An Environmental History Perspective of the Cape Verde Islands'. *Environment and History* 2, no. 3 (October): 271–90.

Lobban, Richard. 1995. *Cape Verde: Crioulu Colony to Independent Nation*. Boulder, CO: Westview.

Lobo, Andrea. 2012. '"Making Families": Child Mobility and Familiar Organization in Cape Verde'. Scientific Electronic Library Online. https://www.scielo.br/j/vb/a/D6VqJqNth6jL5nyNXC9tg4C/?lang=en#.

Lopes de Lima, José Joaquim. 1844a. *Ensaio sobre a statistica das ilhas de Cabo Verde no Mar Atlantico*, vol. 1 of *Ensaios sobre a statistica das possessões portuguezas na África occidental e oriental; na Asia occidental; na China, e na Oceania* ... Lisbon: Imprensa Nacional.

Lopes de Lima, José Joaquim. 1844b. *Ensaio sobre a statistica das ilhas de S. Tomé e Príncipe*, vol. 2 of *Ensaios sobre a statistica das possessões portuguezas na África occidental e oriental; na Asia occidental; na China, e na Oceania* ... Lisbon: Imprensa Nacional.

Lowenthal, David. 1992. 'Small Tropical Islands: A General Overview'. In Malyn Newitt and Helen Hintjens, eds., *The Political Economy of Small Tropical Islands: The Importance of Being Small*, 18–30. Exeter: University of Exeter Press.

Lucas, Patricia Gomes. 2015. 'The Demography of São Tomé and Príncipe (1758–1822): Preliminary Approaches to an Insular Slave Society'. *Anais de História de Além-Mar* 16: 52–73.

Lyall, Archibald. 1938. *Black and White Make Brown*. London: Heinemann.

Macaronesian. n.d. 'Islands and Biodiversity. Geology of Cape Verde'. http://www.macaronesian.org/en/show/geologia-de-cabo-verde.

Macedo, Donaldo. 2003. 'Literacy in Post-colonial Cape Verde'. In *Cape Verde: Language, Literature and Music*, 393–410. Dartmouth: Centre for Portuguese Studies and Culture, University of Massachusetts.

Macedo, Tânia. 2003. 'Tilôbe, personagem das estórias tradicionais caboverdianas'. In *Cape Verde: Language, Literature and Music*, 103–8. Dartmouth: Centre for Portuguese Studies and Culture, University of Massachusetts.

MacGregor, Marilla. 2022. 'Confronting Different Realities: Libraries in Cabo Verde and the Case for Comparative Librarianship'. *E-Journal of Portuguese History* 20.

Machado, João de Sousa. 1891. *Estudo sobre o commercio do carvão no Porto Grande da ilha de S. Vicente e no Porto da Luz em Gran Canaria*. Lisbon: Imprensa Nacional.

MacQueen, Norrie. 1988. *The Decolonization of Portuguese Africa*. Harlow: Longman.

Madeira, João Paulo. 2016. 'Cape Verde: Dimensions in Nation-Building'. *Humania del Sur* 11, no. 20: 93–105.

Madeira, João Paulo and Bruno Carriço Reis. 2018. 'The Construction of Democracy in Cape Verde: From Portuguese Colonial Conditionalism to International Recognition'. *Observare* 9: 176–91.

Mann, Kristin. 2001. 'Shifting Paradigms in the Study of the African Diaspora and of Atlantic History and Culture'. In Kristin Mann and Edna Bay, *Rethinking the African Diaspora*, 3–21. London: Cass.

Mann, Kristin and Edna Bay. 2001. *Rethinking the African Diaspora*. London: Cass.

Mark, Peter. 2002. *Portuguese Style and Luso-African Identity: Precolonial Senegambia, Sixteenth–Nineteenth Centuries*. Bloomington: Indiana University Press.

Mark, Peter. 2014. 'African Meanings and European-African Discourse: Iconography and Semantics in Seventeenth-Century Salt Cellars from Sierra Leone'. In Francesca Trivellato, Leon Halevi and Catia Antunes, eds., *Religion and Trade: Cross-Cultural Exchanges in World History, 1000–1900*, 236–66. Oxford: Oxford University Press.

Massa, Françoise and Jean-Michel Massa. 2001. *Dictionnaire encyclopedique et bilingue. Cabo Verde / Cap-Vert*. Rennes: Edpal.

Medina, Lia. 2009. 'Evolução demográfica da ilha de São Vicente do descobrimento a 1950'. Master's thesis, ISCTE.

Nabolsy, Zeyad el-. 2020. 'Amílcar Cabral's Modernist Philosophy of Culture and Cultural Liberation'. *Journal of African Cultural Studies* 32: 1–20.

Naro, Nancy Priscilla. 2007. 'Colonial Aspirations: Connecting Three Points of the Portuguese Black Atlantic'. In Nancy Naro, Roger Sansi-Roca and David Treece, *Cultures of the Lusophone Black Atlantic*, 129–46. Basingstoke: Palgrave Macmillan.

Naro, Nancy Priscilla, Roger Sansi-Roca and David Treece. 2007. *Cultures of the Lusophone Black Atlantic*. Basingstoke: Palgrave Macmillan.

Narra, Rita Lucas. 2024. '"If You Want to Call It Marxism, You May Call It Marxism": Amilcar Cabral on Class and National Liberation'. In Rui

Lopes and Natalia Telepneva, eds., *Globalizing Independence Struggles of Lusophone Africa*, 63–79. London: Zed Books.
Nascimento, Augusto. 1999. 'A Liga dos Interesses Indígenas de S. Tomé e Príncipe (1910–1926)'. *Arquipélago História* 3: 417–32.
Nascimento, Augusto. 2008. 'Cape Verdeans in São Tomé and Príncipe'. In Jørgen Carling and Luís Batalha, eds., *Transnational Archipelago: Perspectives on Cape Verdean Migration and Diaspora*, 55–60. Amsterdam: Amsterdam University Press.
Newitt, Malyn. 1996–8. 'São Tomé and Príncipe'. *Africa Contemporary Record* 26: B290–8.
Newitt, Malyn. 2010. *The Portuguese in West Africa, 1415–1670*. Cambridge: Cambridge University Press.
Newitt, Malyn. 2015a. *Emigration and the Sea*. London: Hurst.
Newitt, Malyn. 2015b. 'The Portuguese African Colonies during the Second World War'. In Judith Byfield, Carolyn A. Brown, Timothy Parsons and Ahmad Alawad Sikainga, eds., *Africa and World War II*, 220–37. Cambridge: Cambridge University Press.
Newitt, Malyn. 2017. 'Africa and the Wider World: Creole Communities in the Atlantic and Indian Ocean'. *Tempo* (Brazil) 23: 465–81.
Newitt, Malyn. 2019a. 'The Rise and Decline of Porto Grande (Cabo Verde): A Microcosm of Anglo-Portuguese Relations'. *Revista de Estudos Anglo-Portugueses* 28: 163–90.
Newitt, Malyn. 2019b. *The Braganzas: The Rise and Fall of the Ruling Dynasties of Portugal and Brazil, 1640–1910*. London: Reaktion Books.
Newitt, Malyn. 2023. *Navigations*. London: Reaktion Books.
Newitt, Malyn and Helen Hintjens. 1992. *The Political Economy of Small Tropical Islands: The Importance of Being Small*. Exeter: University of Exeter Press.
Newitt, Malyn and Tony Hodges. 1988. *São Tomé and Príncipe*. Boulder, CO: Westview Press.
Oliveira, Cândido de. 1974. *Tarrafal. O pântano da morte*. Lisbon: Editorial República.
Paiva de Carvalho, Jerónimo. 1912. *Alma negra!* Porto: Tipografia Progresso.
Parsons, Elsie Clews. 1921. 'Folk-Lore of the Cape Verde Islanders'. *Journal of American Folklore* 34: 89–109.
Parsons, Elsie Clews. 1923. *Folk-Lore from the Cape Verde Islands*, part 1. Cambridge, MA: American Folk-Lore Society.
Patterson, K. David. 1988. 'Epidemics, Famines and Population in the Cape Verde Islands, 1580–1900'. *International Journal of African Historical Studies* 21: 291–313.

REFERENCES

Pereira, Daniel A. 1964. *A situção da ilha de Santiago no 1° quartel do século XVIII*, 2nd edn. Praia: Alfa-Comunicações.
Pereira, Daniel A. 2004. *A importância histórica da Cidade Velha*. Praia: Alfa-Comunicações.
Pinto, Paulo Tormenta and Rogério Vieira de Almeida. 2015. 'Territorial Development in the Cape Verde Archipelago under the Estado Novo Dictatorship (1953–1974)'. *Planning Perspectives* 30: 597–623. https://doi.org/10.1080/02665433.2014.1000946.
Prata, Ana. 2014. 'Porto Grande of S. Vicente: The Coal Business on an Atlantic Island'. In Miguel Suárez Bosa, ed., *Atlantic Ports and the First Globalisation, c. 1850–1930*, 49–69. Basingstoke: Palgrave Macmillan.
Purchas, Samuel. 1905. *Hakluytus Posthumus; or, Purchas His Pilgrimes: Contayning a History of the World in Sea Voyages and Lande Travells by Englishmen and Others*. Glasgow: Hakluyt Society.
Ramalho, R. 2010. 'Traces of Uplift and Subsidence in the Cape Verde Archipelago'. *Journal of the Geological Society* 167: 519–38.
Rendall, John. 2004. *Guide des îles du Cap-Vert*. Rennes: PCLL. French translation and original English version of *A Guide to the Cap de Verd Islands*. 1856. London: C. Wilson.
República de Cabo Verde. 1984. *Linhas gerais da história do desenvolvimento urbano da cidade de Mindelo*. Lisbon: Fundo de Desenvolvimento Nacional, Ministério da Economia e das Finanças.
Resende-Santos, João. 2019. 'Cape Verde and the Risks of Tourism Specialisation: The Tourism Option for Africa's Small States'. *Journal of Contemporary African Studies* 37: 148–68.
RFI. 2021. 'A história de Armand Montrond na ilha do Fogo'. https://www.rfi.fr/pt/cabo-verde/20211021-a-história-de-armand-montrond-na-ilha-do-fogo.
Ribeiro, Orlando. 1997. *A ilha do Fogo e as suas erupções*. Lisbon: Comissão Nacional para as Comemorações dos Descobrimentos Portugueses.
Russell, P. E. 1995. 'New Light on the Text of Eustache de la Fosse's *Voiaige à la Guinée* (1479–1480)'. In P. E. Russell, *Portugal, Spain and the African Atlantic, 1343–1490: Chivalry and Crusade from John of Gaunt to Henry the Navigator*. London: Aldershot.
Russell-Wood, A. J. R. 2007. 'Atlantic Bridge and Atlantic Divide: Africans and Creoles in Late Colonial Brazil'. In Philip Havik and Malyn Newitt, eds., *Creole Societies in the Portuguese Colonial Empire*, 171–218. Lusophone Studies no. 6. Bristol: Department of Hispanic, Portuguese and Latin American Studies, University of Bristol.
Saint-Pierre, Jacques-Henri Bernardin de. 1788. *Paul et Virginie*. Paris.
Sansi-Roca, Roger. 2007. 'The Fetish in the Lusophone Atlantic'. In Nancy

Naro, Roger Sansi-Roca and David Treece, eds., *Cultures of the Lusophone Black Atlantic*, 19–39. Basingstoke: Palgrave.
Santos, Danilo. 2017. *A imagem do cabo-verdiano nos textos portugueses, 1784–1844*. Lisbon: Pedro Cardoso Livraria.
Sapega, Ellen W. 2003. 'Notes on the Historical Context of *Claridade*'. In *Cape Verde: Language, Literature and Music*, 159–69. Dartmouth: Centre for Portuguese Studies and Culture, University of Massachusetts.
Schonhorn, Manuel. 1975. 'Defoe's *Four Years Voyages of Capt. George Roberts* and Ashton's *Memorial*'. *Texas Studies in Literature and Language* 17: 93–102.
Seibert, Gerhard. 1999. *Comrades, Clients and Cousins*. Leiden: CNSW.
Seibert, Gerhard. 2007. 'Castaways, Autochthons, or Maroons? The Debate on the *Angolares* of São Tomé Island'. In Philip Havik and Malyn Newitt, eds., *Creole Societies in the Portuguese Colonial Empire*, 105–26. Lusophone Studies no. 6. Bristol: Department of Hispanic, Portuguese and Latin American Studies, University of Bristol.
Seibert, Gerhard. 2009. 'Carlo Magno no equador. A introdução do Tchiloli em São Tomé'. *Latitudes* 36: 16–20. https://tchiloli.com/documentos/gerhard-seibert/.
Seibert, Gerhard. 2010. 'São Tomé's Great Slave Revolt of 1595: Background, Consequences and Misperceptions of One of the Largest Slave Uprisings in Atlantic History'. *Portuguese Studies Review* 18: 29–49.
Seibert Gerhard. 2012. 'Creolization and Creole Communities in the Portuguese Atlantic: São Tomé, Cape Verde, the Rivers of Guinea and Central Africa in Comparison'. In Toby Green, ed., *Brokers of Change: Atlantic Commerce and Cultures in Pre-colonial Western Africa*, 28–51. Oxford: Oxford University Press.
Seibert, Gerhard. 2024. *The Wealth of History of the Small African Twin-Island State of São Tomé and Príncipe*. Newcastle upon Tyne: Cambridge Scholars.
Seibert, Gerhard. Forthcoming. 'São Tomé's Popular Tchiloli: The Persistence of Unproven Claims of Its Sixteenth-Century Introduction'. In Shihan da Silva Jayasuriya and Stefan Halikowski Smith, eds., *Global Portuguese*. Leiden: Brill.
Semedo, José Maria. 2003. 'The Construction of Natural-Geographical Space'. In *Cape Verde: Language, Literature and Music*, 25–40. Dartmouth: Centre for Portuguese Studies and Culture, University of Massachusetts.
Senna Barcellos, Christiano José de. 2003 [1900]. *Subsídios para a história de Cabo Verde e Guiné*, 4 vols. Praia: Instituto Biblioteca Nacional do Livro.
Silva, Tomé Varela. 1998. 'Croyances et religions'. In José Maria Almeida,

REFERENCES

Descoberta das ilhas de Cabo Verde / Découverte des îles du Cap-Vert, 141–62. Praia: Arquivo Histórico Nacional.

Silva Andrade, Elisa. 1996. *Les îles du Cap-Verte de la découverte à l'indépendance nationale (1460–1975)*. Paris: L'Harmattan.

Silva Andrade, Elisa. 2002. 'Cape Verde'. In Patrick Chabal, ed., *A History of Postcolonial Lusophone Africa*, 264–90. London: Hurst.

Smith, William. 1745. *A New Voyage to Guinea*. London: John Nourse.

Soares, Maria João. 2011. 'The British Presence on the Cape Verdean Archipelago (Sixteenth to Eighteenth Centuries)'. *African Economic History* 39: 129–46.

Sweet, James H. 2003. *Recreating Africa*. Chapel Hill: University of North Carolina Press.

Tenreiro, Francisco. 1961. *A ilha de São Tomé*. Lisbon: Junta de Investigações do Ultramar.

Thomas, Charles. 1860. *Adventures and Observations on the West Coast of Africa and Its Islands*. New York: Derby and Jackson.

Tognetti, Sergio. 2005. 'The Trade in Black African Slaves in Fifteenth Century Florence'. In T. F. Earle and K. J. P. Lowe, eds., *Black Africans in Renaissance Europe*. Cambridge: Cambridge University Press.

Tomás, António. 2021. *Amílcar Cabral: The Life of a Reluctant Nationalist*. London: Hurst.

Trans-Atlantic Slave Trade Database. https://www.slavevoyages.org/voyage/database.

Travassos Valdez, Francisco. 1861. *Six Years of a Traveller's Life in Western Africa*, 2 vols. London: Hurst and Blackett.

Tuck, Michael W. 2012. 'Everyday Commodities, the Rivers of Guinea, and the Atlantic World: The Beeswax Export Trade, c. 1450–c. 1800'. In Toby Green, ed., *Brokers of Change: Atlantic Commerce and Culture in Pre-colonial Western Africa*, 285–303. London: British Academy.

Valkhoff, Marius. 1975. 'A Socio-linguistic Enquiry into Cabo-Verdiano Creole'. In Marius Valkhoff, ed., *Miscelânea Luso-Africana*, 41–58. Lisbon: Junta de Investigações Científicas do Ultramar.

Veiga, Manuel. 1998. 'O crioulo de Cabo Verde. Emergência e afirmçao'. In José Maria Almeida, ed., *Descoberta das ilhas de Cabo Verde / Découverte des îles du Cap-Vert*, 109–26. Praia: Arquivo Histórico Nacional.

Vieira, Nina, Cristina Brito, Ana Catarina Garcia and Hilario da Luz. 2020. 'The Whale in the Cape Verde Islands: Seascapes as a Cultural Construction from the Viewpoint of History, Literature, Local Art and Heritage'. *Humanities* 9, no. 3: 90.

Wikipedia. n.d. 'Cape Verde Islands, Dry Forests'. https://en.wikipedia.org/wiki/Cape_Verde_Islands_dry_forests.

Williams, Rosa. 2007. 'Migration and Miscegenation: Maintaining Boundaries of Whiteness in the Narratives of the Angolan Colonial State, 1875–1912'. In Philip Havik and Malyn Newitt, eds., *Creole Societies in the Portuguese Colonial Empire*, 127–41. Lusophone Studies no. 6. Bristol: Department of Hispanic, Portuguese and Latin American Studies, University of Bristol.

Film

Rabelados. 2001. Film by Ana Rocha Fernandes and Torsten Truscheit, shown at the Freiburger Filmforum.

INDEX

A Guide to the Cap de Verd Islands 109, 134
A Imagem do Cabo-Verdiano nos textos Portugueses 120
A Modern Slavery 151
ADI 215
Afonso, Diogo 25, 34, 201
Afonso V, king of Portugal 25, 28, 29
Afonso, Infante, son of D. João II 35
Afonso, king of Kongo 81
African Development Bank 205, 209
African influence in the creole world 219, 220, 248, 249, 260, 261, 262
African nationalism 188, 189, 191, 192, 270–1
Afro-Brazilians 261
Afro-Portuguese 30, 75, 119, 232, 234, 256, 257, 258, 267
  brokers 256, 257, 268
agriculture 11, 14, 25, 27, 40, 42, 43, 79, 92–4, 113, 172, 173, 183, 188, 202, 204, 256
  Board of Agricultural Improvement 128

Agua Izé, baron. 150, 229
Agua Izé report 178–80
Ajuda 265
Alcaçovas, treaty 28, 29, 30, 35, 80
Alcatrazes. 26, 34
Alma Negra 151
Almeida, Germano 239
almoxarife 87
Álvares, Manoel 34
Amador revolt 56, 70, 88
Amarilis, Orlanda, 242
Amazonia 20
Ambaca 119, 266
ambergris 46, 115
Americanos 145, 146
amulets 74, 261
Andrade, Elise Silva 198, 221
Anglo-Portuguese alliance 162
Angola 15, 19, 20, 56, 68, 73, 82–6, 88, 119, 124, 149, 151, 152, 153, 167, 168, 177, 188, 189, 213, 214, 257, 259, 263, 266
  and Brazil 265–6
  creole families in 119, 265, 266, 269, 270, 271

INDEX

Angolares 71, 100, 223, 228, 242
Ano Bom 2, 15,16, 29, 49, 50, 99, 243
Anonymous pilot 37, 41, 45, 50, 68–9, 99
António, Dom, Prior of Crato 54
Antwerp 49
Argentina 20, 134, 174
Arguin. 26, 30
Aruba 243
Ascension island 3
Ashanti War 163
Asia 63, 75, 78
  unofficial Portuguese settlements in 63
asientistas 68
Assembly of God 236
asses/donkeys 46, 93, 111, 112, 113, 131, 132
assimilados 270
Atlantic ocean 1, 4, 8, 20, 35, 39, 88, 122, 132, 138, 212
  creole culture of 22, 190
  economy 76, 77, 78, 79, 85, 86, 88, 89
  islands 4, 21, 36, 87, 117, 124, 134, 141, 263
  trade 1, 18, 56, 57, 60, 61, 86, 89, 110
Augustinians 83
Auto de Floripes 251
Aveiro 54
aviation/airports 3, 17, 18, 170, 173, 180, 194, 205, 207, 212
Axim 21, 30
Axis powers 168–9
Azambuja, Diogo de 29
Azores 2, 3, 14, 25, 28, 42, 46, 61, 124, 137, 141, 142, 143, 144, 145, 146, 165, 168, 174, 194, 253, 263

air base in 171
population of 141

Bahia 95, 259, 264
Balanta 189
Baltimore 92
bananas 43, 100, 104
Banco Nacional Ultramarino 118, 141, 150
Barbot, Jean 109
bark cloth 30, 61, 81
Barlavento islands 8, 9, 10, 108, 222
Barotseland 119
Barreno, Maria Isabel 132
Barrow, John 93, 122–3
Batalha, Luís 200
Batepá massacre 101, 180–2
Bathurst 137
batuque/batuko 179, 223, 246, 247, 249
Bay, Edna 255
beeswax 86
Belgium 151
Bengal famine 131
Benguela 85, 119, 257, 260, 266
Benin 86
Bentley Duncan, T. 2, 3, 4
Bioko 2, 15,16
  see also Fernando Pó
bishoprics 39, 83, 96, 97, 128–9
Bissau 188, 196
Black Death 58
Black Sea 58
Boa Vista island 8, 9, 10, 11,13, 14, 15,16, 24, 44, 45, 91, 107–09, 124, 126, 127, 129, 131, 132, 200, 239, 247
  Fernandes description of 12
  tourism in 207
boats 106
Boletim Official 128

INDEX

bolsa de Mandingo 237
Bonaire, 243
Bonfim, count 120
Boulégue, Jean 36
Braganzas 262
Brasileiros 146
Brava island 5–6, 8, 27, 46, 107, 119, 127, 129, 133, 138, 142, 143, 222, 233, 234, 236, 240
   Fernandes account of 13
   Population 107, 144–5
   US connection 127, 138, 140
Bravo Botelho 101, 102, 116
Brazil/Brazilians 10, 20, 21, 28, 39, 52, 56, 62, 72, 85, 88, 90, 91, 94, 101, 113, 115, 119, 120, 132, 134, 141, 142, 147, 148, 162, 174, 228, 235, 240, 268
   and Africa 263–5
   bans slave trade 139, 262
   creolisation in 254, 259–63
   Dutch in 89, 95
   European immigration 268
   independence 118, 123, 187
   influence in Angola 85, 263, 265–6
   influence in creole culture 220
   music 246, 247, 268
   relations with Guinea islands 99
   slave rebellion 265
   slavery abolished 268
Breamore House 260
Britain/British 124, 131, 134, 138, 160, 262, 264
   Empire 162, 262, 270
   Foreign Office 133, 134
   in Mindelo 137, 156–8, 160
   report on São Tomé 150
   scramble for Africa 269
   slave trade suppression 139, 148, 269
   steamship companies 135
   see also England
British African colonies
   independence 187
British policy in Second World War 168–9
bronze casters 86
brotherhoods 261
Bullen, Frank 142
Butler, British vice-consul 158
buzios 61

Cabo Verde economy 184
Cabo Verde islands ix, 4, 19, 29, 41–44, 45, 47, 52, 53, 57, 62, 63, 71, 79, 81, 84, 85, 88, 89, 94, 95, 104, 117, 120, 124, 126, 132, 138, 143, 147, 183, 219
   administration 33, 34, 64, 118, 127–8, 129, 130
   agriculture in 40, 42, 92
   Alcaçovas treaty 28
   attacks on 51–6
   bishops of 39, 43, 47, 71, 83, 103, 106, 114, 115, 128, 234
   Castile attack on 28
   church in 47, 62, 71, 128
   civil unrest 124–5
   climate of 10, 12, 13, 17, 19, 40, 103
   communities in US 15, 174, 175
   contract labour to São Tomé 121, 148, 149, 152–3, 167, 171, 174, 178
   culture 2, 3, 89, 112, 183, 196, 200, 219, 221, 253
   customs 53, 62, 64, 66, 87

293

defence 19
diaspora 122, 177, 190, 200, 205, 244
discovery of 2, 24–5
education 119, 120, 210
emigration 2, 19, 20, 122, 152
famine relief 130, 46, 161, 171, 172
Fernandes description of 12–13
Frutuoso's description of 43
geography 5, 8–9, 15, 16, 28
geology 8–9, 10
governor of 35
identity 122, 187, 190, 213, 243
independence of 18, 194–6, 231, 247, 271
justice 42
land reform 140–1, 146
marriage in 123, 221
population 19, 31, 32, 36, 38, 41, 44, 106, 117, 122, 123
religion in 129
Ribeira Grande decline 101–04
Roberts description of 6–7
in Second World War 169–71
settlement of 23, 24, 25, 26, 31–, 35, 61
ship owners 144
slavery in 21, 67–9, 70, 72, 89, 91, 106, 132, 139, 140, 222, 227
working class 158–62
see also pirates
Cabo Verde republic 176
  constitution 198, 201, 211
  economy 198, 199, 200, 205, 206, 208–10
  education 210
  elections 195, 196, 199, 200, 209, 211, 212
  flag 200
  GDP 204, 209, 211
  independence 195. 198, 210, 211, 233
  land reform, 118, 199, 202, 203
  National Assembly 200
  one party rule 198
  See also emigration, remittances
Cabo Verde union with Guiné 190. 193, 194, 195, 196–7, 199
Cabo Verdean family 224–30
Cabo Verdeans in colonial administration 167, 184, 188, 190, 213, 270
Cabo Verdean music 2, 221, 223, 247, 248
Cabral, Amílcar 188, 189–94, 196, 197, 199, 200, 220, 225, 233, 243
  political ideas 192–3
  symbolism of 193–4, 201
Cabral, Juvenal 188, 225
Cabral, Luís 191, 195, 196–7
cacao 101, 119, 121, 148–9, 150, 153, 177, 178, 212, 213, 214, 215, 229, 264
Cacheu 35, 257
cachupa 22
Cadamosto, Alvise 11, 24–5, 59, 60
Cadbury, William 151
'Cais do Sodre' 242
Caldera, Arlindo 228, 232
Calouste Gulbenkian Foundation 249, 251
Caminha, Álvaro de 29, 48, 52
Camões, Luís Vaz de 201
Canary islands 2, 3, 8, 28, 45, 162, 176
Candido, Marianna 85
cannibalism 60, 241

INDEX

canoes 30
Cão, Diogo 29, 30, 47, 80
Cape of Good Hope 51, 133
Cape Town 4, 134, 137
capelas 32, 92, 140–1, 227
capitão-mor 102, 106, 133
captaincies 25, 26, 30, 34, 46, 49
    in Angola 83–4
    in Brazil 88, 254
caravels 24, 30, 40, 53, 59, 73, 78
Cardina, Miguel. 193, 233
Caribbean 6, 20, 35, 55, 62, 90, 92, 240, 241, 243
    British 142, 269
Carletti, Francesco 37–8, 64–5, 67–8, 69, 226
Carling, Jørgen 200
Carnegie, Lancelot 163
Carreira, António 59, 67, 102, 125, 139, 152, 168, 171
    on slave supply 76–7
Cartagena 64
Casamance 40, 119, 243, 257
cashew 263
Cassaca conference 189
Cassard, Jacque 90, 102
Casta paintings 259–60
Castile/ Castilians 26, 27, 29, 31, 33, 34, 35, 40, 41, 42, 44, 50, 64, 254
    marriages 35
    war with Portugal 28
    see also Spain
Castilho, José Feliciano de 243
Castro Almeida 178
Catholic church 72, 233, 236, 260, 261, 267, 268
cattle 12, 13,14, 16, 19, 27, 28, 39, 44, 46, 48, 87, 90, 92, 93, 101, 104, 105, 108, 109, 111, 112, 121, 183, 237

Caucasus 58
census 31, 32, 41
Ceuta 58
Chão 207
Chapuzet, João de Mata 128
Chatwin, Bruce 265
Che Guevara 193
Chelmicki, José 129
China 93, 198
Chiquinho 244
Christianity in Central Africa 85
cinnamon 98
Claridade 15, 164–5, 244
climate ix, 13, 17, 40, 219
cloth 14 , 19, 75, 76, 113
    see also panos
cloud forest 115, 126, 208
coal 17, 18, 134, 135–6, 156, 161, 164, 222
    loading 158–9
    price 136, 164
coaling companies 118, 135–6, 156, 157, 159, 160, 161, 206
Cocks, Abraham 69
coconuts 42, 43
coffee 101, 119, 141, 148–9, 150, 177, 178, 264
Coimbra 200
coladeira 247
Cold War 2, 192
colonial reform 180, 184, 185, 186
Columbus, Christopher 35, 62, 263
Companhia da Ilha de Principe 178
Company of Cabo Verde and Cacheu 89
Company of Cacheu 88
Company of Grão-Para e Maranhão 89, 110

Company of Native Labourers 177
CONCP 189
Conde de Frades, *roça* 149
Condent, Christopher 91
Congo Free State 151
Connecticut 146
contraband/smuggling 51, 52, 63, 64, 81, 105, 115, 116, 162, 257
contract labour 140, 149
  see also engagés, serviçais
convicts
  see degredados
cori beads 30, 61, 81
Cornell, Vincent 59
corregidores 34, 42, 50
Correia, Baltahsar 227
Correia e Silva, António 118, 227, 228
Costa Ribeiro, José 227
cotton 12, 13, 19, 27, 31, 40, 43, 44, 46, 52, 61, 92, 96, 110, 115, 147
creole/creolisation 21–2, 32, 33, 36, 56, 75, 85, 86, 100, 117, 119, 124, 177, 245, 264, 269, 271
  in Angola 84, 85–6, 271
  in Brazil 88, 259–63
  commercial agents 53
  culture, 15, 18, 30, 51, 57, 75, 79, 219, 220, 240, 251, 255, 256
  identity ix, 7, 38, 47, 72, 89, 106
  in Kongo 81, 82
  languages 21, 22, 67, 72, 75, 82, 119, 188, 242, 243, 255, 258, 259, 261, 265
  in São Tomé and Príncipe 50, 97

Crioulu 2, 18, 23, 165, 188, 233, 234, 242–5
  dictionary 243
  origins of 243–4
Cuanza river 84
Cuba 197, 198, 247
Cunha Matos, Raimundo José de 100, 101
Curaçao 243
curador 151, 179
currency 61
Curzon, Lord 158

Dahomey, 264, 265
Dakar 10, 136, 162, 167, 174, 245, 258
  see also Senegal
Dampier, William 7, 90, 101, 106, 109–10, 112
danço-congo 251
Dapper, Olfert 232
Darwin, Charles 104, 245–6
Davidson, Basil 225, 230
Davis, Howel 91, 96–7, 113
Defoe, Daniel 6, 105, 238
  see also Roberts
degredados/as 10, 31–2, 44, 45, 48, 74, 84, 101, 104, 122, 124, 168, 269
  numbers 123
  revolt in Cabo Verde 125
  Tarrafal camp 167–8
Del Cano, Sebastián, 51
Delagoa Bay 163
Development Plans in Portuguese Africa 173
Dias, Baltasar 29
Dias, Bartolomeu 59, 80, 83–4
Dias, João José 236
disease 29, 31, 48, 50, 92, 99, 160, 166, 257

diviners 261
Dominicans 83, 270
Donelha, André 74–5
dragon's blood tree (*Dracaena Draco*) 11, 13, 112
Drake, Francis 34, 46, 54–5, 88
drought 10, 11, 14, 19, 20, 92–4, 99, 107, 110, 111, 114, 117, 118, 121, 123, 130, 131, 137, 155, 159, 161, 184, 185, 187, 224, 230, 255
   years 93, 121, 184
   of 1940s 170
Dubois, W.E.B. 177
Duguay-Trouin, René 102
Dutch/Netherlands 19, 88, 90, 91, 106, 115, 119, 133, 256, 265
   Charter companies 66, 88, 95
   war with Spain 54, 55, 89, 95
dyeing industry 31, 105, 108
dyewood 254

East Africa 83
East India Company 66, 134
ECOWAS 201, 220
education 119, 120, 129–30, 164, 166–7, 173, 177, 185, 210, 220, 233, 235, 239, 245
EEZ 5
Ellis, A.B. 126–7
Elmina 21, 29–30, 47, 62, 80, 84, 95
emigration 2, 14, 19, 93, 107, 118, 119, 121, 122, 130, 134, 141, 142, 143, 145, 167, 172, 173–77, 204, 231, 240, 253
   African 176
   barriers to 176
   clandestine 145
   culture of 175–6, 204
   to US 118, 121, 146, 147, 152, 155, 162, 165, 175
Emigration Society of São Tomé 180
engagé labour 149
engenhos 47, 49, 50, 207, 259
England/English 7, 19, 44, 46, 52, 54, 88, 90, 91, 92, 95, 105, 108, 109, 112, 256, 258
   attacks on Cabo Verde 54–5
   East India Company 66, 134
   in Boa vista 108
   in Maio 110
   language 147, 220, 244, 245
   in Mindelo 155
   traders 4, 53, 109, 110
   see also Britain, Fenner
epidemics 130, 135
erosion 13, 121, 172, 202
Escobar, Pero de 29
Espargos 173
Espirito Santo, Carlos 149
Estado da India 254
ethnicity 33, 38, 233
   being 'white' 100, 231–3, 258, 269
EU 194, 202, 208
Europe 17, 18, 20, 21, 78, 85, 86, 93, 105, 122, 146, 199, 234, 248, 253
   and creole world 120, 219
   emigration to 174, 175
   imperialism 253
   population 58
   slave trade to 58, 61, 64
   technology 77–8
   tourism 208
   trade with 49
Évora 46
Évora, Cesária 191, 207, 248
Exxon-Mobil 216

297

INDEX

Eyzaguirre, P.B. 182

Fa d'Ambu 243
fado 246
Faial 46
FAIMO 172
fairs 85
Falkland Islands 3
famine 14, 19, 20, 59, 92–4, 99, 107, 114, 117, 118, 121, 123, 137, 141, 147, 152, 155, 159, 170, 172, 184, 185, 187, 203, 219, 224, 230, 239, 241, 255
   in Bengal 131
   in Ireland 131
   relief 93, 130, 146, 161, 171, 172
   Vice-consul describes 170–1
   years 121
Farr, James 143
fazendas 101, 125, 182
Feijó, João da Silva 10
feitiço/feitiçaria, 237, 242
Fenner, George 43–5, 46, 53
Fernanda, Anna Rocha 236
Fernandes, Valentim 9, 12–13, 48, 65
Fernando, infante 25, 26
Fernando Pó 15
   see also Bioko
Ferreira, Madame 149
fidalgos 31, 33, 46, 208
finaçon 246–7
firearms 78, 85, 86, 119
First World War 130, 133, 136, 146, 163, 168
fish/fishing 50, 68, 88, 98, 109, 110, 115, 116, 223
flamingos 111
Flanders 50, 52
flora 11, 14

Florence 67
FNLA 271
Fogo island 8, 9. 10, 16, 27, 33, 34, 38, 39, 40, 51, 52, 53, 54, 55, 63, 68, 87, 90, 92, 104, 105, 106, 107, 119, 121, 123, 126, 127, 128, 129, 133, 14 1, 145, 170, 172, 185, 200, 201, 222, 229, 232, 240, 247
   descriptions of 12–1, 41–44
   settlement of 25, 31–2, 68
   tourism in 207
   volcanic eruptions on 9–10, 12–13, 15, 44, 55, 92, 107, 131, 207, 239
folk tales 239–42
folklore 165, 222, 239
Fonseca, Francisco de 46
Fonseca, João Gomes 164
Fonseca, Sergio Duarte 195
food crops 86, 110, 253, 263
forced labour 165, 181
   see also serviçais
forros 32, 37, 38, 56, 66, 69, 70, 94, 96, 97, 100, 101, 105, 116, 148, 150, 153, 177, 180, 181, 182, 212, 213, 214, 223, 224, 242, 249, 250, 269, 270
Fortim del Rey 135
France/French 19, 50, 52, 53, 54, 88, 90, 92, 96, 102, 106, 107, 115, 119, 162, 211, 256, 258, 264
   independence of colonies in Africa 187, 188
   language 244, 245
   Revolutionary Wars 107
Franciscans 31, 83, 103
Franco, general 169
Freetown 137
Frelimo 196

INDEX

Freyre, Gilberto 268
Frutuoso, Gaspar 42–3, 46–7
Funchal 39
funcos 221, 232
Furna 107

Gabon, 148, 216
Gambia river 60, 61, 73, 130, 258
Garrett, Almeida 250
Garvey, Marcus 177
General History of the Pyrates 6, 97
Genoa/Genoese 25, 27, 31, 35, 50, 58
geography of islands ix, 9–10, 11
Germany 162, 163
  in Second World War 168–9, 170
Gibraltar 169
global economy 22, 117, 120, 131, 132, 147, 148, 173, 206, 264
Goa 242
goats 12, 13, 14, 27, 28, 39, 44, 45, 46, 48, 49, 52, 87, 93, 108, 109, 111, 115, 116, 121, 183
gold/gold trade 24, 30, 31, 62, 64, 76, 98, 259
  goldsmiths 78
  mines in East Africa 83
Gold Coast 15, 20, 76
  see also Elmina
Gomes, Fernão 26, 29, 80
Gomes, Irineo 231
Gomes, Simone Caputo 247
Gonçalves, Carlos, Felipe 248, 249
Gorgulho, Carlos 180–2
Gough island 3
Gouvea, marquis 115, 116
Gouveia, Francisco SJ. 83
Graça, Joaquim Rodrigues 267–8
Gran Canaria 136, 157
Grand Alliance 90

Green John, 7, 106, 113, 114, 115, 232
Green, Toby 36, 60, 65, 74, 79
Greenland 182
grogue 14, 183, 207
  see also rum
grumetes 255, 264
Gründ, Françoise 250
Guinea-Conakry 188, 191
Guinea islands ix, 3, 4, 8, 14, 15, 16, 21, 23, 29, 37, 47–51, 52, 56, 63, 119, 120, 140, 147, 154, 222–23, 225, 268
  17th-18th centuries 94–101
  climate 17
  geography 15
Guinea rivers 18, 24, 38, 40, 52, 53, 84, 90, 255, 257, 264
Guinea 12, 19, 20, 21, 56, 61, 62, 65, 75, 76, 81, 87, 88, 92, 93, 113, 121, 127, 133, 234, 242, 254, 257, 258, 260
Guinea-Bissau 119, 140, 196,–7, 220, 243, 271
Guiné (Portuguese Guinea) 167, 168, 186, 187, 188, 189, 198, 199, 201
  Independence war 191, 194
Gulf of Guinea 15, 256

Hakluyt, Richard 43
Hall, Trevor 66
Halter, Marilyn 144, 174
Hamilton, Russell 239
Havik, Philip 258
Hawaii 142
Hawkins, John 53
HDI 206
Henrique, infante 25, 166
hides, 27, 44, 6, 104, 113, 115
Hispaniola 64

299

INDEX

Hodges, Tony 214
honey gatherers 86
horses 13, 18, 24, 31, 39, 40, 46, 59, 60, 61, 75, 86, 104

Iberia 24, 63, 254, 270
   in Second World War 169
Independente 128
India 39, 52, 62, 85, 131, 263
   textiles 75
Indian Ocean 17, 22, 78, 90, 211
   Islands 149, 241
   trade 66
indígenas 165, 270
indigo 61, 108
industrialisation 79
Inquisition 36–7, 71, 234
Ireland 131, 146
iron 31, 61, 76
irrigation 199, 203, 204
Isabella the Catholic, queen of Castile 28, 35
Isabella, daughter of Isabella the Catholic 35
Islam 22, 23, 60, 69, 76, 255
Italy/Italians 20, 24, 58, 146, 268
   Cabo Verde emigration to 174
   language 244
ivory 76, 266
   carvings 31, 62, 86

Jaga 82
Jeleén of Waalo 30
Jesuits 83
Jews 18, 20, 23, 29, 32, 33, 35–7, 46, 47, 48, 63, 74, 83, 156, 231, 234, 254
Juana, queen of Castile 28
João II, king of Portual 25, 29, 30, 35, 39, 80
João III, king of Portugal 83
João V, king of Portugal 115
João VI, king of Portugal 262

Keese, Alexander 153, 184, 186, 199
Kimbundu 265
kola nuts 30, 40, 61
Kongo kingdom 20, 21, 30, 79–82, 83, 84, 86, 88, 94, 256, 259
   bishop 82
   Christianity in 80, 81, 82, 256
   culture 80
   embassy to 80
   Jaga invasion 82
   Portuguese relations with 30, 47, 80, 81
   Portuguese settlers in 81
   relations with São Tomé 81–3, 94
   slave trade in 82
korda/korderas, 238
Kriolu 243
Kriston 243

ladinização 67, 72
Lagos 58, 260
lançados 30, 33, 40, 51, 53, 63, 64, 66, 74, 75, 83, 84, 267
   Álvares's description of 34
landownership 33, 183
   see also land reform
land reform 118, 199, 202, 203
languages 22, 220, 243
   see also crioulu
Las Casas, Bartolomé de 270
Las Palmas 163
Law, Robin 264
Leonor, queen of Portugal 39
Leopold, king of the Belgians 151
Leopoldina 133

levadas 199, 203
liceu 166
Liga Africana 177
Liga dos Interesses Indígenas 177
línguas 38, 59, 66, 68
Lisbon 21, 26, 37, 41, 54, 62, 81, 93, 95, 106, 114, 117, 118, 119, 123, 129, 130, 139, 150, 158, 163, 174, 177, 181, 186, 187, 188, 242
literacy 77, 120, 129, 146, 261
literature 206, 220, 246
Livestock Development Station 173
Lobban, Richard 195
Lobo, Andrea 231
London 157
Lopes, Balthasar 165, 244
Lopes de Lima. José Joaquim 14, 101, 120, 126, 129, 131, 140
Louis XIV, king of France 90
Lourenço Marques 137
Lowenthal, David 5
Loyola, Ignatius 83
Luanda. 56, 84, 95, 119, 120, 257, 259, 260, 265, 266, 270
Luso-Africans 266–7
  see also Afro-Portuguese
Luso-Tropicalism 38
Luxembourg 20
  Cabo Verde emigration to 174
Lyall, Archibald 157, 158, 161, 168, 206, 226–7

Macaronesia 2, 3, 201, 220
Macartney, Lord 93
Macedo, Donaldo 233
Macedo, Tânia 241
Machado, Francisco Vieira. 169
Machel, Samora 197
Madagascar 6, 7

Madeira 2, 3, 14, 25, 28, 29, 39, 43, 44, 47, 58, 61, 124, 137, 141, 142, 165, 168, 194, 249, 250
  population of 141
Madeira, João 197
Magellan, Ferdinand 51
magic 242
Maio 8, 9, 11, 27, 45, 54, 62, 90, 91, 104, 109–10, 127, 129, 131, 133
  Fernandes's description of 12, 13
maize 42, 108, 130, 159, 263
malagueta pepper 62
Malanza, viscount 229–30
malaria 160
Mali 10
Malta 136
Malthus, Thomas 123, 224
Mandinka 73, 74
manilhas 61
Mann, Kristin 255
Manuel I, king of Portugal 25, 35, 62, 64, 71
manumission 32, 60, 69, 72, 105, 260
Maria, queen of Portugal 124, 125
maroons 9, 70–1, 88, 100, 223
marriage 21, 72, 73, 123, 176, 221, 222, 224, 225, 226, 227, 228, 229, 231, 255, 258, 264, 267
  of slaves in Brazil 262
Martins, Manuel António 126, 131–2
Marxism 188, 192, 199
Massa, Françoise 8
Massachusetts 146
matriliniality 224, 228, 241
Medina, Lia 164

INDEX

Mediterranean 58, 60, 169
Meneses, Fradique de 215
mestiços 36, 37, 51, 56, 84, 116, 123, 224, 225, 230, 232, 266, 270
Mexico 263
MFA 194
migration 57, 254, 255
Miguel, king of Portugal 124, 125
milho zaburro 42
militia 95, 97, 100, 127, 261
Miller, captain 157
millet 12, 43, 48, 62, 73
Mina coast 260
  see also Elmina
Minas, marquis of 112
Mindelo 109, 118, 119, 128, 134, 135–8, 153, 155–8, 162–4, 173, 185, 201, 202, 205, 210, 248
  British community in 137, 157, 206
  cultural life 138, 164–5
  description of 160
  education in 166, 167
  population 137
  strike 157, 159–60, 163, 164
  working class 158–62
misericórdia 39, 102, 103, 235, 265
missionaries 31, 34, 71–2, 83, 103, 166
Mist, Nathaniel 7
Mixed Commission Court 108–19, 120
MLSTP 212, 213, 214, 215
mocambo 70
Moçamedes 119
modinha 247
moleca 179
Moluccas 51
mondronga 242

Mongols 58
Monte Verde 11, 134, 158
Monteiro, António Mascarenhas 200
Montrond, comte de 207, 229, 230
Moreira, Adriano 202
morgadios 32, 33, 92, 94, 105, 118, 147
  abolition of 138, 140–1, 183
Morison, Samuel Eliot 143
Mormons 236
morna, 246, 247, 248
Morocco 36, 59
mortality 19, 99, 117, 122, 224
Mount Cameroon 15
Mozambique 124, 137, 152, 153, 167, 168, 189, 196, 197, 213, 269, 270, 271
MpD 200, 201, 202, 209, 220, 233
MPLA 188, 213, 271
mules 92, 93, 104, 243–49
music 207, 223, 227, 245–9
  in Brazil 262

Nantucket 143
Napoleonic Wars 148
Naro, Nancy 263
Narra, Rita 192
Native Americans 62, 259, 262, 263
Nazarene church 233, 236
Ndongo 83
Neto, Agostinho 214
Nevinson, Henry 151
New Bedford 143
New Christians 18, 20, 33, 34, 35–7, 46, 47, 53, 83, 85, 231, 234, 254
  and slave trade 63–4
New England 143, 146

Cabo Verdean communities in 175
New Spain 83
New State 153, 165–7, 177, 180, 181, 182, 194, 235, 246
  development plans 171–2
New World 21, 36, 63, 77, 86, 93, 134, 144, 253, 254, 257, 259
  and creole culture 219, 259
  migration to 57, 145
  slave trade to 18, 57, 62, 64, 67, 71, 73, 75, 87
  Spanish conquest 62
Newfoundland 88, 110, 182
Niger delta 15, 256
Nigeria 216
Noli, Antonio di 25, 26, 28, 31, 34
North African trade 24, 58, 59
  slave trade 58
North American colonies 262–3
Nossa Senhora do Rosário 103, 104, 208
Noticia Geográfica e Chronológica 103, 107, 108, 110, 114, 115–16, 133, 226, 230, 235
Nova Sintra 107
Novais, Paulo Dias de 83–4, 85
nzimbu shells 81, 84
Nzinga, queen 86

ODA 205, 206
oil 213, 216–17
Olinda 115, 259
oral tradition/culture 2, 239, 241
  see also folk tales
oranges 42, 46
orchilla 31, 40, 105, 107, 115, 223
Order of Christ 62, 71
O Senhor das Ilhas 132

ouvidor-geral 107, 116

Pacific ocean 51, 57, 211
padroado real 39, 210
PAIGC 186, 188, 189, 190, 193, 194, 195, 196, 197, 198, 199, 211, 271
PAICV 193, 195, 196, 197, 198, 200, 201, 202, 203, 208, 209, 212, 220, 233, 247
palm oil 148, 150, 178
Palma Carlos, Manuel 181
palmatória 179
Pan African Congresses 270
panos. 18, 19, 40, 42, 61–2, 104, 108, 113, 258
  see also cotton cloth
Papal bulls 39
Papel 196
Papiamento 243
Parsons, Elsie Clews 222, 238, 240–2
patrimonialism 213, 216, 217
Patterson, David 122
Paul et Virginie 5
PCD 215
Pedra Lume 110, 117–18, 131, 132, 207
Pedro II, emperor of Brazil 268
Pedro IV, king of Portugal 133
Pentecostal church 236
Pereira, Aristides 195, 196, 200
Pereira, Duarte Pacheco 47
Philip II, king of Spain 3, 54, 55, 153, 208
Philips, Thomas 96
PIDE 168, 181
pigs 48, 49, 100, 116, 238
Pinteado, António Eanes 53
Pinto da Costa, Manuel 213, 215
Pinto da Rocha, Father 181

pirates 23, 52, 53, 54, 89, 90, 91, 92, 96–7, 107, 110, 112, 114, 115, 219
Pires, Gonçalo 48–9
Pires, Pedro 195, 212
Pombal, marquis of 129
pombeiros 85, 267
Pó, Fernão do 29
political prisoners 168
polyandry 228
polygyny 225, 228, 230
pontas 121
Port Said 136
Portalegre, Conde de 46, 87, 112
Porto 53
Porto Grande 114, 115, 118, 132–6, 145, 153, 154, 155, 156, 157, 160, 165, 173, 212
  decline of 163
  recovery plans 163, 164
  shipping in 136, 162, 163
  strike in 157, 159–60, 163, 164
Porto Ingles 108
Portugal/Portuguese 14, 20, 23, 25, 26, 27, 38, 46, 49, 50, 79–80, 85, 106, 129, 130, 131, 137, 145, 146, 148, 155, 156, 157, 171, 174, 199, 201, 210, 254, 257
  church 39, 62, 129
  civil war in 117, 123–4, 125, 127, 140
  Cortes 15
  discovery of Cabo Verde 2
  emigration from 254
  empire 14, 41, 54, 89, 101, 104, 118, 154, 210, 242
  kings of 25, 45, 52
  identity 75, 259, 265, 266, 267
  in São Nicolau 114

independence of Cabo Verde 195, 196
language 59, 72, 233, 261
liberal reforms 118, 123, 124, 125, 127, 140
orders of knights 82
pilots 53
policy in Cabo Verde 33, 34, 36, 51, 53, 62, 63
Republic 157, 159, 165
revolution of 1974. 271
trade monopolies 30, 31, 35, 51, 52, 53, 61–2, 87, 88, 105
Second World War 168–9
settlement of islands ix, 23
Septembrists 134, 135, 139
union of the Crowns 19, 34, 54, 87–8, 90
war with Castile 28–9
Portuguese Colonial Exhibition 164
Portuguese Indian Territories 165
Portuguese influence in Africa 21, 22, 23, 24, 30
Portuguese royal family in Brazil 262
Potosí 83
Povoação Velha 108
Praia 34, 35, 41, 53, 55, 102, 118, 119, 125, 126, 128, 129, 132, 133, 135, 137, 141, 142, 173, 185, 208, 210, 247
  becomes capital 103
  education in 166
presidios 127, 266
Príncipe 2, 3, 15, 29, 47–51, 87, 96–100, 120, 149, 151, 177–83
  description of 96–9
  religion in 98, 99
  white population of 100
printing press 128

INDEX

privatisation 208–10
prostitution 160, 164, 206, 225
Purchas, Samuel 69
Pusich, António 133

Queimadas 114
Quilombos 262
  see also maroons

Rabaka, Reiland 191
Rabelados 9, 223, 236
railways 131, 132, 150
rain 10, 11, 14, 16, 17, 25, 29, 42, 117, 203
Reis, Bruno 197
religion 21, 129, 233–6
  in Kongo 80, 81, 82, 256
  syncretism 74, 99, 234–5, 255, 261, 262
remittances 118, 146, 147, 162, 167, 176–7, 184, 204–05, 206, 211, 212
Renamo 271
Rendall, John 109, 134
Rhode Island 146
Ribeira Brava 113–14
Ribeira Grande 26, 34, 38, 39, 41, 42, 43, 50, 52, 53, 54, 62, 88, 105, 137–8, 208, 226, 235
  cathedral 39, 102, 103, 104, 129, 243
  decline of 101–04
  French attack on 90
  fortress 55
Ribeira Grande (Santo Antão) 116, 127
  education in 166
Ribeiro, Gregório José 149
Ribeiro, Orlando 10, 123, 221, 232–3
rice 12, 62, 73, 159

Rio de Janeiro 102, 259
Rio de la Plata 20, 69
Rio Grande 61, 75
Rio São Domingos 61
roads 173
Robinson Crusoe 6–7
Roberts, captain George 6–7, 8, 11, 90, 93, 94, 103, 105, 106, 108, 113, 222, 234, 237
roças 70, 87, 94, 95, 96, 101, 121, 149–50, 152, 177, 178, 181, 182, 212, 213, 217, 228
  corporal punishment on 178, 179
  decline of 153
  plantation houses 150
  see also Agua Izé, *serviçais*
rocega 161
Rodrigues, André 41
Rodrigues, Inês Nascimento 193, 233
Rolas island 69
Romanceiro 250
Royal Mail Steam Packet Company 134
Royal Navy 91, 96, 110
rum 14, 18, 40, 92, 96
Russia 58

Sá da Bandeira, marquis 201
Sahara 13, 59, 121
  trade across 24, 58, 60, 65
Sal island 8. 9, 10, 11, 27, 54, 62, 91, 93, 104, 117, 126, 127, 131, 132, 140, 17 3, 194, 205
  Fernandes's description of 12
  tourism in 207
Sal Rei 108, 132
Salazar, António Oliveira. 132, 153, 165, 169, 170, 171, 174, 176, 181, 187, 202, 270

INDEX

salt 18, 19, 27, 45, 54, 62, 88, 91, 92, 94, 104, 108, 109, 110, 113, 115, 117, 126, 127, 131, 132, 133, 147, 162
San Ildefonso, treaty 263
San Jon 247
Santa Cruz (Brazil) 262
Santa Cruz dos Angolares 100
Santa Maria 131–2
Santa Maria, João Zuarte 227
Santarem, João de 29
Santiago island 8, 9, 10, 11, 13, 15, 16, 25, 28, 29, 34, 38, 39, 41, 44, 46, 51, 53, 59, 61, 63, 66, 73, 87, 91, 92, 93, 94, 104, 106, 110, 114, 116, 119, 124, 125, 127, 138, 139, 140, 141, 164, 168, 185, 190, 208, 222, 223, 234, 236, 240, 245, 247
   administration of 33
   1466 trade agreement 26, 27
   Fernandes's description of 12
   Frutuoso's decription of 43
   land reclamation in 203
   maroons in 70
   settlement of 31–2
   slave revolt in 125
   slave trade from 65, 66–7, 68
Santo Antão 8, 9, 10, 11, 16, 27, 44, 46, 111, 114, 115–16, 126, 127, 129, 133, 135, 170, 173, 185, 186, 199, 202, 203, 222, 230, 240, 247
   Fernandes's description of 13
   population 116
   senado da câmara 116
   tourism in 207–08
Santo António 98, 99, 100
Santos, Danilo 120
Santos João Resende 206
São Domingos 55, 245
São Filipe 27, 90, 141, 201, 207
São Nicolau 8, 9, 27, 44, 46, 52, 103, 112–14, 119, 127, 128, 129, 142, 164, 168, 170, 222, 240, 247
   Bishop relocates to 114
   education in 129, 166
   Fernandes's description of 13
   population 112, 114
São Tomé 2, 3, 15, 28, 29, 31–2, 37, 38, 47–51, 52, 55, 56, 65, 79, 84, 85, 87, 88, 89, 94–101, 120, 147–53, 177–83, 254, 264, 269, 270
   account of in *General History of the Pyrates*
   Batepá massacre 101, 180–2
   bishopric 39, 49, 71, 82, 83, 95, 96, 97
   Cabo Verde labour in 121
   church in 48, 71
   Cunha Matos's account 100
   descriptions of 41–44
   Dutch occupation 95
   geography of 16, 50,
   labour in 101, 148, 149, 152–3, 167, 171, 174, 178
   maroons in 70
   population of 47, 48, 56, 100, 119–20
   relations with Kongo 81, 82, 94
   seminary 95–6
   senado da câmara 49, 95, 99
   settlement of 35, 36, 48
   urban conditions 150
São Tomé and Príncipe Republic 70, 212–17
   constitution 215
   coup attempts 216
   economy 212, 214, 215, 217
   elections in 212, 216

GDP 214
independence 71, 121, 212
labour supply 214
land reform 216
politics in 215, 216
tourism 216
São Vicente island 8, 9, 10, 11, 18, 44, 46, 105, 114–15, 118, 119, 128, 132, 133–7, 145, 156, 157, 158, 160, 163, 164, 170, 185, 201, 222
   Fernandes's description of 13
Saragossa treaty 51
satellite communications 3, 18
Saudades da Terra. 42
Scotland 146
sea routes 1, 3
Sebastião, king of Portugal 52, 83, 225
Second World War 2, 164, 168–71, 174, 178, 187
Seibert, Gerhard 213, 216
Semedo, José Maria 249
seminário-liceu. 129, 166
senado da Câmara 39, 49, 95, 99, 103, 113, 116
Senegal 17, 24, 30, 40, 61, 71, 73, 162, 174, 243
Senna Barcellos, Christiano José de 102, 227
Serpa Pinto 201
Serradas, Manuel 54
serviçais 149, 150, 152–3, 167, 177, 171, 174, 178, 180
   population 152
   repatriation 151
sesmarias 33, 128
Seville 51
sexual promiscuity 225–6
share-cropping 183
Sherley, Sir Anthony 55

Sierra Leone 23, 24, 40, 61, 71, 86, 258
Silva, Luís Rendall 185
Silva, Nuno da 46
Silva, Tomé Varela 238
Silva Porto, António Francisco Ferreira da 267
Silveira Gonçalo da. 83
silver mines 83, 84
Singapore 136
slave trade ix, 18, 19, 20, 21, 36, 40–1, 43, 48, 53, 55, 56, 57–86, 87, 92, 94, 101, 109, 119, 130, 131, 219, 234, 257, 260
   abolition in Brazil 262
   in Angola 84–5
   as migration 57, 254, 255
   clandestine 63, 64, 65
   in Kongo 81
   numbers 58, 65
   regulation 73
   ship numbers 65, 71
   supply side 77
   suppression of 124, 134, 139, 148
   with sub-Saharan Africa 58
slavery 149, 153, 228, 230
   abolition of 70, 118, 138–41, 268
   in Africa 21
   in Brazil 260–63, 268
   in Cabo Verde 21, 68, 89, 91, 106, 132, 139, 140, 222, 227
   in Príncipe 99
   in São Tomé 97, 149
slaves 2, 18, 21, 23, 24, 30, 31, 32, 37, 38, 40, 41, 42, 44, 48, 50, 51, 58, 59, 87, 88, 91, 94, 97, 99, 102, 105, 116, 118, 120, 133, 138, 140, 148, 223, 243,

246, 254, 264, 266
  baptism of 71–2, 73
  in Brazil 259–63
  prices of 59–60
  revolts 70, 124, 125
  status 60
Smith, William 96, 98
Soares, Maria João 7, 106
Soares, Mário 202
sobas 84
sobrados 141, 208, 232
Soeiro, João 67
Sousa, Francisco Felix de 264
Sousa, Gonçalo de 46
Sousa Machado, João de 156, 158, 159
Sousa Santos, António Policarpo de 185
South Africa 168
South Atlantic ix, 39, 57, 95, 115, 118, 133, 147, 220, 245, 253, 255
Soyo province 80
Spain 3, 19, 23, 42, 51, 54, 59, 62, 63, 67, 88, 90, 95, 157, 210, 257, 263
  Second World War 169
Spanish America 68, 83, 255, 259
  slave trade licensing system 64
  Union of the Crowns 19, 54, 87–8
Spinóla, António de, president of Portugal 194, 195
St Helena 4
steamers 17, 118, 134, 145, 147, 155
submarine cables 17, 118
  see also telegraph
sugar 12, 14, 29, 40, 47, 49, 50, 51, 56, 87, 88, 92, 96, 97, 121, 147, 148, 183, 207, 250, 254
  in Brazil 85, 88, 141
Sweet, James 228–9
Switzerland 20
  Cabo Verde emigration to 174

tabanca 247
tallow 27, 44, 115
tamarind 14
tangomaos, 75
  see also lançados
Tarrafal 41, 94, 167–8, 208
tchiloli 249–50
technology 50, 77–8, 79, 86, 256
telegraph 118, 136, 147, 156, 157, 170, 206
Tenreiro, Francisco 15, 182, 270
The Cruise of the Cachalot 142
'The Tragedy of the Emperor Charlemagne and the Marquis of Mantua' 249
The Viceroy of Ouidah 265
Third Portuguese Empire 89
Thomas, Charles 109, 148–9
tobacco 79, 95, 99, 263, 264
Tocqueville, Alexis de 180
Tomás, António 189, 197
Tongas 152, 179, 214, 242
Tordesillas, treaty 35, 263
Total Oil 216
tourism 3, 4, 5, 9, 20, 201, 205–08, 209, 219, 248
  in São Tomé 216–17
  numbers 206
Towerson, William 16
transnationalism 210–12
Travassos Valdez, Francisco 120–1, 124, 126, 128, 131, 132, 135, 156, 223, 230, 246
Treaty of Friendship and non-Aggression 169
tree planting 202

INDEX

Tristan da Cunha 3
Trovoada, Miguel 215
Trovoada, Patrice 215
Truscheit, Torsten 236
tsetse fly 152
turtles 31, 46, 104, 109–10, 111, 114
Tuscany, Grand Duke of 38, 226
typhoid 160

U-boats 170
UN 191
Union of the Crowns of Portugal and Spain 19, 34, 54, 87–8, 90
UNITA 271
university in Cabo Verde 210
USA 19, 120, 126, 128, 130, 132, 133, 137, 141, 169, 200, 208, 220, 222, 236, 240, 245
   and Cabo Verde independence 195, 198, 199
   Anti-slave trade squadron 109, 135, 149
   Cabo Verdean communities in 175
   Consul, 142
   emigration to 118, 121, 146, 153, 167, 174, 175
   whalers 127, 142–4

Vadios 223
vagrants 131
Valkhoff, Marius 235
Varnhagen, Francisco Adolfo 235
Vatican 82
Vaz Monteiro, Ricardo 182
Veiga, Carlos 198, 200, 212
Veiga, Manuel 244
Venice/Venetians 11, 24, 98
Vieira, 'Nino' 196
Vikings. 58

vinculação 32
vines/vineyards 10, 12, 112, 113, 141, 207, 229
Viseu, duke of 25
Vitoria 51
Viye 267
vizinhos 32
volcanoes/volcanic eruptions. 4, 8, 9–10, 12–13, 15, 131
Voz dámor 248
Voz do Povo 193

Waalo 30
War of the Spanish Succession 90
Warri kindom 256
wars of independence in Africa 168
water supply 91, 107, 113, 115, 134, 159, 173, 199, 202, 203, 204, 229
   for ships 19, 52, 91, 96, 103, 113, 126
weaving 40, 79, 80
West Africa 17, 51, 79, 81, 224, 232, 256, 260, 261, 267
   fairs 61, 73, 85
   economy 76, 77
   trade with 18, 19, 26, 27, 28, 30, 31, 39, 47, 73, 90
West-central Africa 85, 119, 265–7
Western Telegraph Company 137
Westphalia, Treaty 4–5
whales/whaling/whalers 17, 19, 98, 107, 115, 127, 130, 133, 142–4, 146, 222
wheat 43
White Fleet 182–3
Whydah 95, 264–5
wolfram 169
Wolofs 24, 40, 61

INDEX

women 31–2, 36, 38, 41, 51, 59, 96, 108, 113, 214, 224, 226, 228, 229, 231, 245, 246, 247, 248, 258, 268
- emigrants 145, 174
- in Mindelo 159
- in São Tomé 48, 50
- in West Africa 75
- militia in São Tomé 100
- slaves 32, 37, 59, 60, 67, 77

World Bank 214

World Food Proramme 248

Xavier, Francis 83

yams 48, 110
yellow fever, 135, 160
Yoruba 260

Zaire river 15, 30, 80, 87
Zambezi river 83, 85, 119, 266
Zurara, Gomes Eannes 58